The Antiquities Act

The Antiquities Act
A Century of American Archaeology, Historic Preservation, and Nature Conservation

Edited by **David Harmon,**
Francis P. McManamon, and
Dwight T. Pitcaithley

The University of Arizona Press   Tucson

The University of Arizona Press
© 2006 The Arizona Board of Regents

This book is printed on acid-free, archival-quality paper.
Manufactured in the United States of America

11   10   09   08   07   06   6   5   4   3   2   1

Library of Congress Cataloging-in-Publication Data

The Antiquities Act : a century of American archaeology, historic
preservation, and nature conservation / edited by David Harmon,
Francis P. McManamon, and Dwight T. Pitcaithley.
    p. cm.
  Includes bibliographical references and index.
  ISBN-13: 978-0-8165-2560-7 (hardcover : alk. paper)
  ISBN-10: 0-8165-2560-9 (hardcover : alk. paper)
  ISBN-13: 978-0-8165-2561-4 (pbk. : alk. paper)
  ISBN-10: 0-8165-2561-7 (pbk. : alk. paper)
  1. United States. Antiquities Act of 1906. 2. Historic preservation
—Law and legislation—United States. 3. Historic sites—Law and
legislation—United States. 4. Archaeology—Law and legislation—
United States. 5. Indians of North America—Antiquities—Law and
legislation. 6. Nature conservation—Law and legislation—United
States. I. Harmon, David, 1958– II. McManamon, Francis P. III.
Pitcaithley, Dwight T.
  KF4310.A96 2006
  344.73'094–dc22

                                                    2005035156

This book was published from electronic files edited and typeset by the
volume editors.

Contents

Abbreviations

AAA	American Anthropological Association
AAAS	American Association for the Advancement of Science
AFRH	Armed Forces Retirement Home
AIA	Archaeological Institute of America
ANCSA	Alaska Native Claims Settlement Act (1971)
ANILCA	Alaska National Interest Lands Conservation Act
ANWR	Arctic National Wildlife Refuge
ARPA	Archaeological Resources Protection Act (1979)
ASW	Anthropological Society of Washington
BAE	Bureau of American Ethnology
BLM	Bureau of Land Management
CEQ	Council on Environmental Quality
cert. denied	Supreme Court denial of a Writ of Certiorari, i.e., the court's refusal to hear an appeal (in legal citations)
CFR	Code of Federal Regulations (in legal citations)
Cir.	Circuit Court (in legal citations)
cl.	clause (in legal citations)
Cong.	Congress (in legal citations)
D.	Federal District Court (in legal citations)
DOI	U.S. Department of the Interior
EEZ	exclusive economic zone
EIS	environmental impact statement
Env't Rep. Cas.	Environment Reporter–Cases (in legal citations)
EO	executive order (of the president)
F.2d; F.3d	Federal Reporter (in legal citations)
FLPMA	Federal Land Policy and Management Act (1976)
F.Supp.; F.Supp.2d	Federal Supplement (in legal citations)
GLO	General Land Office
H.R.	House Resolution (in legal citations)
I.D.	Interior Department Decisions (in legal citations)
IUCN	International Union for Conservation of Nature and Natural Resources (now known as IUCN–The World Conservation Union)
NEPA	National Environmental Policy Act (1969)
NHPA	National Historic Preservation Act (1966)
NLCS	National Landscape Conservation System
NOAA	National Oceanic and Atmospheric Administration
NPS	National Park Service
NWHICRER	Northwestern Hawaiian Islands Coral Reef Ecosystem Reserve
P.L.	Public Law (in legal citations)

PLLRC	Public Land Law Review Commission
S.	Senate Resolution (in legal citations)
sec., secs.	section(s) (in legal citations)
Sess.	Session (of Congress, in legal citations)
SHSI	State Historical Society of Iowa
SLA	Submerged Lands Act (1953)
Stat.	United States Statutes at Large (in legal citations)
UNCLOS III	United Nations Convention on the Law of the Sea (1982)
UNESCO	United Nations Educational, Scientific, and Cultural Organization
U.S.	United States Reports (in legal citations)
U.S.C.	United States Code (in legal citations)
U.S.C.A.	United States Code Annotated (in legal citations)
USFS	U.S. Forest Service
USFWS	U.S. Fish and Wildlife Service
WL	Westlaw legal database (in legal citations)

Acknowledgments

We thank Janet A. McDonnell, bureau historian with the National Park Service's Washington Office, for reviewing the table in the Appendix. Tom DuRant, archivist with the historic photograph collection at NPS's Harpers Ferry Center, provided invaluable help in locating and reproducing the historic photographs of NPS sites and related activities. Geoff Middaugh, Holly Hampton, Mike Quinn, Colleen Hyde, Neil King, and Anna Hosticka Tamura did the same for some of the contemporary photographs of BLM and NPS national monuments. Brad Barr and Andy Collins provided the photo of the NWHICRER. Carol Gifford and Raymond Harris Thompson located the photographs of Edgar Lee Hewett and John F. Lacey, and we thank the Museum of New Mexico and the State Historical Society of Iowa, respectively, for their permission to use these photos.

Allyson Carter, Anne Keyl, Keith LaBaw, Jason S. Ninneman, Elizabeth Ohm, Alan M. Schroder, Harrison Shaffer, and the rest of the staff at the University of Arizona Press helped speed the book through the production process, enabling us to publish early in the Act's centennial year; we are most grateful for their help.

The chapter by the late Ronald F. Lee is an abridgment made by us of his pioneering history of the Antiquities Act, which originally was published by the National Park Service in 1970 (and reprinted, with a few editorial corrections, in 2000 as part of a special issue of *The Journal of the Southwest* devoted to the Act). The chapter by Raymond Harris Thompson is his own abridgment of his article "Edgar Lee Hewett and the Political Process," which also appeared in that special issue.

Introduction

The Importance of the Antiquities Act

David Harmon, Francis P. McManamon, and Dwight T. Pitcaithley

THE HISTORY OF AMERICAN ARCHAEOLOGY, conservation, and historic preservation often is told in terms of legal milestones, and rightly so. An environmental activist working to expand a nearby park, a historic preservationist trying to save a cherished old building, a volunteer working on a national wilderness campaign, an archaeologist investigating an ancient village site in advance of reservoir construction—all are working from a solid foundation of statutory authorities that, law by law, have expanded protections for archaeological resources, historic structures, and natural areas. There are many laws that mark critical junctures in our national conservation policy, yet what is arguably one of the most important of them all remains little known outside of specialist circles. That law is the Antiquities Act of 1906.

The influence of the Antiquities Act extends far beyond what is suggested by its quaint title. In truth, the name of the Act is downright misleading—or at least seriously deficient, because the law has been used to protect vast natural areas in addition to the kind of well-defined archaeological sites that the word "antiquities" connotes. A mere tangle of terminology? It is that, but also much more. The name signifies the controversy that has swirled around the Act throughout its history: whether the scope of discretionary proclamations as exercised by various presidents has far exceeded what was intended by Congress.

The heart of the controversy is an innocuous clause at the beginning of Section 2 (see text box and following figure). Here, the president is authorized to "declare by public proclamation historic landmarks, historic and prehistoric structures, and other objects of historic or scientific interest that are situated upon the lands owned or controlled by the Government of the United States to be national monuments, and may reserve as a part thereof parcels of land, the limits of which in all cases shall be confined to the smallest area compatible with proper care and management of the objects to be protected...." The key phrases, with emphasis added, are "objects of historic and *scientific* interest" and "confined to the *smallest area* compatible with proper care and management." One reasonable interpretation of these phrases would be that the Act applies only to very specific natural features—a rock formation, say—and that the boundaries of the monument being created should extend very little beyond the feature itself. Another interpretation, which critics of the Act have found highly unreasonable, is that an object of scientific interest can be something as vast as the Grand Canyon, and the smallest area compatible with protection and management can be millions of acres in extent. Yet it is this second, expansionist interpretation that has been adopted by a number of presidents, Republican and Democrat alike, over the past century.

The precedent began with the man who signed "An Act for the Preservation of American Antiquities" into law on June 8, 1906: the larger-than-life *Theodore Rex,* as one of his recent biographers has called him. Congress was well aware of the character of the president into whose hands it was delivering the law, of his sovereign vision of power and his willingness to wield it. And, characteristically, Theodore Roosevelt wasted very little time before making use of the Act. On September 24, 1906, he proclaimed the first national monument: the imposing monolith of Devils Tower in Wyoming. Before he left office in 1909, Roosevelt declared seventeen more, and therein lies the beginning of our story. Many of them, like Devils Tower, conformed to a strict reading of the Act. But several, such as Grand Canyon and Mount Olympus, were Rooseveltian in scope.

TR's dynamic use of the Act set off reverberations that are still being felt today. It was as if he emboldened his successors to dare to match the spirit, if not the sheer volume, of his example. As a result, no other law has had such a wide-ranging influence on the preservation of our nation's cultural and natural heritage. Why is the Antiquities Act so important?

- *Creation of national monuments.* As just noted, the Act gives the president the power to unilaterally declare, independently of Congress, protected national monuments from tracts of existing

An Act for the Preservation of American Antiquities

Be it enacted by the Senate and House of Representatives of the United States of America in Congress assembled, That any person who shall appropriate, excavate, injure, or destroy any historic or prehistoric ruin or monument, or any object of antiquity, situated on lands owned or controlled by the Government of the United States, without the permission of the Secretary of the Department of the Government having jurisdiction over the lands on which said antiquities are situated, shall, upon conviction, be fined in a sum of not more than five hundred dollars or be imprisoned for a period of not more than ninety days, or shall suffer both fine and imprisonment, in the discretion of the court.

Sec. 2. That the President of the United States is hereby authorized, in his discretion, to declare by public proclamation historic landmarks, historic and prehistoric structures, and other objects of historic or scientific interest that are situated upon the lands owned or controlled by the Government of the United States to be national monuments, and may reserve as a part thereof parcels of land, the limits of which in all cases shall be confined to the smallest area compatible with proper care and management of the objects to be protected: *Provided,* That when such objects are situated upon a tract covered by a bona fide unperfected claim or held in private ownership, the tract, or so much thereof as may be necessary for the proper care and management of the object, may be relinquished to the Government, and the Secretary of the Interior is hereby authorized to accept the relinquishment of such tracts in behalf of the Government of the United States.

Sec. 3. That permits for the examination of ruins, the excavation of archaeological sites, and the gathering of objects of antiquity upon the lands under their respective jurisdictions may be granted by the Secretaries of the Interior, Agriculture, and War to institutions which they may deem properly qualified to conduct such examination, excavation, or gathering, subject to such rules and regulation as they may prescribe: *Provided,* That the examinations, excavations, and gatherings are undertaken for the benefit of reputable museums, universities, colleges, or other recognized scientific or educational institutions, with a view to increasing the knowledge of such objects, and that the gatherings shall be made for permanent preservation in public museums.

Sec. 4. That the Secretaries of the Departments aforesaid shall make and publish from time to time uniform rules and regulations for the purpose of carrying out the provisions of this Act.

Approved, June 8, 1906

The signed original of the Antiquities Act, with the handwritten approval of Theodore Roosevelt, as filed with the State Department the following day. Image courtesy of National Park Service Historic Photo Collection, Harpers Ferry Center.

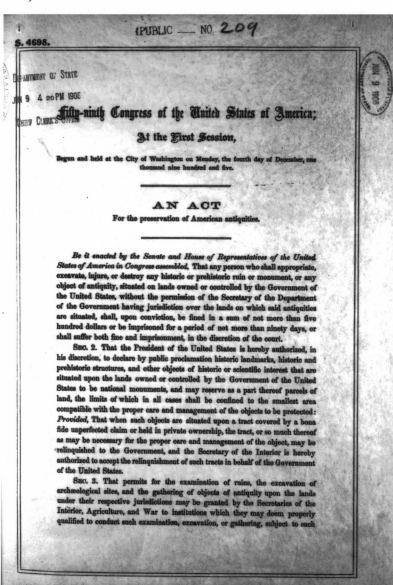

(PUBLIC —— NO. 209

S. 4698.

DEPARTMENT OF STATE

JUN 9 4 20 PM 1906

CHIEF CLERK'S OFFICE

Fifty-ninth Congress of the United States of America;

At the First Session,

Begun and held at the City of Washington on Monday, the fourth day of December, one thousand nine hundred and five.

AN ACT

For the preservation of American antiquities.

Be it enacted by the Senate and House of Representatives of the United States of America in Congress assembled, That any person who shall appropriate, excavate, injure, or destroy any historic or prehistoric ruin or monument, or any object of antiquity, situated on lands owned or controlled by the Government of the United States, without the permission of the Secretary of the Department of the Government having jurisdiction over the lands on which said antiquities are situated, shall, upon conviction, be fined in a sum of not more than five hundred dollars or be imprisoned for a period of not more than ninety days, or shall suffer both fine and imprisonment, in the discretion of the court.

SEC. 2. That the President of the United States is hereby authorized, in his discretion, to declare by public proclamation historic landmarks, historic and prehistoric structures, and other objects of historic or scientific interest that are situated upon the lands owned or controlled by the Government of the United States to be national monuments, and may reserve as a part thereof parcels of land, the limits of which in all cases shall be confined to the smallest area compatible with the proper care and management of the objects to be protected: *Provided,* That when such objects are situated upon a tract covered by a bona fide unperfected claim or held in private ownership, the tract, or so much thereof as may be necessary for the proper care and management of the object, may be relinquished to the Government, and the Secretary of the Interior is hereby authorized to accept the relinquishment of such tracts in behalf of the Government of the United States.

SEC. 3. That permits for the examination of ruins, the excavation of archæological sites, and the gathering of objects of antiquity upon the lands under their respective jurisdictions may be granted by the Secretaries of the Interior, Agriculture, and War to institutions which they may deem properly qualified to conduct such examination, excavation, or gathering, subject to such rules and regulations as they may prescribe: *Provided*, That the examinations, excavations, and gatherings are undertaken for the benefit of reputable museums, universities, colleges, or other recognized scientific or educational institutions, with a view to increasing the knowledge of such objects, and that the gatherings shall be made for permanent preservation in public museums.

SEC. 4. That the Secretaries of the Departments aforesaid shall make and publish from time to time uniform rules and regulations for the purpose of carrying out the provisions of this Act.

[signature]
Speaker of the House of Representatives.

[signature]
Vice-President of the United States and
President of the Senate.

Approved.
June 8, 1906.

Theodore Roosevelt

federal public land. These monuments range from prehistoric ruins and other objects of antiquity (hence the Act's name) all the way up to entire landscapes of ecological and scientific importance, covering thousands or even millions of acres. The Act has been used by thirteen presidents to proclaim new national monuments or expand existing ones.[1] (For a list, see the Appendix.) These monuments, which currently cover over 79,700,000 acres, include world-class protected natural areas, many of which have gone on to receive national park status, and cultural sites of international renown. Of America's twenty World Heritage sites, seven originated as national monuments under the Antiquities Act: Carlsbad Caverns National Park, Chaco Culture National Historical Park, Grand Canyon National Park, Olympic National Park, Statue of Liberty National Monument, Glacier Bay National Park and Preserve, and Wrangell–St. Elias National Park and Preserve.[2]

- *Establishing the primacy of commemorative, educational, and scientific values for archaeological resources.* Section 3 of the Act establishes the regulation of archaeological investigations on public lands and states that such investigations are for "increasing the knowledge of [archaeological sites and] ... objects, and ... for permanent preservation in public museums." In one long sentence, the second half of this section makes clear that archaeological sites and the items removed from them are most important for what we can learn from them with proper study. The objective of archaeological investigations is to study the past through historical and scientific methods, not to retrieve objects for display, exhibit, or sale.[3]
- *A foundation for heritage professionalism.* The Act provides a legal and public policy foundation for public archaeology in the United States, and for public agencies being involved in the preservation of historic places and structures. Its provisions have done much to foster the development of the professions of archaeology, history, and historic preservation in the public sector in this country, and have had an important influence on anthropology and paleontology as well.[4]
- *A scientific basis for nature preservation.* The Act was the first law to systematically enable the creation of large-scale nature reserves for scientific (rather than scenic or economic) reasons.[5] Not only did it therefore prefigure today's emphasis on land-

scape-scale ecosystem conservation by nearly a century, it remains a vital tool for such efforts. In fact, over the past 30 years practically the only big nature reserves created by the federal government have come as the result of monument declarations under the Antiquities Act.

- *An important presidential prerogative.* The Act established the power of the president to proactively preserve important cultural sites and natural areas (up to and including large landscapes of ecological value) that are threatened with degradation or outright destruction. This "one-way" power—the president can unilaterally establish national monuments, but only an act of Congress can abolish them—is an important legal doctrine that has enhanced the strength of the presidency.

Simply put: In shaping public policy to protect a broad array of cultural and natural resources, the impact of the Antiquities Act is unsurpassed.

The year 2006 marks the hundredth anniversary of the Act. The centennial affords an unparalleled opportunity for present-day stewards to reflect on its historic achievements and critique its shortcomings, to remind fellow professionals and the general public of its continuing importance, and to look ahead to its future in the twenty-first century. We attempt to do all three in this book. While the creation of the national monuments occupies center stage in the discussion, we also have made a conscious effort to highlight the Act's other contributions to archaeology, conservation, and historic preservation. The authors whom we invited to contribute to this volume are a mix of scholars and field managers, and their breadth of perspective is very well matched to the wide-ranging accomplishments of the Act.

Our book opens with an abbreviated version of the late Ronald F. Lee's pioneering history of the Act, which was produced for the National Park Service in 1970. In making this abridgment, we have focused on Lee's account of the social history leading up to the Act's passage: the awakening of interest in American archaeology and the growing alarm about pot-hunting and other acts of destruction in the Southwest and elsewhere. Lee's narrative also holds important clues as to why objects of scientific interest came to be included in the Act. The next three chapters delve into the role of three of the fathers of the law, the first two being its principal architects, and the third its precedent-setting first executor. Today the names of Edgar Lee Hewett and John F. Lacey are all but forgotten except by archaeologists and historians of conservation, but their relative obscurity is undeserved. Hewett was an administrator, author, and educator as well as a field archaeologist, whose mix of experience and talent enabled him to forge the compromise that became the final text of the Act. Hewett was one of those invaluable behind-the-scenes brokers without whom most laws would never get through the proverbial sausage factory. As told by Raymond Harris Thompson, the story of how Hewett managed to get squabbling factions to come together behind the language of the Act is one of perseverance mixed with political and professional acumen and flexibility.

Any antiquities bill, no matter how carefully written, faced a major hurdle in the House of Representatives in the form of the Committee on Public Lands, through which all such legislation had to pass. Because the committee was dominated by members from the West who were largely wary of federal power, success for the Antiquities Act depended on the political skill of the committee's chairman, John F. Lacey. Rebecca Conard introduces us to this Iowa congressman, who was a major figure in conservation at the turn of the twentieth century but whose personal background, as she tells us, provides few clues as to what fueled his interest in nature protection. No such mysteries attend our third figure, who occupies an altogether different dimension. Theodore Roosevelt is one of the legends of the White House, an iconic face on Mount Rushmore, and the historical grounds of his interest in conservation have been mapped again and again by his biographers. What Char Miller brings into focus is how much Roosevelt's use of the Antiquities Act was influenced by the doctrines of Progressivism, by its rock-steady faith in the capacity of professional expertise to (paternalistically) improve the American republic. This is a supremely self-confident ideology, daring to do great things, one that meshed perfectly with TR's natural bent. It goes a long way toward explaining why he had no compunction in stretching the language of the Act to its very limits—and perhaps beyond.

If one agrees with the expansive, big-canvas conservationism of a Theodore Roosevelt, then the precedent he set with his monument proclamations is a bold stroke of environmental statesmanship, something to be celebrated. But many local interests, especially in the West, resolutely decline to attend that party, for it is their dreams of commerce that are directly curtailed whenever a new monument is set aside. The second part of the book explores the Act's legacy of controversy. Moving from Theodore to Franklin Roosevelt, the first chapter in this section, by Hal Rothman, recounts how the showdown between FDR and Wyoming politicians over the creation of Jackson Hole National Monument nearly blew apart the Antiquities Act in the 1940s. Had the presidential powers under the Act been emasculated at that time, as many in and around Jackson Hole fervently wished, the most serious repercussions would have been felt two generations later in, of all places, Alaska. That is because in 1978 President Jimmy Carter used the Antiquities Act to preserve tens of millions of acres of the state as national monuments, forestalling the transfer of what was then unassigned national-interest public domain to non-conservation status. The story is told by one of the protagonists, Carter's secretary of the interior, Cecil D. Andrus, along with his colleague at the Andrus Center for Public Policy, John C. Freemuth. They give us an insider's view of what has been called the greatest single act of land preservation in American history. Then we turn to two legal scholars of the Act, each of whom offers a different perspective on its place in American conservation. Mark Squillace, who served in the Clinton administration, is generally supportive of the expansive monument proclamations and analyzes the constitutional and legal issues against the backdrop of the Clinton monuments, some of which engendered controversy almost as virulent as in Jackson Hole. James Rasband gives a dissenting view, arguing that the Act would be fairer if the president's nearly unfettered power to declare monuments were reined in by requiring consultation with state and local groups.

When the Act is in the public eye at all, it is because of controversies such as these. But as we've suggested above, the law is about much more than the proclamation of national monuments. The third part of the book explores how the law has helped create a foundation of public values for commemoration and education, as well as for heritage professionalism and a scientific basis for nature conservation. Francis P. McManamon discusses how the Act has fostered the non-commercial values of archaeological, cultural, and historic resources, and how the Act supported the nascent profession of archaeology in the United States by providing it with an intellectual and ethical foundation of stewardship. In this view, archaeological sites and objects are valued in context for the information and inspiration they provide, and their preservation is a public trust. Jerry L. Rogers shows how the Antiquities Act was not just a radical departure from previous public policy on national heritage, but a lasting one. It proved to be the direct ancestor of the Historic Sites Act of 1935 and the National Historic Preservation Act of 1966; the latter still forms the foundation of most historic preservation in America. Joe Watkins reminds readers of negative ramifications of the Antiquities Act, which by broadening the public control and ownership of ancient archaeological sites alienated Native Americans from their heritage. By limiting legitimate access to the investigation of archaeological sites to experts, the interpretations of non-expert Native Americans about these sites were denigrated and ignored by many. The Act also set a precedent for the use of scientific, rather than scenic or economic, justifications for setting aside large protected natural areas. In the final chapter of this section, David Harmon assesses the ecological accomplishments of the Act by looking at several facets of protection, including World Heritage status and ecoregional representivity.

The next section of the book looks to the future. Much to the consternation of some in the National Park Service, which oversees the vast majority of the monuments as units of the national park system, President Clinton assigned responsibility for most of the monuments he proclaimed to other agencies, the Bureau of Land Management in particular. Almost at a single stroke, the BLM was thrust into a situation where it had to develop a new protected area paradigm that fit into its multiple-use mandate—one very different from the NPS ethos. Elena Daly and Geoffrey B. Middaugh trace the evolution of land protection within the BLM from the early days of the disposition of the public domain, through the passage of the Federal Land Policy and Management Act of 1976 (the BLM's organic act), to the creation of the bureau's National Landscape Conservation System in 2000. Though many consider NPS and BLM strange bedfellows, in two new national monuments they have been given shared management responsibility. This is another new horizon for the Act. From their vantage point as monument co-managers, Darla Sidles and Dennis Curtis give a report from the field on how the experiment is going at Grand Canyon–Parashant National Monument.[6] Next, Brad Barr and Katrina Van Dine discuss the extension of the Act into the last commons: the oceans. They explain the special legal considerations involved in regulating ocean use and how these work both for and against traditional national monument proclamations under the Act.

In the book's final chapter, we try to make sense of it all by highlighting the main themes that have emerged in the preceding chapters, focusing on whether the law has been used justly or not. In closing, we pause to consider what the future may hold, and whether the Act's next century will be as productive as its first.

Notes

1. Confusingly, there are numerous other parks and protected areas, authorized through regular congressional legislation rather than through the Antiquities Act, that are designated "National Monument" (or were at the time of their creation). Examples include Agate Fossil Beds, Badlands (now National Park), Booker T. Washington, Canyon de Chelly, Congaree Swamp (now Congaree National Park), El Malpais, Mount Saint Helens Volcanic (managed by the U.S. Forest Service), and Pecos (now National Historical Park), among many others. Throughout this book, the term "national monument" will be used as a shorthand for any park or protected area, no matter what its current designation, that originated or was expanded through the use of the Antiquities Act—thereby excluding such parks as those listed above.

2. Wrangell–St. Elias and Glacier Bay actually are part of a single World Heritage site made up of a complex of parks, including several in Canada. For more, see the chapter by Harmon in this volume.

3. The primacy of a non-commercial value in United States public policy for other kinds of cultural and historic resources continues from its foundation in Section 3 of the Antiquities Act to the 1935 Historic Sites Act and the 1966 National Historic Preservation Act, the three most important cultural resource statutes of the twentieth century. See the chapter by Rogers in this volume, and also McManamon 1996a.

4. For anthropology, see the chapter by Watkins in this volume. As for paleontology, "[d]espite the conflicting interpretations of whether Congress intended for the phrase 'objects of antiquity' to include paleontological resources, the Antiquities Act served for nearly seventy-five years as the primary authority for the protection and permitting of fossils on lands administered by the Departments of Agriculture and Interior" (Santucci 2005, 1).

5. Before the Antiquities Act was passed, biology played a role in creating Sequoia, Yosemite, and General Grant (now part of Kings Canyon) National Parks, as it did in some early proposals for boundary changes to these and other parks. Still, "evidence that biologic and geologic considera-

tions influenced selection of national monuments is more certain..."
(Shafer 1999, 190).

Once the Act was passed, a related question arose as to the difference
between a national monument and a national park. To some, the monuments were national-parks-in-waiting: "Some confusion has arisen as to the
difference between parks and monuments.... The object of a monument is
the preservation from destruction or spoliation of some object of historic,
scientific, or other interest. The object of a park is that and something more;
namely, the development of the area reserved for its more complete and perfect enjoyment by the people. It might be said that a monument is park raw
material, because many of the existing monuments, in all probability, will
receive park status when their development as parks is practicable"
(Cameron 1922, 8). By 1930, however, NPS was downplaying this distinction: "The national parks and national monuments are so closely allied that
it is difficult to draw a hard and fast line between them. Generally speaking,
national parks are areas preserved in Federal ownership by act of Congress
because of their outstanding scenery, national in character. The national
monuments, on the other hand, are reserved because of their historic, prehistoric, or scientific interest" (NPS 1930).

6. Grand Canyon–Parashant is adjacent to, but administratively separate from, Grand Canyon National Park. The other BLM/NPS co-managed
monument is Craters of the Moon in Idaho.

Part 1

The Origins and Architects of the Act

1

The Origins of the Antiquities Act

Ronald F. Lee

The Beginnings of Concern: 1879

THE ABANDONED AND RUINED DWELLINGS of prehistoric humans in the American West have aroused the interest and comment of explorers and colonizers for centuries. Not until after the Civil War, however, did these ruins, and the continuing discovery of still others, attract the serious attention of the eastern scientific community. Public interest in the continent's ancient civilizations brought about no less than five significant developments portentous for American archaeology in the single year of 1879. They mark 1879 as the beginning of the movement that led, just over a quarter of a century later, to adoption of the Antiquities Act as the first national historic preservation policy for the United States.

First, in this year Congress authorized establishment of the Bureau of Ethnology, later renamed the Bureau of American Ethnology, in the Smithsonian Institution to increase and diffuse knowledge of the American Indian. Major John Wesley Powell, who in 1869 had led his remarkable boat expedition through the Grand Canyon of the Colorado River, was appointed the bureau's first director.[1] He headed it until his death in 1902. During this long period, he and his colleagues became a major force for the protection of antiquities on federal lands.

Second, 1879 marked the appearance of a superbly illustrated book, co-edited by Frederic W. Putnam, devoted to the ruined pueblos of Arizona and New Mexico and the archaeology and ethnology of the Indians of Southern California.[2] Five years earlier, Putnam had begun his long and distinguished career as Curator of the Peabody Museum of American Archaeology and Ethnology at Harvard. Until his death in 1915, Putnam profoundly influenced the rise and development of anthropology in America and served on several committees and boards concerned with federal legislation to protect American antiquities.[3]

Third, in 1879 the American Association for the Advancement of Science for the first time elected an anthropologist as its president. He was Lewis Henry Morgan, then the foremost student in the United States in the comparatively new field of anthropology. During this period the association inaugurated its "Section H," in which growing numbers of students of anthropology gathered each year to read papers and discuss ideas. Eventually the association established an influential committee to work for legislation to protect antiquities on federal lands.

Fourth, on February 10, 1879, the Anthropological Society of Washington was founded.[4] The ASW, as it came to be known, drew support from the anthropologists, ethnologists, and geologists then being brought into the federal government as well as from many other persons active in the life of the national capital.[5] In 1902 members of the ASW formed part of a group that founded the American Anthropological Association, which, in turn, provided crucial support for the Antiquities Act in 1906.

Lastly, in 1879 Charles Eliot Norton, professor of the history of art at Harvard and for a quarter-century one of its most influential scholars and teachers, founded the Archaeological Institute of America with the help of friends and associates in and around Boston.[6] Its purpose was to promote and direct archaeological research, both classical and American. Classical archaeology received substantially the larger support, but the executive committee from the beginning also held the view that "the study of the aboriginal life in America is essential to complete the history of the human race, as well as to gratify a legitimate curiosity concerning the condition of man on this continent previous to its discovery."[7]

In formulating its very first project in the field of American archaeology, the institute turned naturally for advice and assistance to Lewis Henry Morgan. He believed that the most promising field for exploration was the social organization, usages, customs, and architecture of the Pueblo tribes of Indians, especially in the San Juan region (near the point where Colorado, Utah, New Mexico, and Arizona join) and in other parts of New Mexico and Arizona.[8] Morgan drew up a comprehensive plan for such an exploration and suggested that it should be extended to the imposing ruins in Mexico and Central America.

Not only did Morgan outline a program, he recommended an investigator. Adolph F. Bandelier, then forty years old, was born in Berne, Switzerland, but moved with his family to America in 1848 and settled in Illinois. Trained as a geologist, Bandelier turned to the study of history and ethnology and acquired valuable knowledge of several European languages and of linguistics generally. Beginning in 1877, he published several scholarly works on the ancient Mexicans through the Peabody Museum at Harvard and became known to Putnam.[9] With the help of the historian Francis Parkman, Putnam and Morgan persuaded Norton and the institute to engage Bandelier to undertake its first project in America archaeology—an exploration in the Southwest exactly as recommended by Morgan.[10]

The First Responses to Threats, 1880–1889

In August 1880, after calling on John Wesley Powell in Washington, Bandelier journeyed to New Mexico and began a preliminary study of the great ruined pueblo of Pecos, about thirty miles southeast of Santa Fe. Knowledge of relevant Spanish documents persuaded Bandelier that Pecos has first been visited in 1540 by Hernando de Alvarado, Francisco Vázquez de Coronado's lieutenant, during his search for the "Seven Cities of Cibola." Making elaborate architectural measurements of the ruins, Bandelier concluded that Pecos was "probably the largest aboriginal structure within the United States, so far described."[11] In 1881 the institute published accounts of his first season's work.[12] In Bandelier's report appeared these striking sentences on the condition of the great Pecos ruin in 1880:

> Mrs. Kozlowski (wife of a Polish gentleman, living two miles south on the arroyo) informed me that in 1858, when she came to her present home with her husband, the roof of the church was still in existence. Her husband tore it down, and used it for building out-houses; he also attempted to dig out the cornerstone, but failed. In general the vandalism committed in this venerable relic of antiquity defies all description.... All the beams of the old structure are quaintly ... carved ... much scroll work terminating them. Most of this was taken away, chipped into uncouth boxes, and sold, to be scattered everywhere. Not content with this, treasure hunters ... have recklessly and ruthlessly disturbed the abodes of the dead.[13]

Bandelier's revelation of the great historical interest and incredible neglect of Pecos aroused wide interest and deep concern among the members of the Archaeological Institute of America and their friends, who noted that Pecos was of such great antiquity that it was "even older than Boston." Marshall P. Wilder, president of the New England Historic Genealogical Society, and a far-sighted, scholarly, but practical man with a long-standing interest in antiquities, undertook to do something about Pecos.[14] He and others in the society determined to raise in Congress for the first time the whole question of legislation to protect American antiquities on federal lands. They prepared a petition and persuaded Senator George Frisbie Hoar of Massachusetts to present it. The petition stated that

> there are in the Territories of New Mexico and Arizona twenty-six towns of the towns of Pueblos Indians, so called, in all containing about ten thousand inhabitants; that the number of their towns was once very much greater ... that the question of the origin of those Pueblos and the age of their decayed cities, and the use of some of their buildings, now magnificent ruins, constitute one of the leading and most interesting problems of the antiquary and historian of the present age; that relic-hunters have carried away, and scattered wide through America and Europe the remains of these extinct towns, thus making their historic study still more difficult, and, in some particulars, nearly impossible....
>
> Your memorialists therefore pray you honorable body that at least some of these extinct cites or pueblos ... may be withheld from public sale and their antiquities and ruins be preserved, as they furnish invaluable data for the ethnological studies now engaging the attention of our most learned scientific, antiquarian, and historical students.[15]

The issue was new in Congress, and in spite of the high character of the sponsors it received a reserved response. The Southwest contained many similar ruins, it was argued, and it would be impossible for the government to protect them all.[16] The petition was referred to the Committee on Public Lands, where it quickly died. Nonetheless, the issue had been officially raised, and that was a significant first step.

After Senator Hoar's effort failed in 1882, seven years elapsed before another archaeological preservation proposal reached Congress. These years witnessed a steady extension of knowledge and deepening of public interest in American archaeology and ethnology. Bandelier continued his investigations, principally in the Southwest, and Putnam, among many other activities, rescued prehistoric Serpent Mound in Adams County, Ohio, a remarkable 1,300-foot-long earthen effigy of a serpent swallowing an egg. With money raised from the public, the land on which the mound stands was purchased and eventually deeded to the Ohio Archaeological and Historical Society for "perpetual care ... as a free public park forever." This probably was the first archaeological preservation project in the United States.[17]

Under John Wesley Powell's direction, the Bureau of Ethnology was also very active during this period. publishing important annual reports together with special papers on various topics by different scientists attached to its staff.

It was a privately sponsored project, however, that led to the first federal archaeological reservation. Mary Hemenway of Boston was well known for her generosity in supporting a number of important charitable educational and cultural enterprises. Beginning in 1886 and continuing for many years she sponsored the Hemenway Southwestern Archaeological Expedition, which undertook the systematic exploration of Indian antiquities in the Salado and Gila valleys in Arizona.[18] In 1888, the *Boston Herald* carried an account of some of the expedition's discoveries. This account was later published as a pamphlet and helped to crystallize the interest of some of the leading citizens of Massachusetts in Southwestern antiquities.[19]

To these persons, the ancient landmark known as Casa Grande (the "Great House") seemed to be a prime candidate for preservation. So named by the Jesuit Father Eusebio Kino, who said Mass within its walls in 1694, the four-story structure was the principal part of an extensive prehistoric pueblo. Roofless even in Kino's time, Casa Grande continued to slowly decay until the mid-nineteenth century.[20] As it became better known, the rate of its deterioration appears to have sharply accelerated. By 1889, its condition was extremely serious.

On January 30 of that year, fourteen citizens of Boston and vicinity—including such prominent figures as Hemenway, Parkman, Oliver Wendell Holmes, and John Greenleaf Whittier—addressed a petition to Congress urging the enactment of legislation to protect Casa Grande from further destruction.[21] Again they turned to Senator Hoar, who presented it on their behalf in February. Unlike the earlier petition, which called for general legislation affecting all public lands, this one asked only for the preservation of one conspicuous ancient landmark, at small expense.

Congress at once moved to provide for the protection and repair of Casa Grande in an appropriation act approved on March 2.[22] Not only did this legislation appropriate $2,000 to enable the secretary of the interior to repair and protect Casa Grande, it also authorized the president to reserve the land on which the ruin was situated from settlement and sale. Although repair work soon began, it took three years to establish the reservation. On June 22, 1892, President Benjamin Harrison signed an executive order, recommended to him by the secretary of the interior at the request of the director of the Bureau of Ethnology, reserving the Casa Grande Ruin and 480 acres around it for permanent protection because of its archaeological value.[23] Thus was established the first formal national archaeological reservation in U.S. history (Figures 1.1 and 1.2).

The Growth of Interest in Antiquities, 1890–1904

Scholarly interest in American Indian antiquities grew rapidly after 1889. Norton and his associates in the Archaeological Institute of America expanded the organization well beyond Boston by admitting chapters from cities across the country. Members of these flourishing groups came from influential circles, and their articulate support impressed congressional committees when legislation to protect antiquities came before Congress.[24]

Meanwhile, a national organization of anthropologists began to take shape. In 1896, Franz Boas, often called the founder of modern anthropology, organized the Anthropological Club in New York. In 1902 it merged with ASW to become the American Anthropological Association.[25] A committee of the new association was to play a key role in formulating the Antiquities Act.[26] Also during this period, the National Museum substantially enlarged its collection, and public museums of archaeology and ethnology were founded in several other major cities, several in affiliation with universities.

The general public's interest in American archaeology was itself aroused by three widely admired exhibitions. In 1892 the Columbian Historical Exposition was held at Madrid, Spain, to commemorate the four hundredth anniversary of the discovery of America by Christopher Columbus. The exposition exhibited "the greatest collection of Americana ever under one roof" up to that

Figure 1.1. Casa Grande in 1892, the year President Benjamin Harrison made it the country's first protected archaeological site by means of an executive order. Nathan Oakes Murphy, territorial governor of Arizona, is in front. Casa Grande was proclaimed a national monument in 1918. Unattributed image from a glass negative loaned by Henry Hammond Burrell. Courtesy of National Park Service Historic Photo Collection, Harpers Ferry Center.

time. The United States section occupied six rooms, embracing a long list of exhibitors, including the National Museum and the Bureau of Ethnology. One large hall was devoted to collections brought from the American Southwest by the Hemenway Southwestern Archaeological Expedition. Sand pictures and altars were exhibited for the first time with other objects, both ancient and contemporary, from the Hopi tribe representing the sedentary Indians of the Southwestern United States. The exhibit won high praise, and a catalogue was published by the U.S. Government.[27] A much larger public exhibition of American Indian antiquities was featured the next year at the World's Columbia Exposition in Chicago. Collections came from Greenland, Alaska, and Canada; from nearly all the Indian tribes of the United States; and from the West Indies, Yucatan and other parts of Mexico, Honduras, Ecuador, Peru, Bolivia, and even Patagonia. Such an exhibit of the ethnology and antiquities of the New World had never been seen before and excited wide interest. The major portion of the collections remained in Chicago after the exposition closed and formed the foundation of the Field Columbian Museum.[28] The Louisiana Purchase Exposition, held in St. Louis in 1904, provided another highly impressive display of Indian antiquities and whetted public interest still more.

Figure 1.2. Casa Grande with its protective structure in 1929. George Alexander Grant photograph, courtesy of National Park Service Historic Photo Collection, Harpers Ferry Center.

Published reports of new archaeological discoveries further aroused public interest. Some were popular accounts, such as Bandelier's fictionalized account *The Delight Makers* (1890) and *The Land of the Cliff Dweller*, by F. H. Chapin, and *Some Strange Corners of Our Country*, by Charles F. Lummis (both 1892). Equally important were the scholarly publications issued each year by the Bureau of Ethnology (renamed the Bureau of American Ethnology in 1895), the National Museum, and the Peabody Museum, and the professional journals and papers sponsored by the Archaeological Institute of America and the Anthropological Society of Washington and its successors. These and accounts of other antiquities were eagerly read by a growing constituency of anthropologists, curators, and educated laymen.

Vandalism and Commercialism, 1890–1904

Rising public interest in the history and art of the Southwestern Indians in the 1890s was accompanied by a swelling demand for authentic prehistoric objects. The desires and needs of growing numbers of collectors and dealers, exhibitors and curators, teachers and students, added to the native curiosity of cowboys, ranchers, and travelers, created an avid demand for original objects from the cliff dwellings and pueblo ruins of the Southwest. Most of these ruins were situated on public land or Indian reservations. There was no system of protection and no permit was needed to dig. Professional archaeologists were few in number; in America their science was in its infancy and just beginning to be known to the public. The eager seeker for artifacts had one chief worry—that someone else would reach a ruin rich in valuable objects before he did. The result was a rush on prehistoric ruins of the Southwest that went on, largely unchecked, until about 1904.

The early stages of this rush accompanied the spread of prospecting and ranching in Colorado, New Mexico, and Arizona during the 1880s and 1890s. Cowboys pursuing wandering cattle through the mesquite and up remote canyons began to come upon ancient ruins never before seen by white men. In this way, one December day in 1888, ranchers Richard Wetherill and Charles Mason discovered Cliff Palace high on a canyon wall in the Mesa Verde area of southwestern Colorado. This silent, spectacular, many-roomed dwelling, protected by an overhanging cave and the arid climate of the Southwest, had survived almost undisturbed for seven centuries. On the same day, in a nearby canyon, they discovered another large cliff dwelling they named Spruce Tree House. Neither the walls nor the contents of these ruins were to remain intact for long. Richard Wetherill and his brother, Alfred, were soon digging in the rooms. Joined at various times by three other brothers—John, Clayton, and Wynn—they excavated large quantities of decorated pottery, curious implements of stone, bone, and wood, ancient skulls, and other intriguing objects. The Wetherills sold part of their finds to the Historical Society of Colorado but kept a still larger collection.[29]

Word of these spectacular discoveries spread rapidly in America and abroad. Among those whose exploring instincts were aroused was Gustav Nordenskjold, son of Nils A. E. Nordenskjold, the famous Swedish geologist and Arctic explorer. In 1891, when he was twenty-three years old, he determined to see the Mesa Verde country for himself. Arriving in Colorado, he made the Wetherill ranch his headquarters, and with the constant help of Richard and Alfred Wetherill and their workmen, and needing no one's permission, he explored and excavated in Cliff Palace and many other ruins throughout the summer. He took a large collection of prehistoric objects back to Stockholm and in 1893 published a popularly written, handsomely illustrated account of his investigations called *The*

Cliff Dwellers of the Mesa Verde.[30] Nordenskjold's expedition and the loss of a large and valuable collection aroused both admiration and deep resentment among American archaeologists and provided strong arguments in Congress for protective legislation.

The practice of indiscriminate digging went on for years. In 1909, Superintendent Hans Randolph of Mesa Verde National Park described the cumulative vandalism at Cliff Palace (not added to the park until 1913) in these words:

> Probably no cliff dwelling in the Southwest has been more thoroughly dug over in search of pottery and other objects for commercial purposes than Cliff Palace. Parties of "curio seekers" camped on the ruin for several winters, and it is reported that many hundred specimens therefrom have been carried down the mesa and sold to private individuals. Some of these objects are now in museums, but many are forever lost to science. In order to secure this valuable archaeological material, walls were broken down with giant powder often simply to let light into the darker rooms; floors were invariably opened and buried kivas mutilated. To facilitate this work and get rid of the dust, great openings were broken through the five walls which form the front of the ruin. Beams were used for firewood to so great an extent that not a single roof now remains. This work of destruction, added to that resulting from erosion due to rain, left Cliff Palace in a sad condition.[31]

The vandalism so conspicuously illustrated at Mesa Verde spread all over the Southwest, to small ruins and large, in caves and in the open. By the mid-1890s, it was flourishing widely, and a note of alarm began to appear in the writings of professionals working in the field. as is evident in the plea for protective legislation published by J. Walter Fewkes in the *American Anthropologist* for August 1896:

> If this destruction of the cliff-houses of New Mexico, Colorado, and Arizona goes on at the same rate in the next fifty years that it has in the past, these unique dwellings will be practically destroyed, and unless laws are enacted, either by states or by the general government, for their protection, at the close of the twentieth century many of the most interesting monuments of the prehistoric peoples of our Southwest will be little more than mounds of debris at the bases of the cliffs.... Students who follow us, when these cliff-houses have all disappeared and their

instructive objects [been] scattered by the greed of traders, will wonder at our indifference and designate our negligence by its proper name. It would be wise legislation to prevent this vandalism as much as possible and good science to put all excavation of ruins in trained hands.[32]

As early as 1889 the demand for Southwestern antiquities had become so great that forgeries were common. In that year, W. H. Holmes, later chief of the Bureau of American Ethnology, commented on the debasement of Pueblo art. He noted that terra-cotta figurines were being sold in the Pueblo towns of New Mexico "rudely made from clay, not after aboriginal models, but from the suggestions of whites." It was annoying to museum curators to have such objects donated by persons who bought them in good faith, at a good price, believing them to be antiques and who expected them to be cherished and exhibited. "The country is flooded," Holmes said, "with cheap, and scientifically speaking, worthless earthenware made by the Pueblo Indians to supply the tourist trade."[33]

When extensive ruins were found by ranchers on public land that was still open to settlement, applications for homesteads were sometimes filled solely to acquire the ruins, with no intention of practicing agriculture or making improvements. Preservationists charged that such entries were an abuse of the land and fraudulent. In the 1890s, Richard Wetherill, the discoverer of Cliff Palace at Mesa Verde, filed an entry on the great Pueblo Bonito ruin in Chaco Canyon, near Farmington, New Mexico. His unperfected claim on a major ruin became a center of controversy until 1904, when the land was finally withdrawn by the General Land Office from sale or entry, and excavations then in progress were halted.[34]

The responsibility for such indiscriminate pot-hunting and abuse of the homestead laws cannot be put solely onto the shoulders of cowboys and ranchers, whose modest schooling and outdoor life hardly embraced scientific archaeology. The principal demand for authentic prehistoric objects came from private collectors, exhibitors, and museum curators in the East and in Europe. Sometimes handsome objects were purchased by important institutions and not too many questions asked. Even some well-financed and widely publicized expeditions did not escape criticism.

A case in point—and perhaps the most famous case of alleged pot-hunting—was the Hyde Expedition to Chaco Canyon. Here were not merely one or two ancient structures, but the ruins of a dozen great prehistoric communal dwellings together with hundreds of smaller archaeological sites, many of them, with good reason, believed exceptionally rich in artifacts. This extraordinary concentration of ruins had been known since 1849, but it was Richard Wetherill who stimulated the first extensive excavations. Following a visit to the canyon in 1895, he proposed to B. Talbot Hyde and Frederick E. Hyde, Jr., wealthy philanthropists and collectors from New York City, that they sponsor excavations in the Chaco Canyon ruins. The Hydes sought advice from Putnam of Harvard, who agreed to serve as scientific director, and from the American Museum of Natural History, which agreed to accept collections of artifacts. The Hyde Exploring Expedition was formed in 1896. Its principal aim was the exploration of Pueblo Bonito, the most imposing of all the Chaco Canyon ruins, a great semi-circular stone structure covering more than three acres which at its peak of development in the 12th century contained over 800 rooms in an arrangement at least five stories high. Professor Putnam designated George Pepper, one of his students, as field director, and Richard Wetherill as excavation foreman. The digging of Pueblo Bonito proceeded under these arrangements during the summers of the period 1896–1899. Some 198 rooms and kivas were excavated and most of the artifacts, including several complete rooms, were donated by the Hydes to the American Museum of Natural History.[35]

As reports of the extent and nature of these excavations reached the state capital of Santa Fe, and were communicated to New York and Boston, concern developed among interested archaeologists and laymen that irreplaceable antiquities of Chaco Canyon were quite possibly being unscientifically pot-hunted and certainly were being taken out of New Mexico. On November 17, 1900, the Santa Fe Archaeological Society sent a resolution to Secretary of the Interior Ethan Allen Hitchcock urging him to take action to protect the antiquities of Chaco Canyon. An investigation had already been made by the General Land Office, but now Special Agent S. J. Holsinger was assigned to make another and more thorough one. In June 1901 he reported that Richard Wetherill and his brothers had removed entire prehistoric timbers from Pueblo Bonito, dismantled and shipped complete rooms to the American Museum of Natural History, and probably had excavated other prehistoric objects and sold them wherever they could find a market. Holsinger recommended withdrawal of forty townships from settlement preparatory to making Chaco Canyon a national park. Meanwhile, Wetherill had filed his formal homestead claim on the section of Chaco Canyon that included Pueblo Bonito and two other major ruins, Chettro Kettle and Pueblo del Arroyo. This situation, added to numerous additional instances of known or alleged pot-hunting and vandalism, hastened the movement for federal administrative and legislative action to protect antiquities on the public lands.[36]

The Role of the General Land Office, 1891–1906

Until the Antiquities Act was passed in 1906, the chief weapon available to the federal government for protecting antiquities on public land was the power to withdraw specific tracts from sale or entry for a temporary period. As the problem of protection grew and as complaints reached the General Land Office in steadily increasing numbers, this power was exercised more and more frequently. For example, in 1900 the General Land Office withdrew a large area around Frijoles Canyon in northern New Mexico pending a determination of the advisability of setting the region apart as a national park.[37] About this time a movement was started in Denver, Colorado, to save the celebrated cliff dwellings of Mesa Verde as a national park. Pending a determination, the General Land Office withdrew an extensive part of the Mesa Verde area.[38] And in April 1905, Secretary of the Interior Hitchcock finally withdrew those critical portions of the lands in Chaco Canyon which Special Agent Holsinger had recommended in 1901 be protected (Figure 1.3).[39] These important withdrawals were made during the tenures of two enlightened commissioners of the General Land Office: Binger Hermann and W. A. Richards. The total effect of the withdrawals, along with other measures, was considerable.

Yet the problem remained of how to permanently protect the sites. The solution, as it happened, was modeled on recently granted presidential authority to declare timber reserves. Beginning in 1891, timber resources on the public lands benefited from an amendment to the General Land Revision Act that granted the president authority to create permanent forest reserves by executive proclamation. By 1901, under this authority, 41 forest reserves had been set aside containing over 48 million acres. In his first year as President, Theodore Roosevelt created 13 new forests containing more than 15 million additional acres.[40] Until 1905 these forest reservations were administered by the General Land Office. When the problem of permanently protecting selected prehistoric ruins on the public lands

Figure 1.3. Restoration efforts at Chaco Canyon, ca. early 1900s. The area had been withdrawn from homestead claims by the secretary of the interior in 1905 and was proclaimed a national monument by Theodore Roosevelt in 1907. Unattributed photograph, courtesy of National Park Service Historic Photo Collection, Harpers Ferry Center.

arose, it was natural for officials of this agency, who were familiar with timber protection procedures, to propose that the president be granted similar authority to create archaeological reservations, citing congressional authority for forest reservations as a precedent.

But in their view the authority should go further than antiquities and include permanent protection of scenic and scientific resources on public lands as well. Interesting discoveries were constantly being made of caves, craters, mineral springs, unusual geological formations, and other scientific features that appeared to merit special protection by the nation. Bill after bill was introduced in Congress to set aside one or another such area as a public reservation, to be permanently protected for the public benefit. Because no other designation seemed as appropriate, these proposals usually called for establishing the feature as a national park. The General Land Office made investigations of many such proposals. From 1900 to 1906 Commissioners Hermann and Richards consistently recommended general legislation to authorize the president to establish prehistoric and scientific resources on the public lands as national parks.[41] Their actions proved to be the final prelude to the passage of the Antiquities Act.

The Final Push, 1899–1906

Late in 1899 the American Association for the Advancement of Science established a committee to promote a bill in Congress for the permanent preservation of aboriginal antiquities situated on federal lands.[42] The same year the Archaeological Institute of America set up a Standing Committee on American Archaeology, and soon the two committees agreed to combine their efforts.[43]

They began by drafting a bill authorizing the president to "set apart and reserve for use as public parks on reservations, in the same manner as now provided by law for forestry reservations, any public lands upon which are monuments, cliff-dwellings, cemeteries, graves, mounds, forts, or any other work of prehistoric, primitive, or aboriginal man, and also any natural formation of scientific or scenic value of interest, or natural wonder or curiosity, together with such additional area of land surrounding or adjoining the same, as he may deem necessary for the proper preservation and subsequent investigation of said prehistoric work or remains."[44] This is the first link between historic and natural areas in the history of federal preservation legislation. In an explanation accompanying the bill, much emphasis was placed on the sharp contrast between the excellent protection afforded antiquities by most European governments and the almost total absence of such protection in the United States. After some revision, the bill was introduced into the House of Representatives in February 1900.

Now that the antiquities issue had been raised in Congress, competing viewpoints were quickly made known, and within a month two other bills of lesser scope were introduced. All three were referred for consideration to the House Committee on the Public Lands, whose chairman was Representative John F. Lacey of Iowa. He sent them to Secretary of the Interior Hitchcock, who promptly referred them to GLO Commissioner Hermann. He found all three of the pending bills unsatisfactory, and instead proposed a substitute bill. For the next six years, with some modifications, this bill "to establish and administer national parks, and for other purposes" embodied the views of the Department of the Interior on the form antiquities legislation should take. Its first section authorized the president to reserve tracts of public land because of "their scenic beauty, natural wonders or curiosities, ancient ruins or relics, or other objects of scientific or historic interest" and provided "that such reservations shall be known as national parks and shall be under the exclusive control of the Secretary of the Interior, who is hereby empowered to prescribe such rules and regulations and establish such services as he shall deem necessary for the care and management of the same." In this language, one may perhaps discern one of the first expressions of the idea of a National Park Service. The Department of the Interior was plainly seeking broad discretionary authority for the president to reserve a wide range of resources for public use. Historic as well as scenic and scientific resources, it has been well pointed out, were among those added to prehistoric resources for permanent protection.[45]

Interior's proposed bill met with a cool response from the House Committee on Public Lands. The reluctance of the members of the Public Lands Committee, most of them from western public lands states, to grant general authority to the executive branch to create new national parks is understandable in the light of their past experience with the timber reservations act of 1891 and their forebodings of what was still to come. In response, a bill that represented the combined views of the full Committee on Public Lands was introduced. It authorized reservations not to exceed 320 acres, and only in Wyoming, Colorado, New Mexico, and Arizona.[46] Congress, however, took no action on this or any of the other bills. Almost four years were to pass before another set of bills was introduced in Congress, and these too failed, largely because of disagreements between the Department of the Interior and the Smithsonian Institution over who would have authority over the reservations to be created.

This, then, was how matters stood in 1904: there was broad agreement on the need for some kind of federal protection of antiquities and natural wonders, but none on which department was to be in charge. Surveying the bureaucratic impasse, Commissioner Richards of the General Land Office decided that the situation required a new review of the entire antiquities preservation problem on federal lands. To perform this task he turned to Edgar Lee Hewett, a talented young archaeologist with a varied practical background that enabled him to gain alike the confidence of members of Congress, bureau chiefs, staffs of universities and research institutions, and members of professional societies. Hewett immediately launched the first comprehensive review of all the Indian antiquities located on federal lands in four key states. Based on his own observations and those of leading archaeologists, he sketched the characteristics of each district and went on to describe many of the individual ruins, among them the proposed Pajarito National Park (eventually established as Bandelier National Monument), Pecos, Gran Quivira, Aztec, Mesa Verde, Chaco Canyon, Canyon de Chelly, Walnut Canyon, Petrified Forest, El Morro (or Inscription Rock), Montezuma Castle, Casa Grande, and the ruins along the Gila River.[47] Better than any other single document, Hewett's memorandum clearly foreshadowed, in remarkable detail, the system of archaeological national monuments established in the Southwest following passage of the Antiquities Act.

Hewett's political challenge was to mediate the turf war between Interior and the Smithsonian, a task that was further complicated in 1905 when Gifford Pinchot, the chief of the Bureau of Forestry in the Department of Agriculture, succeeded in getting the existing forest reserves transferred from the General Land Office in the Department of the Interior to his own bureau. Nonetheless, Hewett made progress where others had not. In late 1905 and early 1906, he crafted a bill that reconciled the competing bureaucratic interests and succeeded in getting support from a critical figure: Representative Lacey, chair of the House Committee on Public Lands, who sponsored the legislation. These two men did their jobs so well that the House bill and its Senate companion sailed through virtually unchanged, and on June 8, 1906, the "Act for the Preservation of American Antiquities" was signed into law by President Theodore Roosevelt.

The respective roles of these three key figures—Hewett, Lacey, and Roosevelt—are the subject of the next three chapters, adding depth to this sketch of the birth of the Antiquities Act. It remains here to point out that the Act took care of six important points not adequately covered in any previous proposal.

First, the provisions were made applicable to antiquities situated on any "lands owned or controlled by the Government of the United States." Previous bills applied only to unassigned public lands, leaving their applicability to forest reserves, Indian lands, and military reservations uncertain. Second, the authority of the president to establish public reservations was made to include "historic landmarks, historic and prehistoric structures, and other objects of historic or scientific interest." Some earlier versions had been limited to historic and prehistoric antiquities and made no provision for protecting natural areas. At some point in his discussions with government departments, Hewett was persuaded, probably by officials of the Interior Department, to broaden his draft to include the phrase "other objects of historic or scientific interest." As it later turned out, the single word "scientific" in the Antiquities Act proved sufficient basis to establish dozens of national monuments preserving many kinds of natural areas.

Third, the president's discretion to proclaim national monuments was not limited to a small area of 320 or 640 acres, but rather was "confined to the smallest area compatible with the proper care and management of the objects to be protected." This flexible provision permitting the president to establish larger areas if justifiable was accepted by western members of Congress and proved vital to successful administration of the Act. Fourth, the bill introduced the term "national monument" into the language of conservation. Fifth, the bill authorized the secretary of the interior to accept the donation of lands in private ownership on which were situated historic landmarks, historic and prehistoric structures, and other objects of historic or scientific interest. This authority has been utilized many times since. Lastly, after investing the secretaries of interior, war, and agriculture with authority to grant excavation permits, the bill provided that they make and publish "uniform rules and regulations" to carry out the law's provisions. It seems likely that it was informally understood all around that if the bill passed, the role of the Smithsonian Institution as scientific advisor would be protected and clearly set forth in the uniform rules and regulations, making its definition in the law unnecessary.[48] This may have avoided another controversy over authority.

A whole generation of dedicated effort by scholars, citizens, and members of Congress, which had begun in 1879, culminated in 1906 with the passage of the Antiquities Act. More important, this generation, through its explorations, publications, exhibits, and other activities, awakened the American people to a lasting consciousness of the value of American antiquities, prehistoric and historic. This public understanding, achieved only after persistent effort in the face of much ignorance, vandalism, and indifference, was a necessary foundation for many subsequent conservation achievements.

Editors' note: This chapter is an abridgment of Lee's pioneering administrative history of the Antiquties Act (Lee 1970), incorporating minor editoral corrections made when the work was republished, first in 2000 in The Journal of the Southwest *and, more recently, on-line by the NPS Office of Archeology* (www.cr.nps.gov/archeology/PUBS/LEE/ Index.htm).

Notes

1. Hellman 1967, 105–106.
2. Putnam et al. 1879.
3. Dixon 1928, 15:276–278.
4. Hough 1908, 664.
5. *American Anthropologist* 1, 382–386.
6. Moore 1928, 13:569–572.
7. Norton et al. 1885, 32.
8. Norton et al. 1885, 32.
9. Norton et al. 1885, 33.
10. Lange and Riley 1966, 18.
11. Norton et al. 1885, 34.
12. Bandelier 1883, 1.
13. Bandelier 1883, 42.
14. Johnson 1928, 20:210–211.
15. *Congressional Record,* 47th Cong., 1st Sess. (1882), 3777.
16. *Congressional Record,* 47th Cong., 1st Sess. (1882), 3777. (Statement of Senator Preston H. Plumb, Kansas, chair of the Committee on Public Lands.)
17. "The Serpent Mound, Adams County, Ohio," an unsigned article in *Records of the Past* 5 (1906), 119–128. With other leading anthropologists, Putnam served as a consulting editor of this forgotten periodical after 1905.
18. Johnson 1928, 8:518–519.
19. Van Valkenburgh 1962, 11. This is a very informative article in the journal of the Arizona Archaeological and Historical Society.
20. Van Valkenburgh 1962, 11.
21. *Memorial of Oliver Ames, John G. Whittier, Mary Hemenway, and Others, Praying Legislation for the Protection from Destruction of the Ancient Ruin of the Temple of Casa Grande, Situated in Pinal County, near Florence, Arizona,* Senate Miscellaneous Document no. 80, 50th Cong., 2d Sess. (1889).
22. 25 Stat. 961.
23. Sullivan 1947, 140.
24. *Preservation of American Antiquities,* House Report no. 2224, 59th Cong., 1st Sess., 2.
25. Stocking 1960, 1–17. See also an unsigned article in *American Anthropologist,* n.s., 5 (1903), 178–192.

26. See an unsigned article, "Recent Progress in Anthropology," *American Anthropologist,* n.s., 8 (1906), 504; and Hewett 1906, 109–114.

27. Haynes 1900, 19. See also Hough 1893, 271–272.

28. Haynes 1900, 20–21.

29. Nordenskjold 1893, 12.

30. Nordenskjold 1893, chaps. 1 and 2.

31. Ise 1961, 145, quoting from the annual report of the secretary of the interior for 1909, 486.

32. J. Walter Fewkes, "Two Ruins Recently Discovered in the Red Rock Country, Arizona," *American Anthropologist* 9 (1896), 269–270. Fewkes 1896, 269–270.

33. Holmes 1889, 320.

34. Ise 1961, 145, quoting a letter from Jesse L. Nusbaum to Floyd E. Dotson, March 7, 1956.

35. Pierson 1956, 48–55.

36. Bond 1912, 85–86.

37. *Cliff Dwellers' National Park,* House Report no. 2427, 56th Cong., 2d Sess., 146.

38. Hewett 1904a, 723.

39. Pierson 1956, 49–54.

40. Hays 1959, 47.

41. *Annual Report of the Commissioner of the General Land Office for 1901,* 154; for 1902, 115–117; for 1904, 322–323; for 1905, 40; and for 1906, 47–48. These reports are quoted in Claus 1945.

42. AAAS 1900, xii.

43. *American Journal of Archaeology,* 2nd ser., 3 (1899), 665: see also vol. 6, Supplement (1902); Thomas Wilson to Walter Hough, March 31, 1900, copy in files of Office of Archeology and Historic Preservation, National Park Service, Washington, D.C.

44. Undated, unsigned document entitled "A Bill for the Preservation of Prehistoric Monuments, Ruins, and Objects, and to Prevent their Counterfeiting, and for Other Purposes." Ten pages including explanation of bill. On file at the Office of Archeology and Historic Preservation, National Park Service, Washington, DC.

45. Claus 1945, 5; Rogers 1958, vol. 4, Appendix A (for H.R. 11021); McDermott 1966, 11.

46. Rogers 1958, vol. 4, Appendix A (for H.R. 10451).

47. Hewett's memorandum was published in the *General Land Office Circular Relating to Historic and Prehistoric Ruins of the Southwest and their Preservation* (Hewett 1904b). It also appears as an appendix to Lacey's 1905 report, *Prehistoric Ruins on the Public Lands.* Lacey published it again in March 1906 as part of another report from his committee.

48. Hewett 1906, 110–112.

2

Edgar Lee Hewett and
the Politics of Archaeology

Raymond Harris Thompson

A MAJOR BUT CONTROVERSIAL FIGURE in the history of American archaeology, Edgar Lee Hewett played a critical role in the passage of the Antiquities Act of 1906.[1] Ronald Freeman Lee credits Hewett's "unusual combination of western background, farming and teaching experience, first-hand knowledge of ancient ruins on federal lands in the Southwest, and experience as an archaeologist and administrator,"[2] and Hal Rothman notes that "Hewett succeeded when other more prominent professionals had failed."[3] Hewett brought to the task some special personal qualities: prodigious energy and the ability to use it productively, well-developed organizational skills, a superb sense of timing, an ability to identify quickly and define clearly the key elements in a problem, total but diplomatic perseverance in the pursuit of a goal, and a keen insight into the nature of the human condition. Moreover, Hewett realized more than any of his contemporaries that the lengthy battle for the protection of antiquities was not a scientific problem, but a political one.

From the very beginning, the efforts to preserve the nation's archaeological resources embraced two approaches that were both complementary and competitive. On the one hand, there was a desire to protect all the ruins on federal land, the "general bill" approach, and on the other, the temptation to save a few spectacular places, the "national park" approach. The tension created by these seemingly opposite thrusts helped to prolong the campaign for antiquities legislation. At the same time, these approaches were potentially compatible. Part of Hewett's success stems from his recognition and exploitation of that potential. Hewett began his combined archaeological and political career promoting a proposed

Pajarito Park in New Mexico. He put that experience to good use working for the passage of the Antiquities Act and further demonstrated his political skills by brokering the creation of Mesa Verde National Park.

Hewett's career was a serendipitous result of his marriage in 1891 to Cora Whitford, who shared his love of horses and the outdoors.[4] They spent the summer vacations from his teaching positions at Florence and Greeley in Colorado camping all along the front range of the Rocky Mountains. Unfortunately, not long after they were married Cora became "frail," a turn-of-the-century euphemism for someone with tuberculosis. Her doctor recommended that they spend their summers in the warm, dry climate of New Mexico. The Hewetts followed that advice, headquartering in Santa Fe, but spending most of their time exploring and camping on the Pajarito Plateau west of the city. By 1896, Hewett had moved beyond visiting and camping and began carrying out archaeological survey and mapping. He soon became deeply attached to the Pajarito region both professionally and emotionally and very early got the idea that the entire region should be designated a national park.

In 1898, Hewett was appointed to a five-year term as the first president of the new Normal University (now New Mexico Highlands University) in Las Vegas (Figure 2.1) at the recommendation of Frank Springer, a prominent New Mexican lawyer and a leading authority on crinoids, who became Hewett's lifelong friend and supporter. Hewett developed a curriculum that included a good deal of anthropology and began to involve his students in his summer explorations. In 1899, he stimulated the General Land Office to investigate the park potential of the Pajarito region. In 1900, Land Office Commissioner Binger Hermann withdrew 153,000 acres for a proposed Pajarito National Park. Secretary of the Interior Ethan Allen Hitchcock then submitted proposed legislation for the park to Congressman John Fletcher Lacey, chairman of the Committee on Public Lands of the House. Although Lacey introduced the bill in January 1901, no further progress was made.

By this time Hewett's relationship with Congressman Lacey, which began sometime in 1900, was well established. In order to promote the Pajarito Park bill, Hewett invited Lacey to visit the Southwest, and during a trip in August 1902 Hewett and Lacey developed a lasting relationship of mutual respect and friendship.[5]

However, New Mexico Territorial Governor Miguel Antonio Otero disapproved of Hewett's approach to education, considered

Figure 2.1. Edgar Lee Hewett in 1898, when he was the first president of New Mexico Normal University. Unattributed photograph courtesy of Palace of the Governors (MNM/DCA), negative no. 7324.

his summer archaeology trips a waste of time, and agreed with those who were appalled at the idea of withdrawing huge tracts of land from potential private use. Otero's supporters on the Normal University's Board of Regents did not renew Hewett's appointment as president in 1903. Not only was Hewett unemployed, but his dreams of a Pajarito Park soon faded away.

In 1904, many acres of timber land were removed from the area proposed for Pajarito Park and added to the proposed Rio Jemez Forest Reserve (now Santa Fe National Forest), reducing the park to about a quarter of its originally proposed size. In July 1905, President Theodore Roosevelt gave even more land slated for Pajarito Park to Santa Clara Pueblo. A greatly amended park bill was introduced, and Lacey reported it favorably, but no further action was taken. Although Hewett lost the battle for Pajarito Park, he established solid working relations with Congress and the Department of the Interior, gained professional credibility, and learned a lot about the political process. In many ways this early work on the Pajarito Plateau was a defining experience for Hewett. He returned to those early haunts physically, intellectually, and emotionally throughout his life.

These setbacks caused him to re-evaluate his own goals. He found that he was now much more interested in archaeology than in pedagogy and realized that he would need some formal training to facilitate this career shift. During the late nineteenth and early twentieth centuries, many Americans went to European universities for their doctorates. Hewett went to Switzerland to attend the University of Geneva (from which he would receive a doctorate in 1908). While he was busy arranging further education in Switzerland, he was also anxious to find a source of income that would enable him to finish his fieldwork on the Pajarito Plateau and prepare an exhaustive report on it.

When Hewett returned from Europe in August 1904, his friends in Washington, especially William Henry Holmes, the chief of the Bureau of American Ethnology (BAE), had not only arranged such support for him, but also other responsibilities that went well beyond the completion of his Pajarito research. His employment under these conditions was evidence of the emergence of a new political coalition for archaeological conservation that Charles Fletcher Lummis called the "antiquities bill alliance."[6] The Department of the Interior, the Smithsonian Institution, and the archaeological community were beginning to pay attention to the basic principles of the political process.

When William Afton Richards became the Land Office commissioner in 1903, he noted that repeated requests for antiquities legislation were not getting the desired results, because Congress was reluctant to choose between competing bills of similar intent but involving conflicting approaches. He realized that he had to become more proactive and that he needed the advice of credible experts outside of the General Land Office.

When Hewett returned from Europe, Richards requested that he prepare a report on the archaeological resources in the Southwest. Six weeks later, on September 3, 1904, Hewett submitted his cele-brated *Memorandum Concerning the Historic and Prehistoric Ruins of Arizona, New Mexico, Colorado and Utah, and Their Preservation.*[7] He also provided Richards with an assessment of the various bills then before Congress. Hewett's *Memorandum* was given wide distribution with the financial assistance of the Committee on American Archae-ology of the Archaeological Institute of America (AIA). The pam-phlet printed with this subvention included illustrations of ruins and letters from officials of several government agencies document-ing steps taken to protect ruins, demonstrating that at least part of the solution to the archaeological problem was already being carried out successfully by Executive agencies. Important as Hewett's *Memorandum* was, it had its limitations. It was a purposely brief administrative document designed to highlight the magnitude of the problem, to support the preservation efforts of the General Land Office, and to urge the Congress to take action. It did not include detailed definitions and thorough discussions of the problems. Therefore, Hewett published almost immediately a more extended treatment of the material in the *Memorandum* in a paper, "General View of the Archaeology of the Pueblo Region."[8]

Although Hewett spent the summer of 1905 completing his field research on the Pajarito Plateau, he continued to advise Richards and Holmes and to work with Congress and the arch-aeological community. By 1905, when he was appointed to the American Anthropological Association (AAA) Committee on the Preservation of American Antiquities, chaired by Holmes, he was well aware of the unproductive bickering and competitiveness among the various proponents of archaeological legislation that had caused several previous bills to fail. As this committee and a similar one from the AIA began to work together to try to rescue the disas-ter of the previous session of Congress, Hewett quietly moved into a leadership position. He became secretary of the combined com-mittee effort and the informal leader of the "antiquities bill alliance." He was an obvious choice because he had been in Europe during the earlier battles and he had no emotional, historical, polit-ical, or institutional commitments to any of the pending bills. The joint AIA–AAA committee prepared new draft legislation that was submitted to Congressman Lacey on January 16, 1905, but Congress adjourned before it could be brought to a vote. In brokering the new draft Hewett had demonstrated that proposed legislation could be gradually adapted to shifts in thinking and to changing political climates, instead of being abandoned and replaced by new and different bills promoting various special interests. Nevertheless, the unwillingness of the various groups to work together continued to be the primary road block. The Department of the Interior still favored the park approach, while Hewett and the archaeological community were increasingly more interested in the protection of archaeological sites.

It was clear that a new approach was needed. However, no bill can survive the political process if all it does is to declare that a particular goal is both good and noble. It appears that advice from Lacey was critical at this stage of the campaign. A successful veteran of congressional battles who was approaching the end of his long political career, Lacey fully understood that lawmakers normally try to solve problems rather than state policies. For example, his landmark 1900 wildlife act (still known informally as the "Lacey Act") did not declare that the federal government ought to protect birds and game, for that responsibility belonged to the states. However, interstate commerce is the responsibility of the federal government, so Lacey could protect birds and game indirectly by prohibiting interstate (and international) transport of wild birds and game in violation of state law. By passing that bill, Congress indirectly established a federal responsibility for wildlife, and from that has come the nation's wildlife protection policy.

Hewett followed Lacey's example and employed the indirect technique. He did not ask Congress to make the federal government responsible for protecting sites on federal land by declaration of that abstract principle. Rather, his draft implied that responsibility by making it illegal for anyone to damage ruins on federal land. Such a prohibition is something that every law-abiding citizen can comprehend. It is difficult to object to such a prohibition for it is, after all, against the law to damage, destroy, or steal the property of others. Hewett developed a simple and non-threatening way to establish indirectly the principle that the federal government must safeguard the archaeological sites on its lands.

At the same time, there was widespread recognition that there were a few unique places that were so spectacular that they deserved special treatment and permanent protection. It was this type of site that the General Land Office had sought to protect by its temporary withdrawal policy. However, Congress had displayed little enthusiasm for establishing national parks. Therefore, Section Two of Hewett's draft authorized the president to set aside the unique places as national monuments. Hewett made no mention of parks in his draft, which made his wording less threatening than earlier efforts to combine the general and the park approaches. Moreover, by placing the national monument idea in Section Two he avoided having land withdrawal appear in the first sentence or in the title of his draft. Nor did he compare his proposed monument approach with the existing authority to create forest reserves, a feature of earlier drafts that was offensive to many westerners.

Hewett, with his western experience, was for a long time almost alone in recognizing both the nature of the federal landholdings and the importance of the land-managing agencies.[9] Early on he noted that while "public land" and "public domain" were used in the vernacular to refer to government land, the legal system restricted the meaning of those terms to the unappropriated lands available for entry under the Homestead and other acts. Indian reservations, forest reserves, and military establishments were not considered "public lands." To solve this problem, Hewett inserted the phrase "lands owned or controlled by the Government of the United States" in Section One of his draft. He also emphasized the role of the land-managing agencies as custodians of the ruins on their lands. Hewett placed the responsibility for ruins on the land managers, simplified the role of government, and alleviated some of the fears of academic archaeologists by removing all reference to the Smithsonian and the BAE, which were not land-management agencies.

One of the reasons for protecting the ruins was to preserve their educational value. It was expected that information about them would be recovered by properly qualified professionals. These thoughts were reflective of the Progressive Era philosophy that the nation's resources should be centrally managed by competent specialists for the good of the country as a whole. Section Three of Hewett's draft followed similar sections of earlier bills in authorizing the issuance of excavation permits to institutionally based archaeologists. The permits were to be issued by the same land-managing agencies that were responsible for protecting the ruins from the vandalism prohibited in Section One. These agencies would also develop and administer the rules and regulations called for in Section Four of Hewett's draft, because he had seen how bickering over procedural details had hindered earlier attempts to pass antiquities legislation.

The issuing of permits under controlled conditions protected the research interests of the archaeological community, but academic archaeologists were anxious to exercise control over those conditions and were opposed to giving permitting authority to any government official.[10] Frederic Ward Putnam at Harvard, Franz Boas at Columbia, and others lobbied against giving any control over either permits or research to federal bureaucrats, especially those in the Smithsonian Institution. Their concern stemmed from the failure of the university-based scholars to recognize that the Smithsonian was a unique governmental body and not just another competing research and collecting institution that happened to be in Washington. Putnam and Boas employed very different lobbying techniques. Putnam, following an old tradition established in the 1880s when New England preservationists proposed the protection of the Casa Grande Ruin in Arizona, used a well-established old boy network and wrote to Senator George Frisbie Hoar with a copy to Lacey.[11] Expecting favorable action, Putnam did not follow up with arguments to support his request. Boas acted similarly but used a more authoritarian and hierarchical approach probably derived from his German upbringing. He simply wrote to his superior, President Nicholas Murray Butler of Columbia University, expecting him to make the case to Congress.[12] Neither approach recognized the changing nature of the political process or the growing political influence of the western region of the country. The academics, who preferred control by a non-governmental commission of academic archaeologists (that is, themselves) failed to distinguish between the conduct of research on federal land and the management of that land and its resources.

Hewett attended the joint annual meeting of the AIA and AAA in Ithaca, New York, in late December 1905, where he presented a paper on the progress of the "antiquities bill alliance." He had written to Holmes before the meeting: "It is exceedingly important that all the interested parties should be of one mind with reference to the proposed legislation and I am increasingly hopeful that this may be brought about at the Ithaca meeting."[13] That is exactly what happened. He gave his paper on December 28 and that evening at a joint business meeting, the two professional groups unanimously accepted his draft and also adopted a resolution calling for the establishment of Mesa Verde National Park. Hewett had successfully transformed the earlier AIA–AAA draft into an entirely new bill that satisfied both the governmental agencies and the professional community.

Hewett submitted the approved draft to Lacey, who introduced it into the House on January 9, 1906. At Lacey's request, Thomas MacDonald Patterson of Colorado introduced it in the Senate. Patterson was also the Senate sponsor of the Mesa Verde Park bill. Lacey had been embarrassed the year before when several archaeologists unsuccessfully brought pressure on the autocratic speaker of the House, Joseph Gurney Cannon of Illinois, to reverse his decision not to bring the pending antiquities legislation to the floor during the last few days of the previous Congress. Hoping this time to avoid outside interference in the legislative process, Lacey let Hewett know that further letter writing to him and to the speaker was unnecessary. Clearly, Lacey had everything under control and wanted to allow what Hewett called "the great machinery of Congress" to do its work. Throughout the several months before the bill passed, Lacey reassured Hewett periodically and Hewett passed that encouragement on to others. In the end, both houses of Congress passed his draft Antiquities Act without changing a word, the Senate on May 24 and the House on June 5. It was signed by President Roosevelt on June 8, 1906.

In the meantime, a separate bill to create Mesa Verde National Park, introduced by Congressman Herschel Millard Hogg from Telluride, Colorado, was in trouble. It was not clear where the great cliff dwellings were in relation to the southern boundary of the proposed park except that some of the most spectacular ones were known to be on the Ute Indian Reservation. Congress was typically unwilling to consider withdrawal of land without established boundaries. In an effort to resolve the problem, Assistant Secretary of the Interior Thomas Ryan, Land Commissioner Richards, and BAE Chief Holmes arranged to have Hewett assist in a resurvey of the boundary between the proposed park and the Ute Reservation. The survey contract had been awarded to George Mills, one of Hewett's friends from Mancos, Colorado, who had done the previous survey by means of triangulation only. The resurvey was to follow the boundary on the ground, with Hewett locating and identifying the ruins to be included.

Hewett, however, recognized that the real problem was not the lack of good survey information. The survey that Mills and he carried out basically confirmed the earlier one. The problem stemmed from the fact that the major cliff dwellings, such as Cliff Palace, were on Indian land and not inside the proposed park boundaries. Combining his political acumen with the fact that the federal government controlled unpatented Indian land, Hewett drafted an amendment to Hogg's bill that placed all ruins within five miles of the park boundary under the control of park authorities. His amendment was accepted by the Commissioner of Indian Affairs, Francis Ellington Leupp, and the House Committee on Public Lands. The amended Mesa Verde bill passed and was signed by President Roosevelt on June 29, just three weeks after the Antiquities Act.

Ironically, Hewett was not even in the country for either of these triumphs, for in the meantime he had begun a lengthy field trip into Mexico. While Hewett was in the field, Lacey and Holmes both relayed the good news to him. He responded from his camp on the headwaters of the Yaqui River in eastern Sonora, "*estoy muy contento.*"[14] The passage of the Antiquities Act was testimony to the important role that the "antiquities bill alliance" played in the political process, but the alliance was successful in large part because of Hewett's unique understanding of the political process and his relationship with Lacey.

Much of the literature on the Antiquities Act appropriately emphasizes the importance of the authority to create national monuments, natural and scenic as well as archaeological and historical, but the primary purpose of the act was to "preserve American antiquities." As Emil Walter Haury has pointed out, "each of the places set aside for its natural wonders ... has its own wealth of ruins and a human story to tell."[15] Protecting archaeological sites was a clearly articulated purpose based on sound principles that have given structure to the development of the nation's archaeological policies ever since.

One of these principles concerns the nature of archaeological evidence. Hewett's approach did not focus on saving artifacts. Rather, he advocated saving the sites that contained both the artifacts and associated information about the past. He described the archaeological record of the Southwest as a "vast treasury of information" and frequently emphasized the value of artifacts in context. The idea that ruins were treasuries of information, rather than rich repositories of loot, resonated well with both political trends and public opinion in the first decade of the twentieth century.

A second principle underlying the Antiquities Act is the assertion of a public interest in the federal ruins and the congressional acceptance of the responsibility to protect the public's interest. This definition of statutory responsibility for the archaeological resources on federal lands is basic to the nation's historic preservation policy. If the ruins belonged to the public, then the government had a duty to protect them. The Antiquities Act forbade not only looting and destruction of the ruins, but also selling the artifacts found in them for commercial and private gain. Archaeological resources, like all other public resources, were to be managed according to the Progressive philosophy that Gifford Pinchot, the first chief of the Forest Service, succinctly described as "the greatest good to the greatest number for the longest time."[16] Hewett clearly intended the Antiquities Act to identify archaeological resources as public property that the government had a duty to protect. Nevertheless, his indirect approach and turn-of-the-century language began to cause problems in prosecuting offenders as the nation's legal systems became more precise. Therefore, when the Archaeological Resources Protection Act was passed in 1979, very explicit language was included to reinforce the already accepted principle that the ruins and their contents belonged to the government, a principle that Hewett had worked so hard to establish.[17]

Because Hewett emphasized the research potential of sites, he recognized a third important principle: once a site has given up its information, it no longer needs to be preserved. His twofold classification of sites included places worthy of becoming national parks and others that should be protected until all information of importance has been recovered. He anticipated the basic ideas behind what later became salvage archaeology and ultimately cultural resource management, because he gave priority to the information in the site rather than to the site itself. This principle has been of inestimable value to archaeology ever since. It has enabled archaeologists to relate in a rational way to economic and political realities, because they do not have to insist on saving "everything." They can focus instead on recovering the information that makes the ruins valuable in the first place.

The most fundamental of these principles is a very simple one: the federal government has a statutory responsibility for the archaeological resources on the land it owns or controls. At first it seemed that the government had only to protect the ruins from the depredations of others. Gradually, however, it became clear that the government's own land-modification activities also threatened the archaeological resources. Responsibility took on new meaning as archaeology was included in the economic development programs of the Great Depression.[18] As in the case of the Antiquities Act, the Executive agencies took the first action, with Congress following up later with statutory support. After the Second World War, more indirect federal actions, such as permits, grants, tax incentives, and loan guarantees, broadened the nature of the federal responsibility even more. Today, the United States of America has expanded upon the principles embedded by Hewett in the Antiquities Act of 1906 to create an effective body of historic preservation law and policy supported by appropriate rules and regulations.

Hewett's role in the passage of the Antiquities Act marks the beginning of his long, influential, and controversial career in Southwestern archaeology, during which he gained both loyal supporters and persistent detractors.[19] Although the controversies that surrounded him in the first half of the twentieth century are still debated today, there can be no doubt that the Antiquities Act was passed 100 years ago because of the political acumen of that astute pioneer lobbyist, Edgar Lee Hewett.

Editors' note: This chapter is a much abbreviated version of Thompson 2000.

Notes

1. Chauvenet 1983; Walter 1947.
2. Lee 1970, 68 [2000, 236].
3. Rothman 1989, 48–49.
4. Ferdon 1993, 12.
5. Lacey, "The Pajarito: An Outing with the Archaeologists," in Pammel 1915, 210.
6. Charles Fletcher Lummis to Thomas Day Seymour, 16 September 1905, AIA Archives.

7. Hewett 1904b.

8. Hewett 1905.

9. Hewett 1905, 593–594.

10. Mark 1980, 78; Seymour to Committee, 15 June 1904, AIA Archives.

11. Frederic Ward Putnam to George Frisbie Hoar and John Fletcher Lacey, 20 April 1904, AIA Archives.

12. Franz Boas to Nicolas Murray Butler, 7 March 1904, AIA Archives.

13. Hewett to William Henry Holmes, 18 December 1905, National Anthropological Archives.

14. Hewett to William Henry Holmes, 3 July 1906, National Anthropological Archives.

15. Haury 1983, 8.

16. Pinchot 1910, 48.

17. Fowler and Malinkey 2005.

18. Fagette 1996; Lyon 1996; Wendorf and Thompson 2002.

19. Fowler 2000, 261–274; Snead 2001.

3

John F. Lacey

Conservation's Public Servant

Rebecca Conard

JOHN LACEY DID NOT HUNT GAME; he did not fish; he did not even hike or watch birds. Yet, in April 1902 the Boone and Crockett Club elected the Republican congressman from Iowa to associate membership.[1] Certainly Lacey understood this to be a gesture of political coziness, but honorary membership in the exclusive club of eastern sportsmen may have been what prompted him to invite Gifford Pinchot, one of the Boone and Crockett inner circle, to accompany him to New Mexico a few months later. At the invitation of Edgar Lee Hewett, he had arranged to visit the cliff dwellings of the Pajarito region. Lacey and Hewett had met in 1900 when Hewett traveled to Washington, D.C., to develop political contacts, and the 1901 failure of the Pajarito National Park bill possibly led Hewett to invite Lacey to see the place for himself.[2] Lacey, for his part, realized he had an opportunity to study the broader issue of preserving antiquities and natural wonders on public lands in the company of an expert. Throughout the 1890s, the House Committee on Public Lands, which Lacey chaired, had considered an increasing number of bills to create national parks, and Lacey demonstrated a special interest in preserving the petrified forests of Arizona as a national park.[3] Pinchot, as it turned out, declined the invitation to accompany him, as did C. Hart Merriam and T. S. Palmer of the U.S. Department of Agriculture's Biological Survey.[4] Nonetheless, the fact that Lacey sought the company of these three conservation-minded men working within the federal government indicates the sense of purpose he attached to his New Mexico trip. So, too, do the three journal-like letters he sent to his family in Oskaloosa, with a request that they be saved.[5]

Although his purpose was to "see for myself the necessity and propriety of the enactment of a law to protect and preserve the ancient aboriginal ruins of the Southwest," Lacey also sought to observe the effects of acculturation through Indian boarding schools and farming allotments.[6] This is not surprising considering his tenure on the House Committee on Indian Affairs, exceeded only by his tenure on the House Committee on Public Lands. He spent as much time visiting pueblos as he did exploring ruins during his nine-day trip, enough to sense, or project, an overall air of progress that he attributed to the Indians' boarding school education, and he believed that "gradually the life on the farm will supplant the pueblo and people will stay on the farm the year round."[7]

The cliff dwellings, however, were the primary objects of his interest. During Lacey's first term in office (1889–1891), Congress passed legislation giving the president authority to set aside public land to preserve the ruins of Casa Grande. As he was a member of the House Committee on Public Lands, this may be where he learned of the uncontrolled destruction of archaeological sites in the Southwest. However, when the preservation of antiquities on public lands began to heat up as a legislative issue in 1900, Lacey was primarily focused on securing passage of the game and bird protection act that would bear his name. Still, he took the antiquities issue seriously. His committee considered competing bills that year, the first introduced by Representative Jonathan Prentiss Dolliver, another member of the Iowa delegation and also a personal friend of Lacey's. Dolliver's bill, introduced at the behest of the American Association for the Advancement of Science, gave the president broad authority to set aside as national parks or reservations any public lands that contained historic works of human creation or natural "formations" that were of scientific or scenic value—the "generalist" approach as it came to be called. Colorado Representative John Franklin Shafroth, a fellow member of the Public Lands Committee, followed with two bills focused more narrowly on ruins in certain western states and specified reserves not to exceed 320 acres. Lacey himself, at the request of the Department of the Interior, introduced a modified version of Dolliver's bill to accomplish virtually the same end, although H.R. 11021 gave slightly more emphasis to areas of "scenic beauty and natural wonders."[8] None of these bills had a chance of passing. By 1901, three presidents had withdrawn more than 46 million acres for forest reserves under the 1891 Forest Reserve Act, and western interests were poised to thwart any extension of executive power to withdraw large tracts of public land for broad-brush purposes.

Lacey's three letters from late August and early September 1902 are devoid of sentiment about the people and landscape of New Mexico but full of observations that reveal a keen mind absorbing information for later reflection. He describes the cliff and cave dwellings at Puye Mesa in detail, including a sketch of the "ink bottle"-shaped opening to the "cliff cave" where on August 26 he and Edgar Hewett talked and watched the night sky and then "slept well and did not dream of the dead nation which once inhabited the cliff side and mesa above." Unfortunately, he did not record the details of his conversations with Hewett that night, or at any time during their several days together. The next day he and Hewett and the other two members of the party, New Mexico Congressman B. S. Rodey and Land Commissioner A. A. Keen, "climbed up the moccasin worn stairway to the mesa ... and there found the ruins of a communal dwelling" of many hundred rooms arranged around a courtyard. On the 28th, the party continued exploring the Pajarito region to inspect more cliff and cave dwellings, then returned to Santa Fe.

After resting their horses, they traveled on to Cochiti Pueblo, west of Santa Fe. Here, Lacey toured two kivas "in complete order and in present use," the "just discontinued" Indian day school affiliated with the Santa Fe Indian School, and "the old church" occasionally served by a priest from Peña Blanca. Arising at 4:00 AM the next morning, the party made a "hot and weary journey" to a painted cave located in a high recess of a canyon wall. Lacey found the images "quaint and interesting" but questioned the antiquity others had ascribed to them: "There are some improbable human figures and some impossible birds, snakes and beasts. Some antiquarians have supposed the beasts were of an extinct species. One of them has been classed as a mammoth, but I think is clearly a wolf. A man on horseback with bridle on the horse and the reins in his hand shows that the pictures are junior to the Spanish invasion which introduced the horse to the aborigines." He found more compelling two lions carved from a single sandstone boulder, located atop a mesa and encircled by stones. Lacey spent some time sketching the site and contemplating the view from the mesa, from where he could see the cliff dwelling complexes the party had recently inspected. "No doubt," he wrote, "the cave and the lions have both been places of religious interest in the past. Even now it is almost impossible to get an Indian guide to visit the lions."

After two more stops at Laguna and Acoma, Lacey departed by train from Albuquerque so that he could make it to the Republican state conference at Des Moines on September 4. It was, after all, an election year, and he faced mounting opposition from within his own party. Steadfast in his support for high tariffs and sound money, Lacey had become a political liability for Governor Albert Cummins, who was more in step with Republican progressives. Intra-party machinations at the state level would unseat Lacey in the 1906 election, making the Antiquities Act the last major piece of conservation legislation he navigated to passage.

The Antiquities Act is sometimes referred to as the "Lacey Act," although this eponym typically means the 1900 act prohibiting the interstate trafficking of game taken in violation of state laws. In any event, even though Lacey was a key player in securing the Antiquities Act, he was only one of many in that effort, and it has remained something of a puzzle as to why his name in particular also was attached to this act and, more generally, what motivated him to take up the cause of conservation. His long chairmanship of the House Committee on Public Lands is not answer enough. Two things are certain. One is that the voters in Iowa's Sixth District, who elected him eight times to serve as their representative in the U. S. Congress, expressed no interest in conservation, at least not in writing. The second is that there is almost nothing in John Lacey's early background to suggest that he was personally drawn to conservation.

Lacey's constituent mail reveals a constant stream of incoming requests for patronage or intervention on behalf of pension claims, and opinions regarding tariffs, taxation, or temperance—standard money and morality issues of the time—but no constituent demands for conservation. There is, in addition, a curious disconnect between Lacey's political life in Washington, the persona he presented to his constituents, and the devoted husband, father, and brother his family knew. Lacey seems to have compartmentalized the various aspects of his life.[9] This is especially apparent in the many letters he exchanged with his brother Will, who also was his law partner and most trusted confidant. Their correspondence is rich in the minutiae of local legal matters and business affairs but contains no hint of what was going on in the halls of Congress.[10]

Lacey's early life is similarly devoid of clues. Born in 1841, Lacey grew up on the banks of the Ohio River at New Martinsville in what was then western Virginia (later West Virginia). When he was twelve, his parents moved the family to Wheeling, and two years later they moved west, settling in 1855 in Mahaska County, Iowa. In the relentless march of 19th-century westward migration, the place that John Lacey would thereafter call "home" was simply where the Lacey family came to rest, on a farm along the Des Moines River a few miles from Oskaloosa. John Lacey actually spent little time on that farm and never seems to have formed an attachment to the land. He was bookish, even though he had no formal schooling until the family moved to Wheeling. His mother taught him to read and write, and by the time he was twelve he had read every book in New Martinsville that he could borrow, or so he claimed. He pursued a more formal education on his own once the family settled in Iowa. Between 1855 and 1861, he worked on the farm during planting season and attended private academies during winter months. Beginning in 1858, he taught school during the winter and also continued his own studies.[11]

This seasonally determined pattern of his life changed abruptly when civil war erupted. After spring planting in 1861, he and his brother James literally left the fields to volunteer for service. At the battle of Blue Mills' Landing, John was taken prisoner but later released and then discharged. In the winter of 1861, back in Oskaloosa, he began reading law under the tutelage of Samuel A. Rice, a local attorney who was then serving as the state's attorney general. Shortly thereafter, his brother, suffering from consumption, was sent home to die. After James died in February 1862, Lacey helped his father with spring planting and then enlisted again, this time serving under his law mentor, Samuel Rice, who was commissioned as commanding officer of Lacey's regiment. Lacey quickly moved up the ranks and was Rice's acting adjutant-general when Rice was fatally wounded in the Battle of Jenkins' Ferry. Lacey then joined the staff of General Frederick Steele and in 1864 became Steele's adjutant-general, a post he held for the remainder of his military service. Toward the end of the war, he resumed reading law books, even reading in his tent at night during the siege of Mobile: "I found it good mental training, for if one could read a dry book under the fire of siege guns he could study law almost anywhere." Lacey mustered out of service in 1865 bearing the rank of Brevet Major, returned directly to Oskaloosa, was promptly admitted to the Iowa bar, opened a private law office, and married Martha Newell, to whom he had been engaged for three years.[12]

In the span of four years, between the ages of twenty and twenty-four, John Lacey lost a brother, lost his mentor, and educated himself in the law; and for three of those years, he was intimately involved in the military strategy of the western theater of the Civil War. For the rest of his life, he would be addressed as "Major Lacey." He seems never to have discouraged this gesture of remembrance and respect. More to the point, he seems to have forged certain values and habits during this critical period of his life, notably a deep sense of duty to his country and an ability to concentrate under pressure.

Lacey practiced law in Oskaloosa from the mid-1860s to the late 1880s, during which time he dabbled in politics, serving one term in the Iowa General Assembly (1870–1872). He also continued to study law, compiling and publishing a compendium of Iowa Supreme Court decisions as well as a two-volume encyclopedia of railway law. *Lacey's Railway Digest,* a widely used reference work, considerably enhanced his practice by bringing in many railroad companies as clients. Still, he maintained a private, general practice because he "liked a multitude of clients" and the challenge of trying diverse cases. "There is scarcely any kind of a case, civil or criminal, that I have not tried," he wrote in 1900.

> It has been my custom in every case to go to the bottom of it. If it involved an injury to an arm I studied the anatomy of the arm as carefully as any surgeon would have done. If it involved a question of insanity I obtained and read every work on the subject. In short it has been a pleasure for me, for

Figure 3.1. John Fletcher Lacey in an undated portrait. Unattributed photograph courtesy of the State Historical Society of Iowa, Des Moines; negative no. 291.

I loved work, to study every question that might arise in the progress of each case as it came up.[13]

His success as an attorney allowed the Laceys to live a comfortable life. Before and after he was elected to Congress, he enjoyed traveling throughout Europe, Mexico, Cuba, and Puerto Rico. His letters and accounts from these trips reveal the same inclination that is evident in his 1902 letters from New Mexico: a tendency to approach travel as an educational experience rather than a leisure activity.[14] Lacey actually traveled rather extensively throughout the western United States and Alaska; he knew the vastness of the country firsthand. Travel was both a manifestation of his expanding world view and a means to gather information that he incorporated into his railway digest and his legislative work.

However much travel expanded his knowledge of foreign cultures and current affairs, it did not provide the chief motive for his interest in conservation. That, it seems, came from the way he approached work in general and his legislative career specifically. A brief section of his autobiography, written in 1900, sheds considerable insight on his career strategy as a legislator. In four pages of typescript, Lacey briefly describes his work in Congress from 1889 to 1900. Unfortunately, he did not add to it after he left Congress. Nonetheless, these four pages, covering his first ten years in the House, reveal a relish for committee work. He established his credentials as an effective legislator during his first term, the 51st Congress (1889–1891).

As a member of the House Committee on Public Lands, he participated in drafting the 1891 Forest Reserve Act and, as he noted, "secured the passage of a law for the inspection of coal mines and protection of the lives of the miners in the territories."[15] Lacey was proud of the 1891 Mine Safety Act, aimed at improving mines in the Indian Territory where underground gases created especially dangerous working conditions. His approach to the crafting of law replicated his approach to the practice of law: "I got copies of all the mining laws in all the states and territories and also of England and her colonies, and then prepared a short but effective bill for the territories."[16]

Defeated in his first re-election bid, Lacey was returned to office in 1892 as a member of the 53rd Congress. He was reassigned to Public Lands, this time as "the head of the Republican membership."[17] During his second term, Lacey secured passage of the Yellowstone Park Protection Act (1894), legislation of which he was also proud.[18] In the 54th Congress, he became chairman of the Committee on Public Lands, a position he held for twelve years until he was defeated in the 1906 election. During the 54th Congress, he also served on the Committee on Railroads, and in the 55th and 56th Congresses, he served on the Committee on Indian Affairs. "It has been my policy," he wrote, "to remain with one committee so as to obtain rank there by long service, and to change my assignment on other committees so as to give a wide range of service, for in Congress Committee work is the great educator."[19]

Lacey studied his congressional colleagues with as much care as he studied legislation. He devoted at least twenty pages of his autobiography to character-revealing anecdotes about fellow House members, an intriguing glimpse into the interpersonal dynamics of Congress during the 1890s. No doubt he cleaned up the stories for posterity, but overall they convey the degree to which oration and verbal wit sparked partisan politics in the legislative process. His anecdotes also reveal equal respect for members of both parties and an ability to poke fun at members of his own. In none of these stories does he appear as the protagonist, at least not explicitly, but in the aggregate they suggest that he knew how to influence his colleagues in the cloakroom and on the House floor.

Lacey approached legislative issues as legal challenges. As a skilled attorney, he knew that he did not have to believe in any cause in order to serve as an effective advocate. In fact, the only personal passions that John Lacey mixed with professional practice were reading and travel. For instance, the Mine Safety Act pertained only to mines in the territories, where the federal government and not the states had jurisdiction. Politically, however, it signaled legitimate concern for the coal miners of southeast Iowa, some of whom voted in his district. Similarly, the Yellowstone

Park Protection Act firmly established the principle of exclusive federal jurisdiction in national parks by placing Yellowstone in a specific federal judicial district and directing the secretary of the interior to protect the timber, mineral deposits, wildlife, and natural wonders therein from human destruction.[20] As his legislative career progressed, Lacey's name became more prominently associated with conservation legislation.[21] By 1896 he had achieved a national reputation as a congressman supportive of western interests yet protective of the public domain. As a case in point, Lacey explained in stark political terms his role in suspending President Cleveland's order of 1897 to place 21 million acres in forest reserves:

> I am heartily for the forest reserve system, and do not want it destroyed. The Senate wanted to annul Mr. Cleveland's order. I urged the House to suspend it only and authorize Mr. McKinley to modify it. The House thus far has agreed to my views and having been chairman of the Comm. on Public Lands they look to me for information. To attempt to uphold the Cleveland order as a whole would have led to failure and hence I have tried to save the reserves by having the lines corrected.[22]

Lacey's interest in conservation came not from personal influences, but from his broad knowledge of law, the intergovernmental nature of legal issues that attended land use in the developing West, and, of course, his fortuitous assignment to the House Committee on Public Lands. Like many intelligent people of his day, he was appalled by the destructive side of human nature, but he did not blame industrialization, capitalism, or immigration. He took these forces as givens. Instead, he became a strong advocate of federal responsibility for resource conservation in the public domain.

With the 1900 Lacey Bird and Game Act, he made a calculated legal move to expand the authority of the federal government through a narrow, but enforceable, interpretation of the commerce clause. The Lacey Act opened a constitutional path for the federal government to protect wildlife outside public lands by prohibiting the interstate transportation of wild animals or birds killed in violation of state laws. It earned him wide respect among sportsmen and federal officials, and he regarded the 1900 law "as one of the most useful of all my Congressional acts."[23] However, he and others quickly realized its limitations, and in 1905 he drafted a bill designed to test the constitutionality of the general welfare clause by extending federal authority to protect migratory "creatures"—specifically birds but also fish—during "temporary sojourn or transit."[24] Lacey was not in Congress to participate in the triumphal passage of the Weeks–McLean Migratory Bird Act, which accomplished in 1913 the strategy he proposed in 1905, but he followed its legislative progress closely.[25]

The Antiquities Act was to be his last major legislative accomplishment. Lacey's paper trail, like Hewett's, does not clearly reveal the extent of his contribution to the political process. Nonetheless, it is worth considering the legal talent that Lacey brought to legislating. Ronald F. Lee, Hal Rothman, and Raymond Harris Thompson, among others, have meticulously pieced together the act's legislative history and defined Edgar Lee Hewett's role.[26] Lacey's voluminous personal papers contain nothing to dispute what has been established, but in the context of his overall legislative record, two letters in particular indicate that Lacey was more than a power broker.

One is a lengthy letter written by W J McGee in April 1904, during the heat of controversy over the Rodenberg–Lodge and Cullom–Hitt bills—two competing versions of antiquities legislation. Both defined "antiquities" as human-made features, but they differed significantly in legislative intent. The Rodenberg–Lodge Bill would have placed custody of antiquities on public lands with the secretary of the interior along with authority to grant excavation and collecting permits to qualified institutions. The Cullom–Hitt Bill, also known as the Smithsonian Bill, also would have placed control with the secretary of the interior, but the Smithsonian Institution would have had supervisory authority over excavations and collections. Lacey sent copies of both bills, along with his own bill, H. R. 13478 (identical to his 1900 bill, H.R. 11021) to McGee for comment. McGee, then serving as chief of the Department of Anthropology for the 1904 St. Louis exposition, wrote several pages in response. He strongly disapproved of the Cullom–Hitt Bill, and although he found the Rodenberg–Lodge Bill less objectionable, he felt that it, too, "would so far subordinate all other museums and educational institutions to the National Museum as to retard the advance of science and develop friction between public institutions." Regarding Lacey's bill, introduced for the Department of the Interior, McGee suggested a number of revisions, most notably that tracts set aside to preserve "relics" not be confused with national parks: "I am in some doubt as to the expediency of introducing the phrase 'national parks' . . . since it is conceivable that the reservations might be too small or otherwise unfitted for 'parks' in the customary sense of the term." McGee also counseled Lacey not to specify the Smithsonian Institution as the sole supervisor, "partly for the reason that its status is undefined . . . [and] partly because other institutions such as that recently founded by Carnegie approach the Smithsonian status near enough to make the distinction sound invidious." Overall, however, he noted that H. R. 13478 was "in conformity with resolutions, memorials, and other actions taken by various scientific organizations in this country during the last twenty years. In my judgment the measure would have the support of educational and scientific institutions generally, and would be supported by nine-tenths of the archeologists and ethnologists in the country." He closed by stating that it was "too late to secure endorsement of the measure in time for use during the present session," but if action could be deferred to the next session he would use his influence among scientific institutions and professional organizations to pass the bill, an offer he reiterated two years later.[27]

Despite McGee's objections to the Rodenberg–Lodge Bill, Lacey's committee reported it favorably. It is not clear, however, that Lacey himself was willing to work for its passage. The bill had strong support and many thought it would become law, but this did not happen. It would be too much to claim that McGee was instrumental in delaying action, although Lacey clearly was seeking his counsel off the record. Moreover, in McGee's detailed letter, Lacey received informed opinion that undoubtedly helped him get a better sense of where the legislative process should go next.

The process would have played out much differently had Edgar Lee Hewett not stepped back into the picture in the summer of 1904. Throughout late 1904 and 1905, Hewett worked closely with Lacey, the Bureau of American Ethnology, and the General Land Office to hammer out a bill that would satisfy western congressmen opposed to large public land withdrawals, federal agencies protective of their own jurisdictions, and the needs of responsible scholarship. The resulting bill, which Hewett crafted and Lacey introduced, was a masterpiece of legislative compromise. In the process of working with Lacey, however, Hewett appears to have changed his mind about the efficacy of establishing national parks to preserve discrete sites. In May 1906, Hewett traveled from Santa Fe to Mesa Verde to assist the surveyor who was trying to establish legal boundaries for what would become Mesa Verde National Park. Upon his return, he wrote to Lacey that he found "almost everywhere important ruins, and almost every settler a pot hunter." Of the Pajarito region, which Lacey had visited in 1902, Hewett reported, "everything is all right there. The ruins are all being looked after by the forest ranger. But there is renewed activity everywhere on government lands and the custodianship on Indian reservations is worthless." By then Hewett had come to the position that geographically specific legislation such as the Mesa Verde bill was flawed: "Your general bill is the only solution for the problem."[28]

A final note concerns the language of the act that broadened the definition of antiquities to include "objects of scientific interest" as well as historic and prehistoric ruins. Ronald Lee speculated that Hewett probably was persuaded by officials of the Interior Department to broaden the language in order to protect natural areas as well as archaeological sites, using language from H.R. 11021, the 1900 bill that Lacey introduced for Interior. Curiously, an undated and unattributed summary of Lacey's legislative record, buried in his papers, asserts that "Mr. Lacey inserted the words 'scenic and scientific' in the bill particularly to save the

Petrified Forest of Arizona."[29] Lacey's own published account of his 1902 trip more modestly states: "It was this trip that led to the introduction and passage of my bill for the preservation of aboriginal ruins and places of scenic and scientific interest upon the public domain, under which the Petrified Forest, the Olympic Range Elk Reserve and about two hundred places of ethnological interest have been designed as 'monuments' and preserved to the public."[30]

As a congressman, Lacey had tried repeatedly to establish the Petrified Forest as a national park and to create wildlife refuges in forest reserves. In July 1906, President Roosevelt wrote a personal note to tell Lacey that "certain gentlemen" had expressed to him "their deep sense of obligation to you for all that you have done in Congress" to further conservation, and had proposed "presenting some memorial to you."[31] In November 1906, Lacey lost his bid for a ninth term in Congress. In December 1906, the Petrified Forest was designated as a national monument. As much as we know about the complex history of the Antiquities Act, some aspects of its creation remain tantalizing mysteries.

Notes

1. Alden Sampson to John F. Lacey, April 8, 1902, John F. Lacey Papers, State Historical Society of Iowa (SHSI), State Archives, Des Moines (hereinafter cited as Lacey Papers). Lacey did not routinely keep copies of his outgoing correspondence—an unfortunate circumstance that limits the usefulness of his collected papers.

2. See Thompson 2000, 271–318. See also John F. Lacey, "Cliff Dwellers' National Park" (Lacey's 1901 report from the Committee on Public Lands), and his essay "The Pajarito: An Outing with the Archaeologists," both collected in the *Major John F. Lacey Memorial Volume* (cited in the bibliography as Pammel 1915; see pp. 220–223 and 210–219, respectively).

3. "Preserving Petrified Forests," reprinted in Pammel 1915, 207–209 (originally delivered as a speech before the House of Representatives, May 19, 1900); "The Petrified Forest National Park of Arizona," in Pammel 1915, 203–206.

4. Letters from T. S. Palmer, July 18, 1902; from Gifford Pinchot, July 24, 1902; and from C. Hart Merriam, August 10, 1902 (Lacey Papers).

5. The letters, dated August 26–29, [August] 30, and September 1–2, 1902 (Lacey Papers), are preserved as transcriptions of the original handwrit-

ten versions, edited by Lacey to include several small freehand drawings. Lacey later incorporated details from the letters into his essay, "The Pajarito," which he may have written specifically for the *Memorial Volume*.

6. "The Pajarito," in Pammel 1915, 210; W. A. Jones, Commissioner, Office of Indian Affairs, to "All Indian Agents," July 2, 1900, directing them to allow Lacey "freedom of the reservation" so that he could "study the conditions of the Indians" (Lacey Papers).

7. Quotes from his entry dated September 1, 1902.

8. It is worth noting that Lacey's preserved correspondence for 1900 (Box 251) does not contain any letters from the Department of the Interior referencing the antiquities bill, although he received many letters concerning the bird and game bill.

9. Lacey's personal correspondence contains both incoming and outgoing letters from and to family members, making it possible to get a more complete sense of his relationship with some of them, especially his brother, Will, and his son-in-law, J. B. Brewster.

10. Personal correspondence, 1900–1906, passim (Lacey Papers).

11. "Excerpts from the Autobiography of John F. Lacey," compiled by Harriette S. Kellogg for the *Memorial Volume* (Pammel 1915, 381–392).

12. Pammel 1915, 392–416 (quote, 414).

13. Pammel 1915, 419.

14. These letters were bound as diaries and collected in the Lacey Papers.

15. Lacey, "Autobiography," 84, 87.

16. Lacey, "Autobiography," 111. Lacey devoted forty pages of his typewritten autobiography to his congressional work through 1900; Harriette S. Kellogg excerpted only the few pages covering the Mine Safety Act to include in the published *Memorial Volume*.

17. Lacey, "Autobiography," 86.

18. Lacey, "Autobiography," 86. Lacey's entry on p. 86 is confusing because he conflates passage of the Mine Safety Act and the Yellowstone Park Protection Act with action taken by the 51st Congress, but this conflation suggests that he may have perceived both laws to be equally important. The Yellowstone Park Protection Act was passed May 7, 1894; see Tolson 1933, 30–33.

19. Lacey, "Autobiography," 88.

20. Tolson, 30–33; see also "Lacey's Legacy," on-line at www.nps.gov/yell/may-12pr.htm (accessed 1 January 2005).

21. Lacey's collected addresses and other writings, published in the *Memorial Volume*, document his increasing concern for forest and wildlife conservation, as does his political correspondence from 1896 on. See also L[ouis] H. Pammel, "Major John F. Lacey and the Conservation of Our Natural Resources" in Pammel 1915, 36–47; Gallagher 1981, 9–22.

22. Lacey to Charles Aldrich, May 17, 1897, Records of the Iowa Historical, Memorial and Art Department, SHSI.

23. Lacey, "Autobiography" (typescript), 122–123.

24. Lacey to J. W. Wadsworth, Chairman, House Committee on Agriculture, December 11, 1905, with "Proposed Draft of Bill;" see also Lacey to John W. Weeks, December 3, 1910, published in the *Memorial Volume* (Pammel 1915, 185–186).

25. The Weeks–McLean Act took effect in March 1913; Lacey died September 29, 1913.

26. Lee 1970; Rothman 1989; Thompson 2000.

27. W J McGee to Lacey, April 8, 1904; see also McGee to Lacey, April 9, 1904, and January 24, 1906 (Lacey Papers).

28. Hewett to Lacey, May 3, 1906 (Lacey Papers).

29. Typescript entitled "Legislation Secured by Major Lacey" (Lacey Papers), is mixed with miscellaneous materials dated 1908 through 1913. Inasmuch as the document is written in the third person, it is unlikely that Lacey wrote it even though it echoes language of "The Pajarito." The legislative summary may have been written by Louis Pammel when he was gathering information for what would become the *Memorial Volume.*

30. "The Pajarito," in Pammel 1915, 210.

31. Theodore Roosevelt to Lacey, July 16, 1906 (Lacey Papers).

4

Landmark Decision

The Antiquities Act, Big-Stick Conservation, and the Modern State

Char Miller

ROY NEARY COULD NOT HELP HIMSELF; at dinner, he played with his mashed potatoes. Had he been a child, no one would have much minded, but he was a father, and his wife and three children anxiously watched his meal-time antics. Ever since that fearsome night when the power was suddenly cut off, he had become evermore reclusive and odd, so much so that at dinner the kids had scooted closer to their mother. From that remove they watched, furtively, as he molded the white mound topped with melting margarine into a small peak; and then, with ill-disguised fear, as he lunged across the table, grabbed the bowl of steaming spuds, and began ladling gob after gob on to his plate. That's when, "like a mad potter, Neary started to knead the white mush with his hands into some kind of shape," which emerged into a rough approximation of Devils Tower. That's when we know the aliens made him do it.[1]

But why did Steven Spielberg frame his sci-fi thriller *Close Encounters of the Third Kind* (1977) around that remote Wyoming landmark? Why, in a later scene, have a half-crazed Neary upgrade his food-art project into a hardened nine-foot exact replica of the haunting land form; and then, after a harrowing journey, have him come face-to-face with the object of his desire, before which he stood speechless: "The Tower stood alone, unique, something so one-of-a-kind that Neary felt a chill across his shoulders at the thought he was able to reproduce it in sculpture without even knowing it existed." Why that place?[2]

Perhaps for some of the same reasons that several Northern Plains tribes have been drawn to what they revere as Mateo Tipi,

Bears Lodge, though they were (and remain) more voluble in their appreciation of its formidable power than was the tongue-tied Neary. The monolith has played a formative role in legends of the Arapaho and Cheyenne, Crow, Kiowa, and Sioux. Several of these, transcribed in the 1930s, used bears' claws scratching at the tower's surface to explain its deeply grooved sides. Its soaring height is said to be a consequence of the Great Spirit's lifting ground-level rocks into its present elevated form to save children from marauding bruins. Other tales explain the creation of the constellation Pleiades by evoking the plight of seven sisters, saved from earthly demise—once more at the claws of bears—by godly intervention. For the Plains peoples, Bears Lodge occupies a special dimension, a spiritual portal between this world and the otherworldly.

So it also functioned for Steven Spielberg, who closed his film with a now-obsessed Roy Neary walking across a hastily constructed "cosmic port of call" at the tower's base and toward a massive intergalactic spacecraft. Forever alienated from his family, he does not hesitate to step into this "fiery heart of the mystery," and as its gateway closes after him, the craft lifts off into a "scaffold of light," a "brilliant stairway up to the heavens," transported into the night sky where it becomes the "brightest of the brightest stars."[3]

A divine domain, Devils Tower is also a massive, perpendicular obelisk, formed of molten rock and estimated to be more than 50 million years old, lodged within a human—that is, political—environment (Figure 4.1). Designated a national monument, its use is now regulated by the National Park Service in the Department of the Interior, a bureaucratic reification of legal status it gained in September 1906 when President Theodore Roosevelt signed a piece of paper absorbing it into the American polity (Figure 4.2). He did so by invoking the Antiquities Act, passed that same year; congressional legislation that granted the presidency extraordinary powers to preserve "historic landmarks, historic and prehistoric structures, and other objects of historic or scientific interest that are situated upon the lands owned or controlled by the Government of the United States...." However prosaic, Roosevelt's stroke of the pen marked an iconic moment: Devils Tower became the first national monument.

The landmark's political ascension has had earth-bound consequences. Because its modern history has been linked to the Antiquities Act, an initiative emblematic of the Progressive Era in which it

Figure 4.1. A contemporary view of the monolith. Unattributed photograph, courtesy of National Park Service Digital Image Archives.

was crafted, Devils Tower has contributed to the development of a new form of land management in the American West, the realignment of the relative power of the executive and legislative branches of the federal government, and the implementation of a hitherto-untested preservationist ethos on a frontier landscape. Through a secular legislative act, the nation-state, at Devils Tower and elsewhere, created a new kind of sacred space—national in name, sweep, and scope—a legacy of unparalleled significance.

Progressive Aspirations

To understand why Congress passed the Antiquities Act, it is essential to recognize that those who called themselves "Progressives" believed deeply in the capacity of government to mold the com-

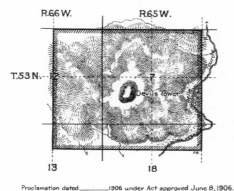

DEVILS TOWER
NATIONAL MONUMENT
Embracing Sec. 7 and the N½ of NE¼, the
NE¼ of NW¼ and lot No. 1 of Sec. 18 in T. 53N.,
R. 65 ; the E½ of Sec. 12 and the N½ of NE¼
of Sec. 13 in T.53 N., R.66 all West of the
6™ Principal Meridian,
WYOMING.
Containing 1152.91 acres.

Proclamation dated_____1906 under Act approved June 8, 1906.

DEPARTMENT OF THE INTERIOR,
GENERAL LAND OFFICE,
W.A.Richards, Commissioner.

Figure 4.2. General Land Office map of Devils Tower National Monument prepared in anticipation of Roosevelt's December 1906 proclamation (note the blank in the date line beneath the map). Like many early monuments—and national parks, for that matter—the boundaries of Devils Tower were drawn without regard for ecological considerations; hence, the Belle Fourche River coursed in and out of the monument. Image courtesy of National Park Service Historic Photo Collection, Harpers Ferry Center.

monweal, present and future. Sharing that faith with Roosevelt was the act's central framer, Representative John F. Lacey of Iowa, and its leading advocates, notably Edgar Lee Hewett, W. H. Holmes, and the Reverend Henry Mason Baum. Emerging out of the late nineteenth century, and buffeted by, while benefiting from, the industrial revolution, this cohort of like-minded reformers drew heavily on European social idealism to shape their perspectives on the necessity of a strong central state. So pervasive was this belief in its preeminence that historian Daniel Rodgers has argued that it is the era's defining feature. Lasting well into the twentieth century, this reconfiguration of American society was ineluctably linked to "movements of politics and ideas throughout the North Atlantic world that trade and capitalism had tied together," he notes. "This was not an abstract realization, slumbering in the recesses of consciousness. Tap into the debates that swirled throughout the United States and industrialized Europe over the problems and miseries of 'great city' life, the insecurities of wage work, the social backwardness of the countryside, or the instabilities of the market itself, and one finds oneself pulled into an intense, transnational traffic in reform ideas, policies, and legislative devices." Making this "Atlantic era in social politics" possible was the creation of a "new set of institutional connections" with European societies, and influential go-betweens or brokers who facilitated the vital traffic in intellectual commerce. This was as true for child-welfare advocates as it was for foresters; for politicians as well as for ethnologists; as much for Jane Addams and Gifford Pinchot as for Roosevelt and the Smithsonian's W. H. Holmes. The key to a more Progressive society, they affirmed, was the establishment of a more paternal nation-state; this European import, shorn of its monarchical trappings, would be the foundation of a potent Republic.[4]

As they imagined a new society, they dreamed of a new social type: the professional. Well trained in the relevant graduate-school programs, and bearing away hard-won knowledge and a crucial credential (the requisite terminal degree in their field), these experts would commit themselves to resolving nagging social ills, from urban poverty to rural immiseration, from political malfeasance to timber theft and relic poaching. That these seemingly disparate issues were of a piece to this generation of American reformers, many of whom received their post-graduate education in Europe or at the new U.S. universities modeled after continental norms, was critical to their Progressivism, an ideal that was global in reach and local in application. Because their "talents meshed with others in a national scheme," historian Robert H. Wiebe has observed, this generation felt encouraged "to look outward confidently." And it was their "earnest desire to remake the world upon their private models" and professional ambitions that "testified to the deep satisfaction accompanying this revolution in identity."[5]

But the identity politics of the late nineteenth century, particularly for those of the urban middle class from which many of the

Progressives came, was fraught with complications. Products of the new order they hoped to impose on what they perceived to be an unruly society and unkempt culture, they were also children of an earlier era. These sons and daughters came of age amid the tumultuous upheaval accompanying the shift from an agricultural to an industrial economy, a nation at once bucolic and citified, still torn in its grief over a brutal civil war, as uncertain about how to incorporate its newly liberated African-American citizens as it would be wary in its welcome of millions of new immigrants. These divisions, sharp, ragged, and painful, animated the late-nineteenth-century political arena that nurtured Progressive visions, giving visionaries cause and context for their work. Convinced that through the scientific method and bureaucratic means they would be able to reconstruct society, these young reformers had "enough insight into their lives to recognize that the old ways and old values would no longer suffice," Wiebe argues. "Often confused, they were still the ones with the determination to fight those confusions and mark a new route into the modern world." And who did they tap to shepherd them to the promised land but a figure emblematic of eastern aristocracy and western rough-and-tumble: "Seeking a new urban leader for modern America, many gave their hearts to a man almost invariably pictured in a cowboy hat, Theodore Roosevelt."[6]

The Coming of Conservationism

In retrospect, it almost seems predictable that a crusading President Roosevelt would affix his signature on the Act for the Preservation of American Antiquities. As a child, he had tramped through forest and marsh in search of bird, mammal, and fish, preternaturally fascinated with the wild and its mysteries, convinced that by collecting specimens, and studying his finds, he could penetrate a fecund world beyond himself. Coming into knowledge of it, and displaying his insights, was also part of his precocious commitment to science, very much on display when, at age eight, he spotted a dead seal in front of a New York shop. As biographer Paul Cutright relates the tale, young Teddy was transfixed, day after day returning to the scene, measuring its length, width, and girth, recording its shape, color, and anatomy, and, in the intervals, perhaps begging his resistant parents to let him purchase the by-now rotting corpse. If his goal had been to secure the full skeleton, he failed, but he came away with its skull, an achievement, Cutright writes, that sparked "two decisions, each of which would importantly shape his future. He determined, first, that he would become a naturalist, and, next, that he would found his own museum, using the seal skull as a nucleus."[7]

Young Teddy pursued both ventures with great success, and because of his skills as collector and taxidermist the grandly titled Roosevelt Museum of Natural History exploded in size, becoming home to thousands of expertly stuffed animals. Within five years, he made the first of his donations to New York's American Museum of Natural History (which his father helped establish), and later presented the bulk to the Smithsonian Institution, which kept hundreds of unique contributions, sending duplicate specimens to museums around the country. Long before he became the nation's twenty-sixth president, Roosevelt had demonstrated his preservationist instinct and pedagogic impulse.[8]

To save and teach: those aspirations were at the heart of the conservationist credo he began to adopt (and model) in the coming years. "His active outdoor life, as boy and man, had made him thoroughly alive to the value of timberland and its essential relation to soil, flood control, and water conservation," Cutright notes. Later, his years in the American West would offer up new lessons, "abundant opportunities to observe firsthand the rapid destruction of the buffalo, elk and other large game, and, in the more arid lands— including the barren, exposed walls of the Badlands' canyons—he ... became more deeply aware of the effects of perennial, unchecked erosion." This devastation of fauna and landform was troubling. It also brought to a climax a mythic moment. The evidence on the ground appeared to confirm for Roosevelt, and those who joined him in the Boone and Crockett Club, among other conservationist ventures, that contemporary historian Frederick Jackson Turner was correct: by 1890, the American frontier had closed.[9]

With it went the masculinized landscape of exploration and survey, contest and conquest, a rugged terrain against which Roosevelt had tested himself. There were compensations, and one of them was conservation, as an idea and an act. Framed around scientific methodologies, Hal K. Rothman avers in *Preserving Different Pasts*, conservationism "gave the nation a way to counter the anxiety created" by the disappearance of frontier and wilderness; because it "allowed for the planning for the future through goals of increased efficiency and equitable distribution" it was an antidote to this cultural unease and a prescription for a healthier body politic. Through a sustained application of this Progressive balm, the nation's forests would be regenerated, its battered lands reinvigorated, and its prehistoric past reclaimed—heroic work for a modernist generation.[10]

A Monumental Achievement

That antiquities-advocate Edgar Hewett recognized the connections between various Progressive reform efforts is reflected in his 1904 comment—published, appropriately, in *Science*—that a "system of governmental protection of archaeological remains is manifestly an accomplished fact, as much so and after the same manner as is the protection of timber on public lands." His claim was premature; a system of protection was not yet the "accomplished fact" he proclaimed it to be, nor would it be fully realized when, two years later, the Antiquities Act became law. But the need for systematic public control of and protection for the remnants of ancient civilizations in the West was much touted in the late nineteenth century. Every subsequent retelling of the origins of the Antiquities Act, drawing on contemporary congressional testimony and journalistic exposés, recounts the increased number of thieves scouring Southwestern canyons in search of relics, describes the inability of well-meaning local and state organizations to defend these sites or to think beyond regional interests, and analyzes the emerging consensus among an eastern elite that a national perspective, defined and enforced by federal authority, was required to stop vandals from pilfering the nation's archaeological heritage.[11]

This is essentially the same narrative spun by contemporaries pressing for regulation of natural resources, and, as Hewett recognized, these shared stories played to and off one another, benefiting each. There was a philosophical reason for this linkage, President Roosevelt asserted in his Fifth Annual Message to Congress in 1905. In it, he attributed the Progressive movement's ideological origins, its hunger for rational restraint, to Edmund Burke, citing his declaration that "[m]en are qualified for civil liberty in exact proportion to their disposition to put moral chains on their own appetites"; this being so, the eighteenth-century political theorist asserted, it is ordained "in the eternal constitution of things that men of intemperate minds cannot be free. Their passions forge their fetters." The

U.S. Forest Service, founded as part of the Department of Agriculture six months before Roosevelt's 1905 address, and the Antiquities Act, gaining congressional sanction six months after his address, were in Roosevelt's mind forged together into an essential chain of self-governance.[12]

Not all shared the president's faith in Burkean principles. Critics of the Antiquities Act (and, by extension, of the Forest Service) charged that Roosevelt and his Progressive allies were concentrating authority in the executive branch, hoping to make it first among equals, the driving engine of a new nation-state. These critics were not wrong. Whether in the Department of the Interior or of Agriculture, the conservation agencies and controls they came to possess over public lands and people's behaviors began to segregate land use and users, and separate parks from forests from monuments. To challenge this system of national management and zoning in the West, contemporaries adopted a Jeffersonian retort to what they perceived to be an ominous federal imperium, unfurling the banner of states' rights.

Their political challenge has found academic favor. The federal government gained greatly from the passage of the Antiquities Act, Rothman has observed. "No piece of legislation invested more power in the presidency," and its "vaguely defined scope, encompassing 'objects of historic or scientific interest,' made it an unparalleled tool" for an expansion-minded chief executive. Consider the Act's apparent concession to congressional worries about the potential size of national monuments, captured in language stipulating that they "be confined to the smallest area compatible with the proper care and management of the objects to be protected." On January 11, 1908, Roosevelt demonstrated just how elastic that terminology could be when he declared the Grand Canyon to be a national monument, and brought within its limits more than 800,000 acres (Figure 4.3). His initiative was as well a vivid illustration of how the Act allowed him "to circumvent the fundamentally languid nature of congressional deliberation and instantaneously achieve results he believed were in the public interest."[13]

In setting a critical precedent that many of his successors would employ, Roosevelt's use of the Antiquities Act in its own way contributed to what Arthur M. Schlesinger, Jr., and, more recently, Stephen Grauband, have denounced as the "Imperial Presidency": the origins of a chief executive freed from, and dismissive of, congres-

Figure 4.3. Theodore Roosevelt (second from left) and party at the Grand Canyon, 1903. Five years later he would proclaim Grand Canyon National Monument. Underwood & Underwood studio photograph, courtesy of National Park Service Historic Photo Collection, Harpers Ferry Center.

sional oversight (and that later would morph into malevolent proportions under Richard M. Nixon), lay in Progressive-era experimentation. Although those latter-day constitutional corrosions were not the ends TR and the Progressives had in mind, their ambitions were imperialistic. So argue Richard Nelson and Sally K. Fairfax: for them, the Age of Roosevelt the First must be understood in the context of the Spanish-American War of 1898 and the colonial possessions that in its aftermath the United States brought to heel. This overseas militarism would find domestic expression in the simultaneous demarcation of landscapes into national forests, monuments, and parks, all protected by uniformed civilian guards, often mounted and armed, signifiers of federal power and national prerogative. Antiquities Act preservationism thus played its part in advancing executive clout at the expense of local control.[14]

For all its compelling power, this argument can be overplayed, for its analytical force depends on a retrospective view, a critique of the excesses of Big Government that emerged in the wake of the second president Roosevelt and his liberal Democratic heirs, Harry S Truman, John F. Kennedy, and Lyndon B. Johnson. Yet the New Deal, and the welfare state it initiated, which reached its zenith with the Great Society legislation of the 1960s, pressed well beyond Progressive-era realities, as is manifestly evident in an examination of the impact of the Antiquities Act in its first twenty years.

Ground Clutter

To suggest that it even had an impact is, in some cases, a stretch. Begin with the letter that Gifford Pinchot, chief of the Forest Service, wrote to his forest officers nearly six months after the Act's passage. "The importance of taking steps to preserve such objects has become very apparent, and as soon as possible I wish you to report specifically upon each ruin or natural object of curiosity in your reserve, recommending for permanent reservation all that will continue to contribute to popular, historic, or scientific interest." Emphasizing that the "areas selected should be compatible with the proper care and management of the objects to be protected," and urging his staff to be mindful of the possibility of these sites "being entered under the mineral laws," the nation's forester said nothing about how these landmarks, once located, identified, and surveyed, would be managed. He had nothing to say because he had no idea of what would constitute good management, and neither did his peers in the Interior Department's General Land Office (GLO), on whose lands national monuments also would be established. In this respect, they were as well informed as the president—but their collective cluelessness did not stop Theodore Roosevelt: after creating Devils Tower National Monument in September 1906, he designated 17 others, totaling more than 1.2 million acres, before he left office in March 1909.[15]

But of what consequence were these designations? Although the Act was written in response to depredations at historic and sacred sites, and granted the relevant agencies the authority to protect their archaeological value and cultural import, none of the first generation of national monuments witnessed sustained supervision until the 1930s, and some not even then. Agents of the GLO and Forest Service rarely visited the landmarks, their offices' already small budgets contained no line items for monument protection, and neither agency constructed a management plan that would have strengthened its sense of responsibility for the properties' care. These guardians' most proactive move was to tack up signs demarcating federal property lines, an action that did not occur at Devils Tower, for example, until 1919, thirteen years after its creation as a national monument![16]

"Warning-sign preservation," in short, did little good. "The pot hunting that had preceded the Antiquities Act remained endemic at archaeological sites, and the influx of people into the Southwest after 1900 increased the potential for scavenging, digging, and callous misuse," Rothman notes. Add to this thievery the casual vandalism, unauthorized hunting, and illegal grazing that occurred beyond the gaze of absentee rangers and officers, to say nothing of the "natural decay of historic and prehistoric features," and the idea of enhanced federal power emanating from Antiquities Act acquisitions becomes laughable. As Frank Bond, chief clerk of the GLO, worried in 1911: "It is only a question of time when [the national monuments] will be secretly attacked and pillaged piecemeal, until there is nothing left to preserve"; they are, he concluded, "a responsibility which we now feel but can not make effective."[17]

Navajo National Monument is a case study in the difficulties associated with defining the legal status of and projecting authority over an ancient religious landscape. An in-holding of the sprawling Navajo reservation in northeastern Arizona, it comprises three noncontiguous segments, separated by considerable distance. It was "awkward and gerrymandered" in size and location, and visitation to the monument "had no place in the thinking of the people" who delineated its boundaries. "They sought to preserve its ruins, apparently assuming that the remote nature of the monument would protect it forever." Off the map in the usual touristic sense—it lacked roads and service facilities until the 1960s—it also was beyond the ken of its governmental administrators. Navajo National Monument, Rothman concludes, "had no advocates or constituents save archaeologists, no one who could argue that it merited the attention of the federal bureaucracy."[18]

The same could be said of Shoshone Cavern in Wyoming or Montana's Lewis and Clark Cavern, Devils Postpile in California or Utah's Mukuntuweap (Zion). Even the much-visited Grand Canyon, with regular rail service from Williams, Arizona, since 1901, received little direct management and no federal investment in tourist infrastructure. Private investors, whose hotels and other service properties often encroached on the fabled monument, were the gatekeepers to and provided interpretation of what Theodore Roosevelt had proclaimed to be the canyon's "wonderful grandeur." With the exception of those few spectacular settings that earned national park status with the advent of the National Park Service in 1916, the rest of the national monuments remained, in Rothman's words, "second-class sites," or, worse, "peripheral oddities" lost in a "system increasingly focused on scenic monumentalism."[19]

Long ignored, the monuments finally gained greater relevance during the Great Depression. President Franklin D. Roosevelt's New Deal initiatives, particularly the escalating appropriations funneled through the Civilian Conservation Corps, helped construct on their grounds a more tourist-friendly landscape. New trails and cabins, scenic overlooks and visitor centers integrated the once-neglected monuments into the larger, national system of recreation; increases in staffing helped too, allowing for much-needed protection of archaeological remnants and cultural resources. An ever-more centralized bureaucratic structure within the Park Service, reflective of Interior Secretary Harold Ickes' top-down management style, also enhanced the monuments' place within the NPS mission. But the most revolutionary change occurred as a result of Executive Order 6166. Drawn up by President Herbert Hoover and signed by Franklin D. Roosevelt on June 10, 1933, the EO instituted new efficiencies in federal governance. One of its mandates was the transfer to the Park Service of all non-Interior Department parks, memorials, and historic sites, as well as all the national monuments that had been created under the Antiquities Act. Included in the transfer were the 10 national monuments that had been assigned to the War Department (from Cabrillo in California to Fort Matanzas in Florida), as well as the 14 national monuments remaining under Forest Service jurisdiction (from Chiricahua on the Coronado National Forest to Wheeler on the Cochetopa & Rio Grande). By his signature, Roosevelt ensured that preservation had become the exclusive purview of the NPS. With that expanding responsibility came a widening of the agency's managerial agenda and the institution of more formal controls over its far-flung properties; its former policy of neglect, at once benign and baleful, became a thing of the past.[20]

Final Frontier

Despite its more muscular presence in and stronger regulation of the national monuments, the National Park Service still sought democratic ends. Access to even the most remote sites accelerated with the construction of roads and services, building over time a more astute and motivated constituency in support of the agency's conception of preservationism. This support in turn strengthened its self-promotional claim of enhancing the nation's appreciation for America the Beautiful, and its unique status as the keeper of a civic religion framed around the West's monumental landscapes. That these sites might be woven into the cultural imagination, becoming part of a national dialogue about what made the United States exceptional, had also appealed to Theodore Roosevelt's conservationist sensibility. That explains why, as he stood on the South Rim of the Grand Canyon in 1903, poised to speak about the "natural wonder" that lay at his feet, the usually loquacious Roosevelt fell silent: "I shall not attempt to describe it, because I cannot. I could not choose the words that would convey or could convey to any outsider what that canyon is." But he would raise his voice in its defense. "Leave it as it is. Man cannot improve on it; not a bit. The ages have been at work on it and man can only mar it." Convinced that his fellow citizens had an obligation to protect the canyon's startling vastness, and certain that this national treasure evoked our virtue, he urged his audience to consider its preservation as a peculiarly American gift to the future: "keep it for your children and your children's children and for all who come after you."[21]

Among those who benefited from Roosevelt's plea, which, three years later, he put into legal force with the signing of the Antiquities Act, was a fictional figure. Like TR, Roy Neary projected his fantasy of democratic self-expression onto a totemic terrain, and from Devils Tower National Monument launched his quest for immortality, his reach for the stars.

Notes

1. Spielberg 1977, 141–142.
2. Spielberg 1977, 181–183.

3. The Plains Indians' legends are collected at www.nps.gov/ deto/stories.htm (accessed on January 19, 2005); Mattison 1955, on-line at www.nps.gov/deto/first50_text.htm (accessed on January 19, 2005); Spielberg 1977, 250–251.

4. Rodgers 1998, 3–4.

5. Wiebe 1967, 113; suggesting the limitations of this new identity is McDonagh 1999, 145–184.

6. Wiebe 1967, 131–132; McDonagh 1999, 171–184.

7. Cutright 1985, 1–2.

8. Cutright 1985, 26, 29–31, 37, 50, 70–71, 139.

9. Cutright 1985, 212–213. On the Boone & Crockett Club, see Reiger 2000.

10. Dalton 2002; Watts 2003; Rothman 1989, 15–16. See also Hays 1959.

11. Lee 1970 [2000], 219–223; Thompson 2000, 271–318; Rothman 1989, 1–30.

12. Theodore Roosevelt, Fifth Annual Message, December 5, 1905. On-line at www.geocities.com/presidentialspeeches/1905htm?200522 (accessed on February 22, 2005).

13. Rothman 1999, 16–18.

14. Schlesinger 1989; Graubard 2005; Nelson 1995; Fairfax 2005.

15. Gifford Pinchot, Forest Reserve Order no. 19, November 21, 1906, Forest History Society archives, with thanks to librarian Cheryl Oakes for its retrieval.

16. Mattison 1955, 6–7.

17. Rothman 1989, 74–76, 82–83.

18. Rothman 1991, 13–49. See also Russell 1992.

19. Rothman 1989, 89–91, 119–20.

20. Lee 1970 [2000], 263–264; Williams 2003, 8–12; Runte 1987; Rothman 1989, 187–209.

21. Theodore Roosevelt, Speech at Grand Canyon, The Coconino Sun (Flagstaff, Ariz.), May 9, 1903, 1, on-line at www.kaibab.org/gc/gcps/teddy.htm (accessed on March 12, 2005).

Part 2

Presidential Audacity and Its Discontents

The Act's Legacy of Controversy

5

Showdown at Jackson Hole

A Monumental Backlash
against the Antiquities Act

Hal Rothman

THE CONTROVERSY OVER THE ESTABLISHMENT of Jackson Hole
National Monument in the Yellowstone–Grand Teton National Park
region in 1943 provided a signal moment in the history of uses of
the Antiquities Act of 1906. Since its passage, the Act had been used
in countless ways for nearly every conceivable purpose. Through a
series of circumstances, its uses had never really been challenged; on
the rare occasions that some controversy emerged, power resided in
the federal agency to which the monument was assigned, and challenges to the Act, in Congress or elsewhere, usually evaporated.
During the Progressive Era, Theodore Roosevelt used the Antiquities
Act indiscriminately, but challenging the idea of the common good
for individual purposes was a long shot at best. During the 1920s,
the Jazz Age climate led to tremendous growth in the national park
system, but with a pliant Congress, the Antiquities Act was not used
in the controversial fashion of the Theodore Roosevelt era. Later, the
Depression so damaged the national economy that federal set-asides
of land passed without comment, and after the beginning of the
New Deal, communities clamored for the life's breath of government programs. National monuments, created under the Antiquities Act, became coveted as part of the response to the hard times of
the era. A national monument might bring a Civilian Conservation
Corps camp, jobs in the new park, and opportunities to sell goods
and services to the government. Such options in dire times muted
opposition, principled or scurrilous, to the federal action.

In Teton County, Wyoming, the climate that arose during
World War II, along with long-simmering resentment of an outsider

buying land, as well as the federal presence in the county, led to a flare-up that affected the power of the Antiquities Act. Typical of portions of the West in its scenic beauty and economic potential, the region acted as a magnet for the desires both of preservationists and the ranching industry. National Park Service (NPS) requests for an extension of Grand Teton National Park began almost as soon as the original park was established in 1929. John D. Rockefeller, Jr., was instrumental in the establishment of the original park, and his Snake River Land Company purchased and managed more than 33,000 additional acres in the area, holding it until the NPS could find a way to include the land in the park. Under Director Arno Cammerer, the NPS had little success in securing an extension; in 1938, opponents calling themselves the Jackson Hole Committee outflanked the agency during a Senate Public Lands Committee hearing in Jackson Hole. The Wyoming congressional delegation dropped the bill from the congressional agenda and no one reintroduced it. The NPS could not persuade Congress to make laws concerning Wyoming lands if representatives of the state did not favor them.[1]

After the debacle in 1938, Rockefeller questioned whether he should continue his support of the project. Rockefeller had become uncomfortable with Cammerer, and the magnate's right-hand man, Kenneth Chorley, echoed Rockefeller's feelings when he remarked that he could not "recall seeing any organization decline as much as the Park Service since Mr. Albright left it." Indeed, the philanthropist had a legitimate complaint. He had been involved in the Grand Teton project since his initial visit to the region in 1927, and all he had to show for his benevolent efforts was an annual tax bill of $13,000. By the early 1940s, Rockefeller felt that the time for action had arrived. On November 27, 1942, he told Secretary of the Interior Harold L. Ickes that if the project did not progress, he had every intention of divesting himself of the property he owned. This was Rockefeller's way of initiating action; his son Laurance later referred to the letter as "undoubtedly more of a bit of maneuver and pressure kind of thing than [an] indication of a change of purpose or policy."[2]

Rockefeller's veiled threat got the response he sought. Ickes and the Park Service suggested the creation of Jackson Hole National Monument as an attempt to circumvent the kind of congressional disapproval they encountered in 1938. Even though Ickes warned President Franklin Delano Roosevelt of the likely uproar, on March

15, 1943, the president proclaimed 221,610 acres, including the tract that Rockefeller owned and more than 179,000 acres from Grand Teton National Forest, as a national monument of historic and scientific significance.[3]

For the first time since the ad hoc creation of Mount Olympus National Monument in 1909, serious opposition appeared to uses of the immense discretionary power of the Antiquities Act. Jackson Hole was the consummate way-station monument, its creation inspired by Park Service desires to include an entire biota instead of just mountain peaks in Grand Teton National Park. Area residents, the Wyoming congressional delegation, and the U.S. Forest Service all objected to the establishment of the monument. At the height of the Second World War, executive discretion on the home front became a controversial issue.

Local and state interests immediately responded. Senator Edward Robertson of Wyoming denounced the proclamation as a "foul, sneaking Pearl Harbor blow."[4] Other members of the legislative delegation, including Congressman Frank Barrett, who lived in the Jackson Hole district, were outraged. The *Jackson Hole Courier,* a traditional nemesis of the Park Service, vilified the proclamation, and newspapers across the state castigated the agency.

Opposition also took other forms. On May 2, 1943, local ranchers, headed by Hollywood actor Wallace Beery, a summer resident of the area, took on the NPS. Heavily armed and lacking the necessary permits, the men drove 550 yearlings across the monument to summer range higher in the mountains, defying the NPS to stop them. Superintendent Charles J. Smith of Grand Teton National Park refused to take the bait and ignored them, but because of Beery's presence, the incident attracted national attention for the burgeoning Jackson Hole controversy.[5]

On May 18 the state of Wyoming also got into the act, filing *State of Wyoming v. Charles J. Smith, et. al.,* a civil suit in federal court that named the Grand Teton National Park superintendent as the primary defendant. The suit charged that the Jackson Hole proclamation was illegal because it was "not authorised by the provisions of law upon which it purports to be based." It also contended that Smith completely excluded state officials from decisions concerning the tract. The state asserted that it had an investment in the property, including highways, game animals, and birds, and contended that because Wyoming had "not given her consent to the acquisition of lands within Wyoming by the United States for monument purposes," the tract was "not a national monument or park, and there is no authority therefor," and that the Park Service had no right to receive donations of private land within the monument. Financial considerations also played an important role in the suit. State officials believed that they would lose important tax revenue, as well as a share of the grazing fees collected in the portion of the monument that used to be a part of Grand Teton National Forest, if the court upheld the monument proclamation.[6]

The suit also had serious implications for the future of the Antiquities Act. It charged that "the proclamation ... has not declared any historic landmark, or any historic or prehistoric structure, or any other object of historic or scientific interest to be a national monument.... The said area itself, does not actually contain any historic landmark, or any historic or prehistoric structure, or any other object of historic or scientific interest."[7] After thirty-seven years of using the Antiquities Act to proclaim whatever it wanted, the Department of the Interior finally was asked to define the boundaries of the national monument category.

The question had never really been formally asked. After the furor surrounding the proclamation of Mount Olympus National Monument in 1909 had subsided, only Ralph Henry Cameron, the political boss of Coconino County, Arizona, and a mine-claim speculator and profiteer active in and around Grand Canyon who later became U.S. senator from Arizona, had attacked the Antiquities Act. He questioned the validity of Grand Canyon National Monument in his lawsuits over mineral claims and property rights in the 1910s and 1920s. Other objections had been confined to public outcry, special-interest lobbying, and congressional carping, mostly by western representatives.[8] Until 1943, the Antiquities Act had escaped legal disputes that stemmed from challenges to federal authority. Cameron had mounted a serious attack, but it so smacked of the use of public office for personal vendetta that it was hard to see a challenge to law in his approach. Jackson Hole was different. "A case of actual controversy exists as to the proper and correct interpretation of the Antiquities Act," the suit contended, and it further requested that the court hold the proclamation of the monument to be null and void.[9] In short, the state asked the federal judiciary to determine the limits of executive power under the Antiquities Act, as well as to abolish Jackson Hole National Monument. The attack contained broader implications that Deputy Attorney General John J. McIntyre, in charge of the case for the state of

Wyoming, apparently did not recognize. The state of Wyoming narrowly perceived the issues, and the Park Service responded with a multifaceted interpretation.

Park Service officials held their ground and addressed the broader implications of the lawsuit. Initially, the agency answered the complaint by denying all charges of substance, including the contention that the agency prevented state officials and local residents from using the disputed area. Superintendent Smith cited his response to Beery and the other publicity-seeking "commandos." He had ignored their presence, making it difficult for the opposition to substantiate its charges.[10] The Office of the United States Attorney General offered assistance, and the agency began to develop the basis of its defense. It needed to define the historical and scientific values to which Roosevelt referred in the proclamation, and to show through precedent the many applications of the word *object* in the Antiquities Act.

The federal legal staff began to work on the defense. On June 17, NPS Solicitor Jackson E. Price offered suggestions for strategy. Price saw three available options. Citing *Colorado vs. Toll,* 268 U.S. 228, he suggested that the suit was an unauthorized challenge to federal authority "since [the] plaintiff seeks to control and interfere with the use and administration of federal property." In another vein, Price believed that the court would not review the "President's express determination" that the area contained significant historical landmarks or objects, nor his implied determination that the area fit the criteria of the Antiquities Act. Price also thought that numerous cases established that "a decision of a head of a Department on a question of fact, rendered in a matter within his jurisdiction, is final and conclusive, binding on the courts and not subject to review." Finally, Price debunked the idea that Jackson Hole represented a deviation from prior uses of the Antiquities Act. He cited the examples of the second Grand Canyon and Zion (Kolob) proclamations as precedents for national monuments located adjacent to existing national parks and which might be later incorporated into them.[11] From the point of view of the Office of the Attorney General of the United States, the state of Wyoming had no real basis for its suit.

As a result, the Park Service requested a summary judgment to dismiss the case. Much to the chagrin of NPS officials, on December 3, 1943, the motion was denied.[12] The Park Service recognized the backlash against federal authority and believed that local politics influenced the decision. Agency officials worried that partisan stances would become a factor in the court case. There was no recourse. The state would have its opportunity to challenge the agency.

Immediately, the acting chief of the NPS Branch of History, Herbert Kahler, began searching for expert witnesses to support the contention that the Jackson Hole area was historically significant. He settled on Dr. Leroy Hafen, the author of a number of books on the fur trade and the West, and chose Dr. Frederic Paxson, of the University of California, as an alternate. Park Service Director Newton B. Drury, who had replaced Cammerer in 1940, suggested the noted scientist Olaus B. Murie as the appropriate person to testify on biological values, and Dr. F. M. Fryxell for geological values. He also enlisted Lawrence Merriam, the assistant director of NPS Region II, which included the Jackson Hole region, to discuss administrative issues.[13]

The Act offered the Park Service great leeway; its inherent ambiguity made it easy to defend in court. The Park Service had only to show that the establishment of Jackson Hole was not an unusual instance. In such an amorphous category, its size did not make it an anomaly. Although there were few nineteenth-century structures in the region, Jackson Hole had historic importance because of its significance for the fur trade. Its unique geological features and important kinds of scarce wildlife became the basis for its scientific value (Figure 5.1). From the perspective of the agency, both values made the establishment of Jackson Hole National Monument a legitimate use of the Antiquities Act. Agency witnesses sought to convince the court of the scientific and historical value of the region. The Park Service's case would be strengthened by evidence that Jackson Hole contained compound cultural and scientific value.

In March 1944 the NPS settled on most of its expert witnesses. The agency chose Fryxell, Hafen, and Murie, along with Merrill J. Mattes of the NPS historical staff; the search for a biologist and geologist outside the agency continued.[14] But confusion continued over how to make the case: the specialists took a narrow view of their responsibilities, and someone had to develop a broadly based integrative approach.

The process of creating a historical justification produced tension within the agency. Mattes felt that the agency wavered on important historical questions. He advocated presenting Jackson Hole as an unequivocal historic landmark, but he contended that the NPS needed to assert conclusively that such mountain men as John Colter, Jedediah Smith, and Jim Bridger traversed the Jackson Hole area. The agency was too tentative, Mattes wrote, asserting that the objective was "to win a lawsuit rather than to write an historical monograph.... Our main job is to prove to the satisfaction of the court that *Jackson Hole does have special historical significance.* If I am wrong in this I am wondering what kind of a case for history we have left."[15] Mattes saw that accepting the pronouncements of historians offered a tactical advantage. He wanted the agency to capitalize on it.

Presenting the comparable values of history and science became the crucial question in pretrial strategy. The agency had to decide which value offered a more credible argument for the court. Assistant Regional Director Howard Baker answered that question in a memo of July 4, 1944, to Director Drury. "It is our opinion," he wrote, "that all of the values contained in the Jackson Hole National Monument should be presented with equal importance, for the composite of all places the monument in the national [significance] category."[16] Baker argued that the most compelling way to make the

Figure 5.1. Jackson Hole as it appeared in 1933, with the valley lands that would be at the heart of the 1940s controversy in the foreground. George Alexander Grant photograph, courtesy of National Park Service Historic Photo Collection, Harpers Ferry Center.

case was to present Jackson Hole as an aggregation of values, equally justifiable historically or scientifically, and certainly secure together. The latitude in the Antiquities Act afforded the NPS that option.

It was sound policy: broaden the issues at stake and overwhelm the state in court. The case was heard August 21–24, 1944, in federal district court in Sheridan, Wyoming, and according to National Park Service accounts, the trial went exactly as the agency planned. The state tried to show that the creation of Jackson Hole National Monument had been a political tactic to extend the boundaries of Grand Teton National Park. As a result, Wyoming Deputy Attorney General McIntyre had to prove that there were no outstanding historic or scientific objects in the region. He presented a series of local and state residents and experts to support his claims.[17]

The Park Service, whose case was overseen by Solicitor Price, countered by presenting its witnesses. Murie testified that Jackson Hole was unique because there were 120 different species of birds and 40 species of mammals in the region. Dr. Harold E. Anthony of the American Museum of Natural History testified that the monument contained objects of interest to scientists and students of natural history, and that the region was "a unique ecological area." He was followed by Mattes, whose testimony, in Price's opinion, "adequately demonstrat[ed] the historical significance of the area." A geologist from the University of Illinois, Dr. Leland Horberg, along with Dr. Rudolph Edmund of the Shell Oil Company, "revealed the importance of the Jackson Hole valley as an outstanding example of a fault-trough, to be considered in connection with the fault-block comprising the Teton Range."[18] According to their testimony, the region also contained examples of three separate stages of glaciation, lending even more significance from a geological perspective.

The NPS succeeded in showing that the area had significance, and Price chose not to present evidence justifying the size of the national monument area. He thought such a tactic unnecessary. Wyoming failed to show that the size of the monument was inappropriate, and Price believed that the court record clearly showed that the Antiquities Act offered sufficient authority to establish the national monument. "Under the recognized authorities," Price wrote in his report of the trial, "the court may not substitute its judgement for that of the President in reviewing the propriety of the action."[19]

The lawsuit challenged the nature of the proclamation as well as its constitutionality, but in the courtroom, the state emphasized the specifics of the case. The NPS counterattacked with a challenge to the right of the state of Wyoming to question the authority of the president. After this tactic, the state appeared to be on shaky ground, barring the kind of partisan judicial interpretation that the NPS officials indicated they feared when they discovered Judge T. Blake Kennedy's close ties to the grazing industry and the local states'-rights-driven Republican party. Judge Kennedy took the case under advisement at the close of the trial. Despite Price's fears, he was confident that the judge planned to vindicate the creation of the monument.[20]

Because Park Service strategists were able to construe the lawsuit as an attack on the Antiquities Act itself as well as on the monument, they built a defensible case. In the more than seventy previous national monument proclamations that employed the Antiquities Act, no one had ever challenged the law itself. Natural areas even larger than Jackson Hole, including the original Grand Canyon, Mount Olympus, and Joshua Tree national monuments, had been proclaimed under its auspices. The representative-area monuments of the 1930s, such as Organ Pipe Cactus National Monument, established a precedent for including flora typical of an area. Proclaimed as scientific monuments, they were additional ammunition in favor of the Park Service's case.

Although the crucial issue appeared to be the limits of the Antiquities Act, Judge Kennedy avoided addressing it when he made his decision. Kennedy dismissed the case on the grounds that it was "a controversy between the legislative and executive branches of the Government in which ... the Court can not interfere."[21] By circumventing the larger issue, the judge refused to rule upon the discretionary power of the president. The establishment of the monument stood, a sizable victory for the agency. The only redress for the state of Wyoming lay in legislative initiative.

The battle over Jackson Hole National Monument was the last of the first generation of conflicts between the interests of conservation/preservation and unregulated use of land. Wyoming pitted its rights as a sovereign state against those of the federal government—a battle not unlike the one Ralph Henry Cameron had fought against the Park Service at the Grand Canyon—and lost. Despite vindication of their position, Park Service officials recognized the importance of good relations with individual states. The agency had further objectives in the region and used the legal victory as a place from which to negotiate a compromise. As a result, the court case served as an indirect prelude to a negotiated abrogation of the Antiquities Act in Wyoming.

During the late 1930s and 1940s, other park projects created controversy in Congress. The Park Service lost much of its support in Congress as a result of weak leadership, attrition of elected officials, and retirement. The need for the development and interpretation of new park areas made the Antiquities Act a less formidable tool for preservation. Coupled with the unfavorable coverage the entire Jackson Hole episode generated, congressional uproar and greater public expectations made agency officials reconsider its assumptions about further expansion of the national park system.

The discovery phase of American preservation ended before the beginning of the New Deal, and the Antiquities Act became a valuable anachronism that recalled the Progressive-era values that shaped the early years of the agency. Between 1906 and 1944, the hegemony that invested the presidency with unlimited authority in federal land reservation matters broke down. The rush to reserve new park areas also dissipated: additions were no longer established just ahead of bulldozers and dam builders. Money for developing areas other than national parks became available. As the Park Service realized the value of all its different categories of areas and developed the kinds of programs that built and sustained an infrastructure, it spread its resources more evenly among the park system. Cooperation with Congress became critical to the future of the system, and the appeal of the Antiquities Act diminished. In an environment where the pronouncement of the establishment of an area meant less than its subsequent development, limits on uses of the Antiquities Act became inevitable.

Although in 1943 Earl Warren, then the governor of California, suggested to a conference of western governors that they work together to abolish the Antiquities Act, and Wyoming senator Joseph O'Mahoney cosponsored a bill in the Senate to that end, the abrogation of the Antiquities Act came only in 1950, and applied only in the state of Wyoming. The heated exchanges of earlier years cooled considerably in the postwar climate, and the participants negotiated an amicable compromise. What the NPS and the president sacrificed to acquire the new and enlarged Grand Teton National Park, which included the disputed Jackson Hole National Monument, was the right to use the Antiquities Act within the boundaries of the state of Wyoming.[22]

The NPS gave up little in the compromise, for the role of the Antiquities Act had already diminished. After the Park Service's division into regions in 1937, the agency gradually ceased to use the designation of an area to determine its value to the national park system. The manner in which an area entered the system became less important than its potential, and because most of the important areas in the public domain had long before been scrutinized for membership in the park system, the legal limits upon its use were no greater than the restrictions the agency placed upon itself.

In the end, the Jackson Hole National Monument controversy was a small battle about a question that has come to loom larger in the American West. The state of Wyoming challenged the monument as a precursor of what a later generation would call a "taking"; the federal court disagreed. Even though in 1943 Wyoming Governor Leslie Miller announced that the future of the state was in recreation instead of commercial resource extraction, the culture of the time and place argued strongly for protection of the right to use land for grazing and even mining. That the Antiquities Act was upheld in the Jackson Hole case sent a signal that the old culture was no longer dominant, and may have initiated the kind of resentment that has been common ever since among groups that represent the traditional economy in the West. In an indirect way, the battle between the Old and New Wests, between service and leisure on one side and commercial extraction on the other, has its roots in the showdown at Jackson Hole.

Notes

1. Righter 1982, 96–97. Senator Henry Ashurst of Arizona stated during the 1933 hearings on the enlargement of Grand Teton National Park that "the other states are not going to put over on Wyoming something that her two Senators do not want."

2. Righter 1982, 105–106, 108.

3. Righter 1982, 108.

4. Righter 1982, 110–111.

5. Righter 1982, 114–115.

6. *State of Wyoming vs. Charles J. Smith et al.*, May 18, 1943, National Archives Record Group 79, Series 7, Jackson Hole National Monument, file 201-06. (Hereafter cited as NA, RG 79.)

7. *State of Wyoming vs. Charles J. Smith et al.*

8. On June 17, 1943, Solicitor Jackson E. Price informed the Attorney

General of the United States that the validity of the Grand Canyon National Monument was an issue in *Cameron vs. U.S.*, 252 U.S. 450. But Cameron only challenged the federal government's right to take title to land to which he had filed a claim (see NA, RG 79, Series 7, Jackson Hole National Monument file 201-06; Shankland 1951, 225–242; NA, RG 79, Series 6, Grand Canyon, file 12-5, and Series 17, Records of Horace M. Albright 1927–1933, Grand Teton file).

9. *State of Wyoming vs. Charles J. Smith et al.*

10. Charles J. Smith, memorandum for the Associate Director, June 2, 1943, NA, RG 79, Series 7, Jackson Hole National Monument, file 201-06.

11. Solicitor Jackson E. Price to Attorney General, June 17, 1943, NA, RG 79, Series 7. Jackson Hole National Monument, file 201-06. The second Grand Canyon National Monument (proclaimed by Herbert Hoover in 1932) was indeed incorporated into the national park in 1975. The second Zion proclamation (covering the Kolob section) was made by FDR in 1937; it became part of the national park in 1956.

12. See letters following the December 3, 1943, decision in the National Archives, RG 79, Series 7, Jackson National Monument, file 201-06, particularly a confidential memo dated December 6, 1943, from Regional Director Lawrence C. Merriam to Paul Franke, who replaced Smith as the superintendent of Grand Teton National Park.

13. Newton B. Drury, memorandum, January 7, 1944, NA, RG 79, Series 7, Jackson Hole National Monument, file 201-06.

14. Hillary A. Tolson, memorandum for the files, March 13, 1944, NA, RG 79, Series 7, Jackson Hole National Monument, file 201-06.

15. Merrill J. Mattes to [NPS] Director, June 30, 1944, NA, RG 79, Series 7, Jackson Hole National Monument, file 201-06.

16. Howard Baker, memorandum to Newton B. Drury, July 4, 1944, NA, RG 79, Series 7, Jackson Hole National Monument, file 201-06.

17. Jackson E. Price, memorandum to Newton B. Drury, August 30, 1944, NA, RG 79, Series 7, Jackson Hole National Monument, file 201-06.

18. Price memorandum to Drury, August 30, 1944.

19. Price memorandum to Drury, August 30, 1944.

20. Paul Franke, memorandum to [NPS] Associate Director, April 19, 1944. NA, RG 79, Series 7, Jackson Hole National Monument. file 201-06.

21. Righter 1982, 119.

22. Righter 1982, 113, 117.

6

President Carter's Coup

An Insider's View of the
1978 Alaska Monument Designations

Cecil D. Andrus and John C. Freemuth

THE 1978 ANTIQUITIES ACT PROCLAMATIONS of President Jimmy Carter have been called the greatest single act of land preservation in American history. At that time Carter set aside, upon recommendation by Secretary of Interior Cecil D. Andrus, 56 million acres of Alaska as national monuments, an action that approximately doubled the size of the national park system. It was not a sudden and arbitrary act, but came towards the end of a twenty-year process. Yet, almost none of the original proclamations remain today as national monuments. Those of us who participated in those withdrawals certainly know why this is so, as do observers of our public land policy. To those who did not, it is a story of politics and power, employed to help bring closure to a contentious chapter of public land policy history, in the name of all of the values proclaimed in the purposes of the Antiquities Act itself.

The size of Alaska astounds. To use one national park example, consider Yellowstone and Wrangell–St. Elias National Park and Preserve. Yellowstone is 2.2 million acres. Wrangell–St. Elias is 13.2 million acres. There are over 54.7 million acres of national park system lands in Alaska, while the entire park system contains about 79 million acres of federal parkland, with another 5.4 million nonfederal acres under National Park Service management. Thus, almost *two-thirds* of the acreage contained in the national park system can be found in Alaska.

The numbers are even more significant for the U.S. Fish and Wildlife Service, as it manages 76 million acres in Alaska out of its nationwide total of 93 million acres. That is over 80% of the national wildlife refuge system. Finally, the federal land estate in

Alaska totals about 236 million acres, which is about 37% of the entire U.S. federal land system.

Although President Carter's Antiquities Act proclamations were sizeable, they were not the first for Alaska. In 1918, President Woodrow Wilson proclaimed Katmai National Monument at slightly less than a million acres. Katmai was enlarged over time to nearly 2.6 million acres by subsequent Antiquities Act actions and was the largest national park system unit for a long while. Today, Katmai National Park and Preserve is over 4 million acres. In 1925, President Calvin Coolidge proclaimed Glacier Bay National Monument. Like Katmai, it was enlarged over the years from around 1.2 million acres to its current size of 3.3 million acres, and is also now designated a national park and preserve.

Setting the Stage: Statehood and Native Claims

Our story begins with Alaska statehood.[1] Alaskans had lobbied for statehood for a number of years and finally received it in 1958. In order, among other things, to ensure its residents some sort of economic future, the state of Alaska was given the right to select approximately 105 million acres of federal land. Wrapped up in this were a number of issues, including a lack of knowledge of resources contained in those lands, and the land claims of Alaskan native peoples left unresolved by the statehood act. Because there had never been treaties negotiated with the various native groups and tribes in Alaska, the status of titles to land was uncertain. The 1958 statehood law did not resolve this issue either but left it up to a later Congress. It has been argued that high-ranking Alaskan officials did not think that the land that would be claimed in the state would amount to much, perhaps ending up simply being the land in and around native villages. A court case put that notion to rest with a much broader interpretation of land use.[2] Thus, the status of the claims, as well as their extent, created huge uncertainty. State selection of lands was slow because of the claims issue and the knowledge gap about what resources actually existed, and where.

As agreed to by Secretary of the Interior Stewart Udall, beginning in December 1966 a freeze was placed on any transfer of ownership on lands claimed by natives until Congress could act. Eventually, due to claims that overlapped with each other, over 380 million acres, an area larger than the state itself, were covered by the freeze.

One more event intervened. In 1968, oil was discovered at Prudhoe Bay up on the north slope of the state. That discovery and the need to transport the oil through a pipeline had the result of "refocusing" people's attention on the land claims. No pipeline could be constructed until the claims were resolved. It has been argued that it was the pipeline, rather than concern for justice for Alaska natives, that led to the passage of the Alaska Native Claims Settlement Act (ANCSA).[3]

The Alaska Native Claims Settlement Act

Passed in 1971, ANCSA finally resolved the native lands question. It conveyed over 44 million acres of land to regional and village native corporations. It also paid almost $1 billion to these groups for the rest of the land in Alaska that they gave up title to. But the law did something else. As with other public land, a question of "national interest" arose. If this land had once belonged to native Alaskans, it now in a key sense belonged to all Americans. While Alaskans themselves would obviously feel that any national policy on those lands would affect them more than most, nonetheless all Americans might have an interest in how those lands were dealt with as well.

The impetus for such a notion came from a federal committee charged with planning in Alaska after the large earthquake in 1964. Joseph Fitzgerald, the chair of the Federal Field Committee for Development Planning in Alaska, and David Hickok, a member of his staff, have been given credit for originating the notion that certain lands in Alaska should be included in the national park and national wildlife refuge systems.[4] Congress debated how to do this and how much land ought to be included. Senator Alan Bible of Nevada introduced a key amendment addressing these concerns. A pro-conservation amendment was introduced in the House by Morris Udall and John Saylor, and barely failed to pass. Instead, the House version that did pass called for extending the Stewart Udall freeze on entry on unreserved lands. The two versions of the settlement act were resolved in conference committee.

The result was ANCSA. It contained two key provisions that addressed the question of lands in the park and refuge systems. The key section, for the purposes of this chapter, was Section 17(d)(2), forevermore known as the part of the law that led to the "(d)(2)" lands debate. Paragraph A of the 17(d)(2) section authorized the secretary of interior to withdraw, within nine months of the passage of

ANSCA, up to *80 million acres* from the unreserved public lands in Alaska, including those that both the state of Alaska and the Natives had already selected. Lands withdrawn under this section would be protected "from all forms of appropriation under the public land laws, including the mining and mineral leasing laws." The purpose of the withdrawals was to allow for the secretary to make recommendations as to the inclusion of these lands in the park, wildlife refuge, wild and scenic river, and national forest systems. The secretary had up to two years to make the recommendations, but had to report on the withdrawals and the recommendations every six months. Another key paragraph of the (d)(2) provision, paragraph D, gave Congress a *five-year period* to act on the secretary's recommendations once they had been made.

What followed next were numerous attempts to meet the stipulations of the (d)(2) provision. On September 13, 1972, Secretary of the Interior Rogers C. B. Morton, after a great deal of study, preliminary withdrawals, and so on, withdrew 79 million acres of land for study for inclusion in the four federal lands systems. On December 17, 1973, his final recommendation to Congress came in at almost 83.5 million acres. The five-year clock had started. And now the action would shift to Congress for a time.

Histories of this period suggest that Congress did not begin hard work on the Alaska question until 1977. The Congress that took office in 1977 had two noted conservationists slated to take key positions. Morris Udall of Arizona would chair the House Interior and Insular Affairs Committee, and John Seiberling of Ohio would chair a new Interior subcommittee on General Oversight and Alaska Lands. The year 1977 was also when the Carter administration took office, with Cecil Andrus as his secretary of the interior. The House led with a strong protection bill (H.R. 39) that Udall styled as a place to start discussions.[5] Udall introduced the committee-passed bill on May 17, 1978.

Andrus, in an early appearance before Seiberling's subcommittee in 1977, asserted that protection of "large land areas" as called for in ANCSA was "the highest environmental priority" of the Carter administration and promised a departmental report on H.R. 39.[6] Andrus also decided that he would recommend more lands be included than those in the Morton proposal. His recommendations (after much study and internal discussions and vetting) came to almost 92 million acres.

On May 19, 1978, H.R. 39 passed the House by a 279–31 vote, adding over 100 million acres to the lands systems. Things would be different in the Senate. Alaska had a strong congressional delegation in its two senators, Ted Stevens and Mike Gravel, and in its sole member of the House, Don Young. The delegation was opposed to any sort of protection measures as wide ranging as those outlined in the House bill. Stevens, the de facto leader of the delegation, had indicated that he wasn't sure a bill would pass before the end of the five-year deadline.[7] Gravel wanted to prevent the passage of any legislation that entire session, which of course would run past the deadline as well. The two senators, however, employed different styles of legislative behavior. Stevens stayed completely involved in all activity of the Senate Committee on Energy and Natural Resources, participating in every mark-up session held on the Senate versions of the various Alaska bills in play, including H.R. 39. Gravel, on the other hand, chose to hardly participate. What eventually passed out of committee was unacceptable to the House and to the Carter administration. It seemed that a conference committee was in order, but seeing as it was October already and an election year, prospects for holding such a conference were dim.

But action did occur. Udall began working with his staff on small changes to the House bill, while Senator Henry Jackson of Washington convened a meeting of key actors, including Seiberling and Stevens, among others. Gravel had indicated that he would support some sort of compromise arrangement. After several days of meetings, Secretary Andrus joined this group on October 11.[8] Gravel muddied the waters by making a number of proposals that other legislators found unacceptable. Gravel again indicated he might compromise. The informal conference group worked frantically to come up with something they all could agree to. In this sort of climate, no one had the time to check every part of what was being worked on. Gravel once again derailed things by asserting that parts of the compromise were unacceptable to him.

He went further than that, though. When the conference group then attempted to extend the (d)(2) protections for one more year, Gravel threatened a filibuster. He claimed that his constituency would not allow for anything else.[9] One might spend some fruitful time analyzing who and what set of events were most to blame for the failure to pass legislation up till then. Gravel clearly seemed to be the one person most others blamed for the failure. As National

Park Service historian G. Frank Williss noted: "Killing the staff 'ad hoc' draft was one thing. Refusing to accept an extension of the d-2 protection was something else." Gravel may have "set into motion a chain of events that would be a major step in the direction" of an Alaska Lands bill.[10]

What followed next should not have been a surprise to Gravel or anyone else. Secretary Andrus had made it clear that he would do whatever he could administratively to protect the national interest lands, should Congress fail to act in time. The White House had requested an analysis of what would happen to the lands if (d)(2) ran into the deadline, and of what options existed to do something about that. The Department of Interior issued a report that listed available options. They included use of the Antiquities Act to proclaim national monuments, as well as provisions of the new Federal Land Policy and Management Act (FLPMA), passed in 1976. That act also gave the secretary of the interior emergency withdrawal powers. Not surprisingly, Gravel and Stevens would try to prohibit the use of the Antiquities Act in Alaska.

It took the state of Alaska to force the issue. The state requested that the freeze be lifted and at the same time filed for a state land selection of over 40 million acres, including 14 million acres that were within the boundaries of proposed conservation units.[11] Andrus considered this to be a violation of a spoken agreement by the state not to do this, but rather to select only lands outside the proposed protected areas. On November 16, his first action was to use provisions of FLMPA to withdraw 110 million acres for a three-year period, preventing state selection from being finalized and protecting the lands from mineral entry. Then came the Antiquities Act proclamation on December 1. Again, it must be remembered that the Park Service had already been working on such a possibility as early as July of that year.

Antiquities Act Action

The moratorium put in place by 17(d)(2) was set to expire in late 1978. Andrus went to Carter with information about the Antiquities Act after coordinating and checking with Stuart Eizenstat, Carter's domestic policy advisor. A "talking points" memo for senior White House staff outlined a number of key themes, discussed below.

Andrus had fended off Alaska's attempts to gain an injunction, but the FLPMA withdrawals were under attack by the state. The

Figure 6.1. Two of the protagonists in the Alaska monuments controversy: Secretary of the Interior Cecil D. Andrus watches as President Jimmy Carter speaks, 1977. Bob Coles photograph, courtesy of DOI and National Park Service Historic Photo Collection, Harpers Ferry Center.

Antiquities Act provided the "best and most unassailable protection" against threats to the conservation lands.[12] The secretary and the president had said they would take some sort of action and needed to be true to that promise. Use of the Act would force people back to the table to work on legislative solutions because large majorities of the American public supported protection, while Alaskan opponents were never supporters of protection. The memo noted that the legal rationale for this being a legitimate use of the Antiquities Act had been researched and found to be sound.[13]

Finally, a memo from Andrus' director of public affairs, Chris Carlson, to the White House's assistant press secretary, Patricia Bario, made it clear that congressional action was still desirable. Antiquities Act designations were considered more inflexible, and the diversity of uses envisioned in the original 1960s planning effort developed by administration resource planners allowed for "subtle shades of management regimes."[14]

In a meeting with the president, Andrus outlined a brief history of the use of the Antiquities Act by former presidents, such as President Theodore Roosevelt's use of the Act to protect Grand Canyon and President Hoover's protection of Death Valley. Andrus suggested that Carter protect the administration-proposed areas, which totaled some 56 million acres. Two large areas would be managed by the U.S. Fish and Wildlife Service. The U.S. Forest Service would manage some of the protected lands as well. The actual exchange between the president and the secretary is one not soon to be forgotten in American conservation history: "Can I do that?" asked the president. "Yes sir, you can, you have the authority," Andrus replied. "Let's do it," responded the president.

Of course, the action caused a loud outcry of protest, similar to that which would later arise after President Bill Clinton announced the creation of Grand Staircase–Escalante National Monument, the first to be administered by the Bureau of Land Management. Court cases were filed against the Carter monument proclamations, all of them unsuccessful. The Antiquities Act proclamations had the effect, though, of protecting proposed parklands intact. Moreover, it brought opponents back to the bargaining table by ensuring that the political tactic of delay would not bear any more fruit. Most importantly, 56 million acres of Alaska land entered the national park and wildlife refuge systems (Figure 6.2; for a full list of the Carter monuments, see the Appendix.)

As expected, Congress took up legislation again, in 1979. Gravel remained opposed and not engaged in the process. The House that met had seen a change in seats, with Republicans the clear gainers. Udall introduced H.R. 39 again. Various alternative bills were also proposed and more pro-development bills gained support, yet the Alaska delegation remained opposed even to the latter, while environmentalists were opposed to them as well, as were Udall and Seiberling.[15]

Udall and Representative John Anderson of Illinois introduced another bill that eventually passed in amended form by a vote of 360–65. Even the issue of gun control entered the picture, as the National Rifle Association claimed that this bill was a gun control measure. It took Pat Williams, congressman from Montana, and an undecided vote on the bill, to defuse that issue.[16]

Andrus kept up the administration's momentum and pressure by ordering twenty-year withdrawals and plans to be drawn up under FLPMA authority. Once the Senate began work, it relied on Senator Jackson's bill as its vehicle (S. 9). Stevens was once again the lead player during the mark-up sessions. Gravel, as usual, threatened filibusters, and debate on the bill was held up until 1980.[17] Once again, Andrus tried to keep things focused by suggesting that he would use FLPMA to protect, for twenty years, another 40 million acres withdrawn temporarily in 1978, which he then proceeded to do.

Figure 6.2. Some of the Alaska national monuments proclaimed by President Carter in December 1978. Clockwise from upper left: Yukon–Charley Rivers National Preserve, Aniakchak National Monument, Kobuk Valley National Park, Lake Clark National Park. Unattributed photographs, courtesy of National Park Service Digital Image Archives (Lake Clark); National Park Service Historic Photo Collection, Harpers Ferry Center (all others).

Back in the Senate, Stevens, sensing that he was on the losing side, slowed things down by introducing a number of amendments. That led to a substitute bill being introduced.[18] Gravel filibustered, but was finally defeated by a cloture vote, 63–25. The substitute bill (Amendment 1961) passed, 72–16.[19]

Again maneuvering began between the two legislative branches. The Senate said it would not accept any changes, while the House, led by Udall, worked on compromise guidelines and hoped for later amendments once the bill was signed.[20] But then the ultimate arbiter intervened: a presidential election. The sweeping victory of Ronald Reagan and the Republican ascendance to the majority in the Senate led the House to accept the Senate bill as the best they could now get.

The law, passed as the Alaska National Interest Lands Conservation Act (ANILCA), had its compromises. Wilderness designations allowed for motorized access in some places.[21] The Arctic National Wildlife Refuge (ANWR) language did not prohibit oil and gas exploration on its coastal plains. Some people thought too many places were designated as "preserves," allowing for hunting, and not enough were designated as "parks."

Still, the scope of what was preserved was breathtaking. Forty-three million acres were added to the park system, 54 million to the wildlife refuge system, and 56 million to the wilderness system. Some of these included the largest ecosystems yet protected in the United States. As part of ANILCA, the original Antiquities Act proclamations that were not legislatively protected were rescinded: "As to all lands not within the boundaries established by this Act of any conservation system unit, national conservation area, national recreation area, or national forest addition, the aforesaid withdrawals and reservations are hereby rescinded on the effective date of this Act."[22]

Postscript: The Arctic National Wildlife Refuge

Given the current and seemingly endless controversy over development of the Arctic National Wildlife Refuge, a word or two about that is in order, because it is part of the Alaska story told here. Recall the role played by Alaska Senator Gravel during the attempt to pass legislation that would resolve the debate over what lands ought to receive protection in Alaska. Gravel used the filibuster on numerous occasions to derail attempts to resolve the issue. Remember that H.R. 39 had passed the House by a vote of 279–31, a clear expression of majoritarian support in that branch. The Senate, of course, followed its own counsel. Senator Stevens fought a hard battle for his perception of the needs and views of Alaska, and the entire series of debates, meetings, and bills clearly showed his imprint. But Senator Gravel took a different tack, threatening *filibusters* during conference committee attempts to resolve differences between the House and Senate. The conference committee included Andrus in its negotiations. Gravel's opposition extended to the extension of the (d)(2) deadline. Of course, the rest is history. Andrus advised the president to bring the Antiquities Act into play.

Fast-forward to the debate over ANWR in 2005. At this writing, the Senate, in a parliamentary maneuver, has placed the authorization to open ANWR for oil and gas development in the fiscal year 2006 budget resolution. This resolution is exempted from a filibuster and subject to a simple majority vote of the Senate. As Senator Stevens—still very much on the scene in 2005—said at the time, this budget resolution "move" was the only way to *avoid* the potential of a filibuster of a straight vote on ANWR development as stand-alone legislation.

The filibuster is a time-honored strategic tool used by impassioned Senate minorities to slow down, if not derail, legislation that they oppose. That was its use by Senator Gravel based on his opposition to ANILCA. It would likely be used that way by senators opposed to the opening of ANWR, if they could.

Conclusion: The Antiquities Act and Alaska

As we have said, the size and abundance of Alaska's natural resources simply astounds. Understandably, people will have different opinions about what uses ought to be made, or not made, of those resources, and by whom. That was the real story of the saga to protect and develop Alaska's lands. The Antiquities Act was an absolutely vital tool in that saga. It was used protectively, as one key land withdrawal action taken by Andrus and Carter to protect some of Alaska's special lands. It was also used strategically to force Congress to deal with a question that it ought to have dealt with all along. None of those uses of the Act can be understood without the others. American environmental history provides plenty of examples of the use of the Act to protect landscapes and resources that Congress could or would not. Some of those areas later became well-known, if not "crown jewel," national parks. The Act's use in Alaska was and remains today the largest act of land protection in American history. In this case, though, we want to remind our readers of how this issue was resolved. The Antiquities Act was used to protect key areas, spurring Congress to finally act. Protection for areas not included in ANILCA was rescinded, a necessary compromise once Congress had acted. One could certainly argue that a different Congress could have chosen to protect more, or less, of the land within the original proclamations, however. All of this happened within the difficult give-and-take of American politics that takes place between the executive and legislative branches.

That struggle continues with the debate over ANWR, this time within Congress. Originally, as we have seen, the filibuster was used to slow down progress with ANILCA. Now members of Congress are trying to neutralize its use to stop the opening of ANWR. As majorities and presidents change, they choose to use the tools at their disposal in different ways. Ultimately, it is up to Congress to decide the future of ANWR. Whether a majority of the American public is happy with this current strategic move to deny the use of the filibuster remains to be seen.

Acknowledgments

We would like to thank Marc Johnson for encouraging us to complete this project and for his support during its writing. We would also like to thank the two anonymous reviewers of this manuscript for their detailed and rigorous review.

Notes

1. A very accessible and readable history of the National Park Service in Alaska is Williss 1985.

2. Haycox 1992, 31.

3. Williss 1985, chapter 2, part B, 4.

4. Williss 1985, chapter 2, part C, 2; Haycox 1992, 31.

5. Williss 1985, chapter 4, part E, 3.

6. Williss 1985, chapter 4, part E, 4.

7. Williss 1985, chapter 4, part F, 5.

8. Williss 1985, chapter 4, part G, page 1.

9. Haycox 1992, 35.

10. Williss 1985, chapter 4, part G, page 3.

11. "Summary of the Alaska National Interest Lands Legislation," prepared by the Department of the Interior (February 1979), 5. Andrus Collection, miscellaneous Alaska files, Boise State University.

12. "Talking Points for 11/28/78 Meeting with Senior White House Staff Re Alaska National Interest Lands," 2. Andrus Collection, miscellaneous Alaska files, Boise State University.

13. "Talking Points," 3–6.

14. Memorandum from Chris Carlson, Assistant to the Secretary of the Interior and director of Public Affairs, to Patricia Bario, Assistant White House Press Secretary, November 28, 1978.

15. Williss 1985, chapter 4, part H, 2.

16. Williss 1985, chapter 4, part H, 3.

17. Williss 1985, chapter 4, part H, 4.

18. Williss 1985, chapter 4, part H, 5.

19. Williss 1985, chapter 4, part H, 5.

20. Williss 1985, chapter 4, part H, 6.

21. Williss 1985, chapter 4, part I, 1.

22. Public Law 96-487, Alaska National Interest Lands Conservation Act (December 2, 1980), section 1322(a).

7

The Antiquities Act and the Exercise of Presidential Power

The Clinton Monuments

Mark Squillace

SCHOLARS WILL LONG DEBATE THE LEGACY of William Jefferson Clinton and his presidency, but it will be hard to ignore the considerable impact that Clinton had on the preservation of public lands and public land resources—especially during his second term in office.[1] If history is any guide, few of Clinton's actions will likely endure as long and as well as his decisions to proclaim twenty-two new or expanded national monuments under the authority of the Antiquities Act of 1906.[2]

The story of the Clinton monuments is largely the story of Clinton's secretary of the interior, former Arizona Governor Bruce Babbitt. Babbitt was a favorite of the media, having endeared himself to the press corps during a brief but unsuccessful run for the Democratic presidential nomination in 1988.[3] Babbitt brought a unique set of skills to the position of interior secretary. As a former Democratic governor of a Republican-leaning state, Babbitt demonstrated an ability to work well with others, including those who might not fully agree with him. As the son of a pioneer ranching family of northern Arizona, Babbitt understood the issues facing ranchers—one of the Department of the Interior's major constituencies—including issues involving water rights, grazing rights, and dealings with the federal government. And as a graduate of the University of Notre Dame and Harvard Law School, Babbitt had honed the intellectual and political skills necessary to manage a major federal bureaucracy.[4]

This chapter begins by describing Grand Staircase–Escalante National Monument and shows how this designation was instrumental in setting the stage for Clinton's subsequent monument decisions. It then looks at the process used by the Clinton White House and the Interior Department to develop and designate additional monuments. This is followed by a brief review of the Clinton monuments and some of the policy issues and practical problems confronted by the administration during the development of monument proposals. In this context, the decision not to designate Arctic National Wildlife Refuge as a monument is considered. Finally, it addresses long-term prospects for the Clinton monuments in light of the continuing controversy over their creation.

The Instrumental Role of
Grand Staircase–Escalante National Monument

During the early history of the Antiquities Act, presidents used the law freely to protect public lands and public land resources that had captured the imagination of government officials and the public at large.[5] Even without the benefit of hindsight, the decisions made in those early years must have seemed obvious. Millions throughout the world have marveled at the massive scale of the Grand Canyon, the towering walls of Zion, the temperate rainforests of the Olympic peninsula, and the coastal beauty of Acadia.[6] By the mid-twentieth century, however, the most obvious places to designate as national monuments had largely been protected or developed. So, with the spectacular exception of the Alaska monuments, designated by President Jimmy Carter in 1978,[7] the Antiquities Act fell into desuetude. The early years of the Clinton Administration brought little change to this state of affairs. The politics of Clinton's re-election bid in 1996, however, coincided with growing pressure from the conservation community to protect some of the remote canyons and deserts of south-central Utah.[8]

Southern Utah is home to the largest concentration of national parks and monuments in the country, including Zion, Bryce Canyon, Capitol Reef, Canyonlands, and Arches National Parks, as well as Cedar Breaks and Natural Bridges National Monuments and Glen Canyon National Recreation Area. But one spectacular area remained unprotected. The Escalante Canyon and its tributaries, and the Kaiparowits Plateau southwest of the canyon area, had long been targeted by conservation groups for protection. These deep and starkly beautiful canyons support vibrant riparian ecosystems, and their remote location and challenging topography make them inaccessible to casual tourists but prized by backpackers and wilderness advocates. But some resource developers prized the area too. The Kaiparowits Plateau, just north of the Colorado River and south and west of the Escalante River, had long been eyed by coal companies eager to exploit its estimated 5–7 billion tons of recoverable coal.[9] As Babbitt surely knew, designation of the monument would effectively kill any chance of developing this coal.[10] Still, the politics of the decision fit neatly into Clinton's re-election strategy.

Declaring a southern Utah monument would not be popular among state and local politicians, but Utah is the quintessential "red" state, and it was plainly not going to support Clinton under any circumstances. Just to the south, however, Babbitt's home state of Arizona was looking more and more like Clinton country. Moreover, Clinton's first-term environmental record disappointed some sectors of the environmental community and he needed their full support to secure his re-election. Clinton's dramatic announcement of the new Grand Staircase–Escalante National Monument—made just two months before the 1996 election while standing on the south rim of the Grand Canyon in Arizona—was great political theater and had just the desired effect (Figure 7.1).[11] The 1.7-million-acre Grand Staircase–Escalante National Monument triggered vehement opposition from Utah politicians, but it was quite popular in other parts of the country, and it sparked a resurgence of interest on both sides of the political fence in what had become a rather moribund law.[12]

Opponents of the Antiquities Act in general, and of Grand Staircase–Escalante National Monument in particular, focused on the lack of notice and the lack of public process in the decision to designate the monument.[13] They sought relief both in the courts and in the halls of Congress. Even after Clinton's re-election in November 1996, some members of the Utah congressional delegation continued to push for reform of the law. But as time passed, opposition to the new monument waned.

Clinton's re-election and the public's support for the Grand Staircase decision opened a window of opportunity to promote other land protection measures. But some congressional opponents of Grand Staircase were pushing proposals that would limit the president's authority under the Antiquities Act, and these efforts counseled against proceeding too precipitously. By 1998, however, Babbitt began thinking about new monument opportunities. He first set

Figure 7.1. President Bill Clinton proclaimed Grand Staircase–Escalante National Monument at a highly publicized event held, not in Utah, but at Grand Canyon National Park in Arizona, September 18, 1996. NPS photograph by Mike Quinn, courtesy of National Park Service.

his sights on the Otay Mountain area near San Diego, California. If the president was going to declare new monuments, California seemed like a relatively safe place to start. Babbitt paid a visit to the area and talked about the possibility of a new monument. To his surprise, the local congressional designation responded with a bill to designate Otay Mountain as a wilderness area.[14] It was most likely this experience that caused Babbitt to realize that simply talking about a possible new monument might be enough to spur local congressional leaders to take action on their own without the need for a presidential proclamation.

Babbitt was emboldened by his experience at Otay Mountain and on November 10, 1998, he secured a letter from the president soliciting "any recommendations you may have for further appropriate exercise of my authority under the Antiquities Act to protect objects of historic or scientific interest on federal lands."[15] This letter achieved two important purposes. First, it put the White House on record as supporting new monument proposals. Second, and importantly, it insulated Babbitt's activities from the procedural burdens of the National Environmental Policy Act.[16] Less than three weeks after receiving the letter, Babbitt was in northern Arizona touring the North Rim of the Grand Canyon around the Shivwits Plateau and setting the stage for what eventually would become the 1.1-million-acre Grand Canyon–Parashant National Monument.[17] By the end of 1999, Babbitt had sent to the White House recommendations for three new national monuments—Grand Canyon–Parashant and Agua Fria in his home state of Arizona, and California Coastal National Monument—and recommended expansion of a fourth, Pinnacles, also in California.

As it became clear that President Clinton was prepared to use the Antiquities Act to help secure his environmental legacy, many more ideas were put forward. Some were first suggested by persons from outside the agency with interests in protecting particular tracts of land, but credit for the astonishing success of Clinton's second-term Antiquities Act campaign must be given to several key people within the Administration. Most important was Babbitt himself. Once it became clear that the White House would support his efforts, Babbitt embraced his role as chief architect and salesman for new monument proposals. His knowledge of western lands, his commitment to protecting special places, and his willingness to travel to every proposed site and meet with affected parties generated widespread public support for the proposals and disarmed his critics. Within the White House, the enthusiastic support of John Podesta, Clinton's chief of staff, was crucial. While much has been made of the claim that Babbitt nudged Clinton into accepting his monument proposals, their value as a key parts of Clinton's legacy was not lost on Podesta, nor for that matter on Clinton himself. Thus, while Babbitt was ready with information to bolster his case, the White House did not resist his entreaties.[18] Back at Interior, the department's chief solicitor, John Leshy—who, like Babbitt, served the entire eight-year Clinton term—also deserves much of the credit for developing a legal strategy that would secure the Administration's decisions from subsequent attacks. Leshy was a key official involved in developing the Alaska monument proposals during the Carter Administration, and this experience gave him a perspective and understanding of the issues that was invaluable. In the end, President Clinton proclaimed 22 new or expanded national monuments during the final year of his administration. In all, the Clinton monuments encompass nearly six million acres of land.

Developing the Clinton-Era Monument Proposals

The Antiquities Act is silent about the process used to develop monument proposals. Monuments are limited in size to the "smallest area compatible" with the protection of the resource, but the Supreme Court's decision in 1920 upholding Theodore Roosevelt's 1908 proclamation of the 800,000-acre Grand Canyon National Monument assured the president broad discretion to set the scope and size of a monument.[19] Beyond the size limitation, the Antiquities Act also limits monuments to "historic landmarks, historic and prehistoric structures, and other objects of historic or scientific interest that are situated upon the lands owned or controlled by the Government of the United States." The breadth of this authority, however, makes it difficult, if not impossible, to challenge a presidential decision to proclaim a national monument.

While the courts have uniformly sustained the myriad uses of the Antiquities Act by various presidents over many years,[20] the Antiquities Act may be more vulnerable to congressional action. The only time the Act has been amended was in response to the designation of Jackson Hole National Monument in Wyoming.[21] That amendment—a compromise that allowed the monument to become part of Grand Teton National Park—prohibits the designation of any new Antiquities Act monuments in Wyoming.[22] As noted above, the Grand Staircase–Escalante designation triggered a new round of debate over amending the Antiquities Act. This time the proposed changes were more fundamental. They included proposals that would have effectively repealed the president's authority to proclaim national monuments, as well as proposals that would require substantial public process and participation before a monument could be designated.[23]

In recommending monument proposals to the president, Secretary Babbitt followed a carefully engineered strategy designed to protect areas deemed worthy of national monument status while at the same time holding congressional opposition at bay. Criticism of the Grand Staircase–Escalante proclamation focused on the administration's failure to consult adequately with state officials, and the statute's failure to establish a public process before a proclamation is issued. As a former governor, Babbitt was sensitive to this criticism, and he committed the administration to a three-part process—which he often described as his "no surprises" policy[24]—before recommending new national monuments. First, he expressed a willingness to visit any area that his office was considering for monument status. Second, he agreed to meet personally with local officials and interested members of the public about different strategies for protecting the area under review.[25] Finally, he agreed to afford local congressmen and senators the opportunity to adopt appropriate legislation to protect the area under consideration for national monument status before making a recommendation to the president. This last concession resulted in legislation protecting several remarkable areas that would not likely have received congressional attention without indications from the secretary that these areas were being considered for national monument status.

Developing proposals for new monuments proved relatively easy. Babbitt's many years of experience in public life, and his long association with the public lands, had put him into contact with the people who were likely to promote monuments and the places where monuments might be proclaimed. Moreover, the conservation community was quick to provide Babbitt's office with its own well-documented proposals, along with thousands of letters supporting them. The federal Bureau of Land Management (BLM) also offered a wealth of information and experience with particular tracts of public lands and proved instrumental in providing logistical and technical support for various proposals.

For those proposals with merit, the secretary's office would make preliminary inquiries with local congressional representatives and state officials to gauge the degree of support or opposition that a proposal might encounter.[26] If at this or any other stage in the process it appeared that legislative action to protect the lands was a possible option, Babbitt would pursue that avenue with the appropriate congressional representatives. He did not shy away from proposals solely because they lacked broad support from the local political establishment, but local concerns were always part of the calculus. Of particular concern to Babbitt was that he not force through proposals that might unnecessarily threaten the Antiquities Act itself. He understood that the law was vulnerable to political attack, and that the more it was used, the more likely it would be that opponents would try to amend or repeal it. It was this concern, for example, that may have led him to resist pressure from the environmental community to recommend the Arctic National Wildlife Refuge for monument status.[27]

If a proposal passed through this filter, Babbitt would schedule one or more visits to the site and associated communities. He would walk the ground and meet with local people, individually and publicly, to discuss their concerns and hopes for the lands.[28] Far from being a mere formality, these encounters would often result in changes to monument proposals.[29]

For proposals that remained viable after this public process, document preparation would begin. This included preparing a draft proclamation, developing maps to describe the area proposed for designation, and preparing appropriate background documents.

From the earliest history of the Antiquities Act, monument proclamations were written simply to describe—often eloquently, and almost always briefly—those objects that were to be protected in the proclamation. The Clinton-era proclamations follow the trend begun by President Carter's Alaska monuments of being substantially more detailed than their predecessors. They describe with particularity the "objects" to be protected and they explain why the lands designated are "the smallest area compatible with the proper care and management of the objects to be protected." They explicitly withdraw the lands from "all forms of entry, location, selection, sale, or leasing or other disposition under the public land laws," including the mining and mineral leasing laws. They also typically "prohibit all motorized and mechanized vehicle use off road" in most circumstances. Where appropriate, they also address whether the monument designation reserves water rights.[30] Otherwise, they follow the historical preference for simplicity.

Map preparation was generally entrusted to the federal land management agency with jurisdiction over the area being considered, whose personnel usually had a good idea of the resources, potential resource conflicts, and topography of the area under consideration. Draft maps were prepared and studied, and potential conflicts or issues with other resources were identified. To the extent possible, conflicts were avoided by carefully drawing monument boundaries.

In addition to containing draft proclamations and maps, Babbitt's recommendation to the president included a detailed memorandum describing the reasons for the recommendation, as well as a bibliography of sources supporting the decision. These were generally developed by the secretary's staff in conjunction with experts from within and outside the agency who were familiar with the landscape, and were made available to the public along with the president's proclamation. A separate memorandum was also prepared for the White House, and though it contained essentially the same language as the public memorandum, the White House would not release this document. Press documents were also prepared that summarized the resources proposed for protection under the Antiquities Act.[31]

When a monument recommendation appeared likely, the secretary's staff would brief the president's staff at the Council on Environmental Quality (CEQ) on the background of the proposal and the possible controversy that the proposal might engender. A recommendation was sent to Clinton only after it had received tentative approval from the CEQ.

The Nature of the Clinton-Era Monuments

Babbitt was willing to entertain a wide variety of proposals, but his penchant was for monuments that would protect large landscapes and unique ecosystems. And he viewed these concepts broadly, to encompass landscapes of archaeological sites.[32] Babbitt believed he could win approval and widespread public support for a substantial number of new monuments by entrusting their management to the existing land manager, which in the case of many of the largest new monuments was the BLM.[33]

The environmental community was skeptical of the BLM's ability to manage lands for conservation purposes. Historically, the BLM had aligned itself with the ranching and mineral industry. Upset by this apparent alliance, environmental groups sometimes tagged the agency with the unflattering sobriquet of the "Bureau of Livestock and Mining." But as Arizona governor, Babbitt had developed good working relationships with the BLM. During the mid-to-late 1980s Babbitt worked closely with the BLM to orchestrate a massive exchange of lands among the BLM, the state of Arizona, and private landowners to consolidate state land holdings and secure protection for critical areas such as the San Pedro River.[34] This experience undoubtedly gave Babbitt a more sympathetic view of the BLM. Moreover, entrusting monument management to the BLM was less likely to arouse significant opposition. Plainly, some within the bureau were ready to assume the conservation mantle and Babbitt shrewdly concluded that providing the BLM with its own unique conservation mission had the potential to transform the agency.

The monument initiative was just the vehicle to steer the agency in this new direction.[35]

Babbitt promoted this new approach to monument management by establishing a new sub-agency within the BLM that is responsible for managing national monuments and other BLM lands with a conservation focus, such as wilderness areas. The National Landscape Conservation System (see the chapter by Daly and Middaugh in this volume) gives the BLM a conservation charge distinct from the other federal land protection agencies, such as the National Park Service. The focus of the NLCS is to manage landscapes and ecosystems and eliminate incompatible uses. In keeping with this aim, units of the NLCS provide opportunities for visitor use, but generally without visitor centers and other facilities in the monument itself. To the extent that such facilities are needed, they will usually be built in nearby communities or on the periphery of the monument.[36]

The BLM also intends to allow a wider range of uses within its NLCS units, to the extent that such uses are consistent with other management authorities, and, in the case of national monuments, with the proclamation establishing the monument. Thus, while new mineral development and new road construction are generally precluded in BLM monuments, hunting and grazing can continue to the extent that such uses are consistent with the management of the objects identified for protection in the proclamation.[37]

It remains to be seen how such notions of multiple use will play themselves out in the context of monument management, especially under the leadership of the current administration, which has shown every sign of favoring more extractive uses on public lands, including national monuments. In March 2001, Secretary of the Interior Gale Norton sent a letter to the governors of Utah and Arizona, host to several new monuments, inviting suggestions about "vehicle use ... grazing and water rights, as well as the wide spectrum of other traditional multiple uses that might be appropriately applied to these [monument] lands."[38] Certainly, some forms of hunting and recreational activities are compatible with the protection of most monument resources, and the proclamations generally leave the state game and fish departments in charge of regulating hunting and fishing activities.[39] But other uses, such as logging and grazing, are more problematic. The U.S. Forest Service, another multiple-use agency that manages the Clinton-designated Giant

Sequoia National Monument, approved a plan in December 2003 that allows logging 7.5 million board-feet of timber annually from the monument, despite language in the presidential proclamation that prohibits tree removal unless "clearly needed" to protect the ecology of the forest or public safety. The California attorney general has sued the Forest Service to block implementation of the plan on the grounds that it violates the terms of the monument proclamation.[40]

In two of the proclamations establishing BLM monuments—Kasha–Katuwe Tent Rocks and Sonoran Desert—President Clinton required the elimination of livestock grazing over much or all of the monument to promote the protection of these areas.[41] The legislation for Steens Mountain (one of the areas protected by an act of Congress in lieu of a Babbitt monument proposal) also provides for elimination of certain livestock grazing, albeit through the vehicle of land exchanges.[42] The proclamation for Cascade–Siskiyou National Monument in Oregon requires the BLM to "study the impacts of livestock grazing on the objects of biological interest in the monument with specific attention to sustaining the natural ecosystem dynamics."[43] At the time of this writing, the study has not been released but it could plainly lead to restrictions on grazing in the monument.

Authorizations for new rights-of-way across monument lands may also raise difficult questions. The broad language in the Clinton monument proclamations withdrew the lands from all forms of disposition under the public land laws, which would appear to include new rights-of-way.[44] The memoranda from the secretary that accompanied the recommendations to Clinton typically addressed rights-of-way in a very general way, noting that "[s]ome existing rights-of-way may include valid existing rights," but indicating that "[t]he exercise of such rights may be regulated to protect the purposes of the proposed monument, but any regulation must respect such rights."[45] New rights-of-way were not generally mentioned. However, when the issue was raised squarely in the context of Sonoran Desert National Monument, the secretary agreed to include an additional sentence in the memorandum written to support the monument allowing new rights-of-way within existing right-of-way corridors, so long as the BLM determines, after NEPA compliance, that such rights-of-way "are consistent with the purposes of protecting the objects for which the monument was established and the monument's management plan."[46] While it thus appears that new rights-of-way under strict conditions might be allowed in Sonoran Desert National Monument, the absence of comparable language in any of the other memoranda may suggest a contrary intent for those other monuments.

For monuments designed to protect broad landscapes or ecosystems, the Clinton proclamations sometimes required the management agency to prepare a management plan to ensure that appropriate actions are taken to protect the objects identified in the proclamation.[47] Such plans will likely be prepared in accordance with the existing land use planning authorities of the various management agencies, whether or not they are specifically required in the proclamation. But the proclamations will clearly limit the management options that would otherwise have been available, especially to agencies such as the BLM. The BLM established an "Interim Management Policy for Newly Created National Monuments,"[48] and completed its management plan for Grand Staircase–Escalante National Monument. If that management plan offers a glimpse into how the BLM will manage its other monuments, then the agency appears well on its way toward achieving the transformation towards conservation that Secretary Babbitt promoted.[49]

The Clinton Monuments

Viewed in isolation, Bill Clinton's record under the Antiquities Act was extraordinary, and compares favorably with the impressive record of Theodore Roosevelt, who was president in 1906 when the Antiquities Act was passed.[50] When viewed from the perspective of history, however, Clinton's record is particularly remarkable because his decisions were made against a backdrop of nearly one hundred years of presidents, legislators, and public land administrators with the prior opportunity to evaluate and recommend lands for protection under the Antiquities Act and a host of other land protection laws. Moreover, every single monument created during the Clinton Administration came at a time when the Republican Party—the opposition party—held control of both houses of Congress. And many of these Republicans were adamantly opposed to the Antiquities Act, and especially to its repeated use by a Democratic president.

The monuments created during the Clinton Administration are a diverse collection (Figure 7.2). They include four small historic sites. President Lincoln and Soldier's Home National Monument includes the Anderson Cottage where President Abraham Lincoln lived with his family during Washington's warm summer months. The Minidoka Internment National Monument is a 72.75-acre tract of land in Idaho that housed a Japanese internment camp during World War II. Pompeys Pillar National Monument encompasses a 51-acre tract of land in Montana and includes a bluff with William Clark's name carved in the wall—the only known tangible evidence of the Lewis and Clark expedition. Governor's Island National Monument—a 20-acre site in New York state—served as an outpost for New York City during the early part of the nineteenth century.[51]

Figure 7.2. Some of the other monuments proclaimed by President Clinton during the latter half of his administration, 1996–2001. Clockwise from upper left: Vermillion Cliffs National Monument, Arizona; Upper Missouri River Breaks National Monument, Montana; Minidoka Internment National Monument, Idaho; Grand Canyon–Parashant National Monument, Arizona. Unattributed photographs, courtesy of Bureau of Land Management, Office of the National Landscape Conservation System (Vermillion Cliffs, Upper Missouri River Breaks); National Park Service (Minidoka Internment; Grand Canyon–Parashant).

Among the more unique of the Clinton monuments are two that consist entirely of submerged lands—the 13,893-acre Virgin Islands Coral Reef National Monument, which lies directly adjacent to the Virgin Islands National Park off the island of St. John, and an 18,135-acre expansion of the Buck Island Reef National Monument off the island of St. Croix. The California Coastal National Monument is another unusual monument, encompassing all unappropriated islands, rocks, pinnacles, and exposed reefs in the jurisdictional waters of the United States for the 841 miles of California coastline within 12 nautical miles from the coast.[52] The monument was set aside to protect the nesting habitat of thousands of seabirds, as well as the tidepools and other resources of these biologically rich coastal lands. One new monument—Giant Sequoia in California—consists of groves of towering giant sequoias, the world's largest trees, interspersed with coniferous forest, mountain meadows, granitic domes, and plunging gorges. Giant Sequoia National Monument will be managed primarily by the U.S. Forest Service, with the National Park Service playing a consultative role.[53] Another monument, Hanford Reach in the state of Washington, protects the last free-flowing nontidal stretch of the Columbia River and is managed primarily by the U.S. Fish and Wildlife Service in cooperation with the Department of Energy.[54] The National Park Service has sole management authority over six of the new or expanded monuments, and co-manages two others with the BLM (Grand Canyon–Parashant and Craters of the Moon).[55]

Finally, fourteen of the Clinton monuments are managed in whole or in part by the Bureau of Land Management. These monuments have special importance, both because of the precedent they set as the first monuments managed by the BLM and because of their sheer size. The first, the largest, and probably the best known of these is Grand Staircase–Escalante. As designated, it encompassed 1.7 million acres of largely undeveloped steep canyons and spectacular geologic features bordering Capitol Reef National Park and Glen Canyon National Recreation Area on its east side, and Bryce Canyon National Park on the west. Legislation adopted after the designation expanded the monument to more than 1.9 million acres, largely due to the exchange of state inholdings within the monument boundaries.[56] The 1,014,000-million-acre Grand Canyon–Parashant National Monument, on the northwest side of Grand Canyon National Park, and the 293,000-acre Vermillion Cliffs National Monument,[57] on the northeastern side of that park, encompass similar landscapes and help to secure the ecology of the Grand Canyon region.

Two of the BLM's new monuments—the 71,000-acre Agua Fria National Monument in Arizona, and the 164,000-acre Canyons of the Ancients National Monument in Colorado—were set aside largely for their archaeological importance. Two others—the 135,000-acre Ironwood Forest National Monument and the 506,513-acre Sonoran Desert National Monument—are designed to protect the unique biological resources of the Sonoran Desert. The 52,947-acre Cascade–Siskiyou National Monument in Oregon was designated primarily to protect its rich biological diversity, and the 504,729-acre Upper Missouri River Breaks National Monument protects biological, geological, and historical objects along the Missouri River running through Montana.[58]

The BLM's five other monuments include the previously described California Coastal National Monument; the 204,107-acre Carrizo Plain National Monument, which protects the largest remnant of what was once a vast grassland habitat near California's San Joaquin Valley; the 4,148-acre Kasha–Katuwe Tent Rocks National Monument, which protects unique cone-shaped geological formations in New Mexico; the previously described 51-acre Pompeys Pillar National Monument on the banks of the Yellowstone River in Montana; and additions to the pre-existing Craters of the Moon National Monument in Idaho, which the National Park Service continues to manage in part.[59]

In addition to these monuments, the Antiquities Act legacy left by the Clinton administration should arguably include several areas that received legislative protection only because Secretary Babbitt indicated that he was considering monument recommendations for these areas.[60] Babbitt was actively involved with each of the legislative proposals, and insisted that they meet certain standards before he would agree not to pursue monument designations.[61] Lands that were protected by legislation in lieu of having monument designations include the Steens Mountain Cooperative Management Area in the high desert environment of eastern Oregon, Colorado Canyons in Colorado, the Santa Rosa and San Jacinto Mountains in California, Black Rock Desert in Nevada, and Las Cienegas in Arizona.[62] In a significant concession to the management precedent established by Secretary Babbitt, all five of these areas are managed by the BLM. In addition to these designations, 84 million acres of submerged lands in the Northwestern Hawaiian Islands were protected by executive order, in consultation with interested members of Congress, under the National Marine Sanctuaries Act, in lieu of granting these lands national monument status.[63]

For all of the monument recommendations he made, Babbitt will also be remembered for a monument that he did not recommend: the Arctic National Wildlife Refuge (ANWR). The decision made good sense on many levels. Most importantly, Clinton could not use the monument designation to withdraw the lands from mineral development because the Alaska National Interest Lands Conservation Act (ANILCA) specifically prohibits the president from making new withdrawals in Alaska in excess of 5,000 acres unless he provides notice in the *Federal Register,* and unless Congress passes a joint resolution approving the withdrawal within one year after receiving notice.[64] Moreover, given the political controversy surrounding ANWR, a monument designation there might well have provided a boost to those seeking to amend the Antiquities Act—an overriding concern for Babbitt. Finally, congressional action was already needed to open ANWR, and if Congress could muster the votes to authorize oil and gas development in ANWR, it presumably could do so whether or not ANWR had been declared a national monument.[65]

Still, in hindsight, it is fair to ask whether the designation might have been worth the risks even given the minimal legal protection it might have offered. In order for leasing to take place in ANWR following a monument designation, Congress would have had to do more than address the restrictions in ANILCA; it would also have had to override a long-standing provision of the Mineral Leasing Act of 1920 that expressly precludes mineral leasing in national monuments.[66] Perhaps this would not have added a significant obstacle. But given the controversy swirling around oil and gas development in ANWR, it is also possible that the conservation community might have marshaled greater political support with an argument that a decision to open a national monument to oil and gas leasing would break with the long-standing precedent established under federal law.

The Long-Term Prospect for the Clinton Monuments

The Congress of the United States has the constitutional responsibility to make all needful rules governing the public lands, and there is no doubt that Congress may use this authority to alter or repeal monument designations created by the president. Yet despite the controversy that frequently surrounds national monument designations, Congress has only rarely reversed or even curtailed presidential decisions establishing national monuments.[67] On the contrary, Congress most often takes action that supports these presidential decisions, and even builds upon them by expanding the protected area or upgrading its status to that of a national park.[68] This has been true even in those cases where an initial designation by Congress may have been inconceivable.

President Clinton's 1996 proclamation of Grand Staircase–Escalante National Monument offers an excellent contemporary example. Protection of this remote area of southern Utah had long been a priority for conservation groups, but the staunch opposition of the Utah congressional delegation made it highly unlikely that protective legislation would have been enacted. After the monument was proclaimed, several unsuccessful attempts were made by Senator Robert Bennett and Congressman Jim Hansen (both of Utah) to enact legislation to undo the decision.[69] Then, in 1998, Congress passed, and the president signed, two pieces of legislation that, far from overturning the monument designation, appeared to effectively ratify it. The first was the Utah School and Lands Exchange Act, which transferred approximately 176,000 acres of school trust lands located within the exterior boundaries of Grand Staircase–Escalante to federal ownership in exchange for a cash payment and a transfer of other federal lands to the State.[70] Subsequently, Congress passed the Automobile National Heritage Act of 1998.[71] Title II of that law is entitled "Grand Staircase–Escalante National Monument" and was designed to correct minor errors in the original proclamation and to make minor boundary adjustments. While a federal district court judge subsequently rejected the government's legal claim that these and other congressional actions had in fact ratified the Grand Staircase–Escalante proclamation,[72] the practical effect of this legislation was to take the wind out of the effort to undo the monument decision.

Given the controversy that surrounded Grand Staircase–Escalante's proclamation, the fact that Congress moved so swiftly to embrace the decision suggests that monument decisions will not be easily overturned. Among the more contentious of the other Clinton monument decisions was the Virgin Islands Coral Reef National Monument, in large part because it banned most fishing activities within the monument boundaries. The Virgin Islands leg-islature adopted a resolution expressing its "disappointment and indignation" over the decision,[73] but threats of congressional action to overturn the decision have thus far not materialized.

Administrative decisions to manage the Clinton monuments in ways that could damage some of their resources may be a more imminent threat. As noted previously, the Bush administration has recently approved plans to allow timber harvesting on the Giant Sequoia National Monument despite language in the proclamation that prohibits tree removal unless "clearly needed" to protect the ecology of the forest or public safety. They have also moved to expand existing oil and gas leases on the Canyons of the Ancients National Monument, despite the prohibition on new leasing in national monuments contained in the Mineral Leasing Act.[74] Finally, as noted above, the Bush administration has expressed interest in revising some of the Clinton proclamations, including, for example, restrictions on grazing and off-road vehicle use. Although presidents have revised monument proclamations in the past, their authority under the Antiquities Act to do so is a matter of some doubt,[75] and the environmental community is not likely to sit by silently if and when development restrictions in monuments are lifted. It thus seems likely that future battles over the use of monu-ment lands will be fought both in the political arena and in the courts.

Several challenges to the Clinton monument decisions them-selves were also filed but, as with challenges over decisions by pre-vious presidents, these lawsuits have not borne fruit. These lawsuits were filed exclusively by groups opposing the designations. The cases raised a myriad of issues—some new, and some seeking to reopen legal questions raised in earlier Antiquities Act cases.[76] The most significant of the lawsuits were two cases filed in federal court in the District of Columbia. One was a generic challenge filed by the Mountain States Legal Foundation—the former employer of Secretary of the Interior Gale Norton. The *Mountain States* lawsuit challenged various aspects of four national monument designa-tions: Canyons of the Ancients, Cascade–Siskiyou, Hanford Reach, and Ironwood. The other was filed by Tulare County and others challenging the Giant Sequoia National Monument. After losing in the district court, the plaintiffs appealed to the Court of Appeals for the District of Columbia Circuit. In decisions handed down on the same day, the court rejected both challenges.[77] In the *Mountain States* case, the court first held that judicial review was available "to ensure that Proclamations are consistent with constitutional principles and the President has not exceeded his statutory authority."[78] Nonetheless, the court rejected Mountain States Legal Foundation's claim that the proclamations exceeded the president's authority under the Property Clause of the Constitution because the president was exercising authority lawfully delegated by Congress in the Antiquities Act. The court also rejected the foundation's claim that the president had included "ineligible items" in the proclamations in light of the Supreme Court's broad reading of the law in *Cameron v. United States*, an early Antiquities Act case involving the Grand Canyon.[79]

The plaintiffs fared no better in the *Tulare County* case. There, the court specifically rejected the plaintiffs' complaints that the president had failed to describe the protected objects with sufficient specificity, and had failed to demonstrate that the area protected was "the smallest area compatible with the proper care and management of the objects to be protected" as required by the Antiquities Act. The court found that the Act does not require any particular level of detail and does not require the secretary of the interior to undertake any particular investigation to identify the proper size of the monument. Moreover, to the extent that the county believed that the president had designated too much land, they had failed to make sufficient factual allegations to support this claim in their complaint. The court also upheld the president's authority to declare monuments for purposes that include the protection of ecosystems and scenic vistas.

The only other significant decision thus far to come out of the Clinton monuments involved three separate lawsuits challenging various aspects of the Grand Staircase–Escalante decision.[80] In *Utah Association of Counties v. Bush*, the federal district court in Utah held that the authority of federal courts to review presidential decisions was extremely narrow. Courts may not review such decisions to determine whether they involve a mere excess or abuse of discretion because "[a] grant of discretion to the President to make particular judgments forecloses judicial review of those judgments altogether."[81] Nonetheless, the court conceded that review was available to determine whether the president acted within the authority granted by Congress under the statute or whether the president's action violated some provision of the Constitution. The court found no such violations in President Clinton's decision to proclaim Grand Staircase–Escalante.

Conclusion

The confluence of circumstances that led to a resurgence in the use of the Antiquities Act during the Clinton Administration—an engaged and well-informed secretary of the interior, a presidential chief of staff with a strong conservation ethic, a president eager to build a lasting legacy, and a conservation community ready and able to seize an opportunity that serendipitously presented itself—may never occur again. But if and when similar circumstances arise, the Clinton administration's experience offers a road map for future success under this remarkable, century-old law.

Notes

1. In addition to declaring or expanding 22 national monuments covering approximately six million acres of land, Clinton must be credited with protecting several areas designated by Congress, 84 million acres of submerged lands around the northwestern Hawaiian Islands, and 55 million acres of roadless lands in the National Forest System. See below for more detail.

2. 16 U.S.C.A. secs. 431–433 (2005).

3. See, for example, LaVor 1993 (noting that Babbitt's "thoughtful 1988 campaign captivated the press and not the public"); Kopkind 1988.

4. A brief biography of Babbitt is on-line at govinfo.library.-unt.edu/npr/library/status/bios/babbit.htm.

5. Squillace 2003, 489–499.

6. Grand Canyon: Proclamation no. 794, 35 Stat. 2175 (1908). Zion (originally Mukuntuweap): Proclamation no. 877, 36 Stat. 2498 (1909). Olympic (originally Mount Olympus): Proclamation no. 869, 35 Stat. 2247 (1909). Acadia (originally Sieur de Monts): Proclamation no. 1339, 39 Stat. 1785 (1916).

7. See the chapter by Andrus and Freemuth in this volume.

8. The politics of the decision to designate Grand Staircase–Escalante National Monument are apparent from the critical report by the members of the Republican staff of the House Resources Committee on the decision: *Behind Closed Doors: The Abuse of Trust and Discretion in the Establishment of the Grand Staircase–Escalante National Monument*, Majority Staff Report, Subcommittee on National Parks and Public Lands, Committee on Resources, U.S. House of Representatives, 105th Cong., 1st Sess. (1997), available on-

line at http://resourcescommittee.house.gov/archives/105cong/parks/stair-case.htm. The report includes reproductions of correspondence primarily within and between the White House (CEQ) and the Interior Department that further illustrate the political nature of the decision.

9. For the BLM's coal estimates, see www.ut.blm.gov/monument/Monu-ment_Management/Initial%20Planning/deis/chapter_3/3_K.html#COAL. In his decision sustaining the Grand Staircase–Escalante proclamation, fed-eral District Court Judge Dee Benson cites a Utah Geological Survey estimate of 62.3 billion tons of coal, of which at least 11.3 billion tons was deemed recoverable. *Utah Ass'n of Counties v. Bush*, 316 F. Supp. 2d 1172, 1181, n. 5 (D. Ut. 2004).

10. See also www.freedom.org/prc/news/19991001/21.html. In the 1960s the BLM had issued coal leases to 23 separate companies that made plans for a massive 5,000-megawatt coal-fired power plant—later scaled back to 3,000 megawatts—on Fourmile Bench. See www.ut.blm.gov/monu-ment/Monument_Management/initial%20planning/deis/chapter_3/3_K.html. Economic concerns and strong opposition from the environmen-tal community eventually led most of the companies to walk away from their leases. Two companies, however, remained; PacifiCorp, holding one coal lease covering approximately 18,000 acres; and Andalex Resources, holding 17 leases containing approximately 36,000 acres. In the early 1990s, Andalex proposed a coal mine 70 miles east of Kanab, Utah. While designa-tion of the monument could not take away the prior rights of the coal lessees, it surely made the prospect for coal development on the Kaiparowits Plateau more complicated and, in 1999, both lessees accepted a cash pay-ment from the government in exchange for their leases.

11. As *Outside* magazine noted: "The fact that the president was speak-ing so glowingly of a place in southern Utah from one in northern Arizona was hardly lost on so knowing a crowd.... The president's decision was immediately denounced as election-year pandering." (Turner 1997). "Many people in Utah believe that President Clinton's decision to designate the Grand Staircase–Escalante as a national monument was politically moti-vated.... It cost him votes in Utah, of course, but he was unlikely to win the state anyway" (Nie 1999, 77–78).

12. As a result of the Utah School and Lands Exchange Act, 112 Stat. 3139 (1998), and the Automobile National Heritage Area Act, 112 Stat. 3247 (1998), discussed below, the monument now contains nearly 1.9 million acres. For reaction to the proclamation, see Benedetto and Kanamine 1996. The political calculus behind the Grand Staircase decision is evident from a memorandum from Katie McGinty, chair of the CEQ, to the president dated August 14, 1996: "Designation of the new monument would create a com-pelling reason for persons who are now disaffected to come around and enthusiastically support the Administration.... [T]he new monument will

have particular appeal in ... coastal California, Oregon, Washington, south-
ern Nevada, the Front Range communities of Colorado, the Taos–
Albuquerque corridor, and the Phoenix–Tucson area." Reproduced in *Behind
Closed Doors*, 23.

13. See *Behind Closed Doors*, 23.

14. On December 11, 1999, Clinton signed the Otay Mountain Wilderness Act, thereby preserving 18,500 acres of the region as wilderness. P.L.
106–145, sec. 3, 113 Stat. 1711. In describing his efforts to promote a land
legacy through the use of the Antiquities Act, Babbitt commented that
"[t]his process, in many ways, began at Otay Mountain...." White House
press briefing by Babbitt and George Frampton, chair of CEQ, December 14,
1999.

15. Letter from Clinton to Babbitt, November 10, 1998 (on file with the
author).

16. NEPA requires that any proposal by a federal agency for "legislation
and other major Federal actions significantly affecting the quality of the
human environment" include a detailed statement of the environmental
impact of that action (an "EIS"); 42 U.S.C. 4332(2)(C) (2005). In *Alaska v.
Carter*, 462 F.Supp. 1155 (D. Alaska 1978), however, the federal district court
in Alaska held that the president is not an agency for purposes of NEPA and
that, accordingly, he is not obliged to prepare an EIS before taking actions
that might significantly impact the environment. Freed from the burden of
having to engage in a lengthy review process, Babbitt followed a standard-
ized approach toward developing monument proposals and preparing the
necessary proclamation and background documents (Squillace 2003,
540–541). A letter similar to the more generic letter of November 10, 1998,
dated on or around July 24, 1996, was apparently prepared in advance of the
recommendation on Grand Staircase–Escalante National Monument as well
(*Behind Closed Doors*, 23).

17. Babbitt's initial proposal was for a "Shivwits Plateau National
Monument" consisting of about 400,000 acres (Yozwiak 1998). The original
proposal was expanded to the north and west all the way to the Nevada border, taking in a portion of Lake Mead National Recreation Area to the west
and the Grand Wash Cliffs to the north, and extending to the border of the
Paiute Wilderness Area.

18. One of the strategies used by Babbitt when he encountered Clinton
was to hand him an index card. On one side of the card was the Antiquities
Act record of Theodore Roosevelt—18 monuments encompassing about 1.5
million acres of land; on the other side was the Clinton record, which until
2000 included only the Grand Staircase–Escalante Monument (Larmer 2001,
1). But Babbitt did not need to sell Clinton on the merits of his proposals.
The cards were used more as a way to help Clinton understand the kind of
legacy he might leave. Ultimately, Clinton surpassed Roosevelt's record by

proclaiming 19 new monuments and expanding three others, thereby protecting nearly six million acres of public land.

19. *Cameron v. United States*, 252 U.S. 450 (1920). A recent decision of the federal district court for Utah suggests that the president's exercise of his discretionary authority under the Antiquities Act is simply not reviewable, although questions regarding the president's compliance with the Act or possible violation of the Constitution remain reviewable. *Utah Association of Counties v. Bush*, 316 F.Supp.2d 1172, 1185–1186 (D. Ut. 2004).

20. See, for example, *Tulare County v. Bush*, 185 F.Supp. 18 (D. D.C. 2001); *Cameron v. United States*.

21. See the chapter by Rothman in this volume.

22. For the Grand Teton compromise, see Squillace 2003, 495–498. But for this amendment, Babbitt might very well have recommended the designation of some portion of the Red Desert in central Wyoming for monument status. See www.doi.gov/news/ archives/001115.html.

23. See, for example, The National Monument Fairness Act of 2001, H.R. 2114, 107th Cong. (2001), requiring that any national monument proclamation that protects more than 50,000 acres of land "shall cease to be effective" two years after it is proclaimed unless approved by Congress; and the National Monument Fairness Act of 1997, S. 477, 105th Cong. (1997), requiring that all monuments in excess of 5,000 acres be approved in advance by the Congress. See also The National Monument NEPA Compliance Act, H.R. 1487, 106th Cong. (1999), requiring preparation of draft and final environmental impact statements on any monument proposal, including a minimum comment period of six months, and a waiting period of at least four months following promulgation of a final EIS before a monument is proclaimed; and The National Monument Public Participation Act, S. 729, 106th Cong. (1999).

24. This should not be confused with another important "no surprises" policy established by Babbitt under the Endangered Species Act. See 63 *Federal Register* 8859 (1998).

25. Babbitt's willingness to meet personally and engage local officials was perhaps his most important and meaningful commitment. His sophisticated understanding of public lands issues, combined with his well-deserved reputation for working cooperatively with local communities to address practical concerns, went a long way toward defusing public criticism for the monuments that were ultimately proclaimed. See Leshy 2001.

26. If it appeared that the resources proposed for protection might be threatened with adverse impacts while the proposal was pending, Babbitt would consider a temporary withdrawal of lands under the authority of Section 204(e) of FLPMA. 43 U.S.C.A. sec. 1714(e) (1994).

27. ANWR was a particularly sensitive political issue. When told that the Administration was considering national monument status for ANWR, Senator Ted Stevens responded, "If they do this, it would be the last straw."

Arctic National Wildlife Refuge Update, Government Affairs Program, American Geological Institute, July 7, 2000, on-line at www.agiweb.org/gap/legis106/anwr.html.

28. During the course of his tenure, Babbitt developed a knack for engaging the public on controversial issues in a personal and highly effective manner. Most notable to this observer was his willingness to respond directly and honestly to questions asked, even when he knew his response would not be well received by the questioner.

29. For example, in the Sonoran Desert National Monument, in response to concerns by the utility industry, language was added in the memorandum supporting the proclamation suggesting that new rights-of-way could be approved through the monument, subject to a requirement that they be consistent with the monument management plan. "Nothing in this proclamation precludes the issuance of new rights-of-way within existing right-of-way corridors, so long as the BLM determines, after NEPA compliance, that such rights-of-way are consistent with the purposes of protecting the objects for which the monument was established and the monument's management plan." See the BLM's "Sonoran Desert National Monument Background Materials," on-line at http://www.az.blm.gov/fr_nlcs.htm. In the same proclamation, at the state of Arizona's request, the monument boundaries were adjusted to exclude state lands along its borders.

30. For withdrawal of mining rights, Sonoran Desert National Monument, Proclamation no. 7397, 66 *Federal Register* 7354 (2001) and Agua Fria National Monument, Proclamation no. 7263, 65 *Federal Register* 2817 (2000). For prohibition of off-road motorized vehicles, see Upper Missouri River Breaks National Monument, Proclamation no. 7398, 66 *Federal Register* 7359 (January 17, 2001) and Cascade–Siskiyou National Monument, Proclamation no. 7318, 65 *Federal Register* 37249 (2000). It is not entirely clear whether this language prohibits new road construction within these monuments, although that appears to have been the intent. Several of the proclamations (e.g., Upper Missouri River Breaks) require preparation of a transportation plan to address road closures and travel restrictions. In other cases, a general management plan is required. For example, see Virgin Islands Coral Reef National Monument, Proclamation no. 7399, 66 *Federal Register* 7364 (2001), requiring the secretary to prepare a management plan "which addresses ... specific actions necessary to protect the objects identified in this proclamation." As for water rights, the Sonoran Desert proclamation, for example, disavows any intent to reserve new water rights; Proclamation no. 7397, 66 *Federal Register* 7354 (2001). By contrast, the Hanford Reach proclamation expressly reserves "a quantity of water in the Columbia River sufficient to fulfill the purposes for which this monument is established"; Proclamation no. 7319, 65 *Federal Register* 37253 (2000). See also Leshy 2001, 278.

31. Although official memoranda to the president were not released, all
of the substantive data contained in the memoranda, including the bibliography, were released to the public at the time that the recommendation to
the president was announced. Although these documents may not be readily available in all cases, many are available on-line. The Arizona BLM office,
in particular, provides access to relevant monument documents on-line at
www.az.blm.gov/ fr_nlcs.htm.

32. Speaking at the Denver University Law School on February 17,
2000, Babbitt spoke eloquently about how archaeological sites ought not to
be viewed in isolation, but rather as part of a landscape or "anthropological
ecosystem." "The real science on these landscapes doesn't come out of digging out a room and extracting a few pots.... The real discoveries today
come from asking the deeper question of 'How did communities live in spiritual and physical equilibrium with the landscape?'" He described the Agua
Fria National Monument as

> [A] defensive community on the ramparts up above Phoenix....
> [T]hey've located [a] line of ... watchtowers and shown how these huge
> Pueblo ruins were built in defensive array around about 100,000 acres.
> The whole landscape is kind of a Masada in central Arizona. As a single
> ruin, it's not a very interesting place. But all of the sudden you think of
> Masada and how this fits together and it's a starburst of revelation and
> the protection is fitted to the landscape.

See "From Grand Staircase to Grand Canyon–Parashant: Is There a Monumental Future for the BLM?", remarks of Babbitt, February 17, 2000, on-line
at www.doi.gov/news/archives/.

33. This also allowed Interior to avoid potentially difficult issues regarding the president's authority to transfer management jurisdiction over
national monument lands. See Squillace 2003, 292–365.

34. See *Congressional Record* 135, S13603, October 18, 1989. This
excerpt, offered by Senator Dennis DeConcini of Arizona, praises the work
of the former Arizona BLM State Director Dean Bibles, and notes among the
latter's accomplishments his work with Babbitt on the land exchange.

35. In his Denver University Law School speech, Babbitt noted that "the
largest [public] land manager [the BLM] ought to have a sense of pride rather
than simply having a bunch of inventory out in the garage that is discovered and given to someone else.... I think you give an institution some
pride and direction, not by stripping it [of] its best assets."

36. Babbitt announced his intention to establish this new sub-agency
in a broadcast to BLM employees on March 24, 2000. The NLCS includes
national monuments, national conservation areas, wilderness areas and
wilderness study areas, national wild and scenic rivers, and national scenic
and historic trails on BLM land. See www.blm.gov:80/nhp/news/releases/
pages/2000/NLCSQ&As.615a.htm. According to this BLM news release,
which accompanied the broadcast, "management will focus on conserva-

tion." Further, "while there will be opportunities for visitation, there will be no major facilities located within these areas. Visitor contact and information facilities will be located in adjacent communities or at the periphery of the units."

37. Babbitt broadcast of March 24, 2000.

38. Congressman Nick Rahall quotes from a Norton letter to the state of Arizona, as follows: "I would like to hear from you about what role these monuments should play in Arizona. Are there boundary adjustments that the Department of Interior should consider recommending? Are there existing uses inside these monuments that we should accommodate?" *Congressional Record* 147, H3418, June 21, 2001 (statement of Representative Rahall).

39. The language of the Upper Missouri River Breaks proclamation is typical: "Nothing in this proclamation shall be deemed to enlarge or diminish the jurisdiction of the State of Montana with respect to fish and wildlife management." Proclamation no. 7398, 66 *Federal Register* 7359 (2001). The state of Arizona has complained, however, that its ability to manage monument lands is unduly restricted. Arizona's complaint arose in the context of an attempt by its Game and Fish Department to chain an area within Grand Canyon–Parashant National Monument to improve wildlife habitat. The BLM refused to allow the chaining because it was contrary to the BLM's policies, which applied irrespective of the national monument status of the lands. Subsequently, when Babbitt proposed to designate the Sonoran Desert National Monument, the state of Arizona sought assurances that it would be allowed to retain its artificial water holes, which are maintained for wildlife purposes. While maintenance of the water holes is somewhat controversial, the BLM does not expect to require removal of existing ones, though it may limit any efforts on the part of the state to install any new ones. See The Wilderness Society, "National Monument Designation in Arizona: Governor Hull's Letter and the Facts at 2," on-line at www.wilderness.org/Library/Documents/upload/HullLetter-Arizona-Monuments-Factsheet.pdf.

40. Proclamation no. 7295, 65 *Federal Register* 24095. See also "Attorney General Lockyer Defends Newly Created Giant Sequoias National Monument in Sierra Nevada," March 20, 2001, on-line at http://ag.ca.gov/news-alerts/release.php?id=1070.

41. Kasha–Katuwe Tent Rocks: Proclamation no. 7397, 66 *Federal Register* 7354 (2001); Sonoran Desert: Proclamation no. 7394, 66 *Federal Register* 7343 (2001).

42. Steens Mountain Cooperative Management and Protection Act of 2000, P.L. 106-399, 114 Stat. 1655 (2000), codified at 16 U.S.C. sec. 460nnn. The statute requires the secretary to cancel certain grazing permits "on Federal lands in the Fish Creek/Big Indian, East Ridge, and South Steens allotments" and prohibits future grazing on these lands. 16 U.S.C. sec. 460nnn-23.

43. Proclamation no. 7318, 65 *Federal Register* 37249 (2000). See also Cascade–Siskiyou National Monument, *Draft Study of Livestock Impacts on the Objects of Biological Interest*, April 2001; on-line at www.or.blm.gov/medford/docs/CSNM_Range_Study.pdf.

44. In 1908, Secretary of the Interior James Garfield addressed several rights-of-way applications that had been filed by the Grand Canyon Scenic Railroad Company through Grand Canyon National Monument. The language of the Grand Canyon proclamation was even broader than that included in the Clinton-era proclamations. It reserved the land "from all forms of appropriation and use of all kinds under all of the public land laws, subject to all prior, valid adverse claims." Proclamation no. 794, reprinted in 35 Stat. 2175 (1908). Garfield held that Interior was "without authority to approve [the] applications for rights-of-way." 36 I.D. 394 (1908).

45. See, for example, Bureau of Land Management, "Grand Canyon–Parashant National Monument Background Materials" (January 11, 2000), on-line at www.az.blm.gov/parashant/bkgdp.htm, containing the background memorandum issued by Babbitt in conjunction with the monument proclamation.

46. The memorandum is on-line at www.az.blm.gov/sonoran/sdbkgd.htm.

47. See, for example, Sonoran Desert National Monument, Proclamation no. 7397, 66 *Federal Register* 7354 (2001).

48. The policy is on-line at www.az.blm.gov/interimgt.htm.

49. The final management plan sets aside 65% of the monument in a "primitive" zone. The BLM plans to provide no facilities in this zone and will post only such signs as are necessary for public safety or resource protection. No motorized or mechanized vehicles (including bicycles) are authorized in this zone. Approximately 4% of the land will be in the "frontcountry" zone, which will be the "focal point of visitation," although visitor centers themselves will be placed outside of the monument and in the local communities. The "passage" zone encompasses 2% of the monument and includes the main travel routes. The remaining 29% of the land is in the "outback" zone where motorized and mechanized access will be accommodated, but only on designated routes. The entire management plan is available on-line at www.ut.blm.gov/monument/Monument_Management/monument_management.html.

50. Roosevelt was president when Congress passed the Antiquities Act, and he quickly asserted his new authority, declaring Devils Tower in Wyoming as the nation's first monument. In all, Roosevelt designated 18 monuments covering 1.5 million acres of land. Among his most important monuments were Grand Canyon and Mount Olympus. His most enduring contribution to the Antiquities Act, however, was his bold interpretation of the phrase "objects of scientific interest" to encompass geological and bio-

logical features covering large landscapes. It was this precedent that made possible virtually all of the large Clinton monuments.

51. Lincoln and Soldier's Home: Proclamation no. 7329, 65 *Federal Register* 43673 (2001). Minidoka Internment: Proclamation no. 7395, 66 *Federal Register* 7347 (2001). Pompeys Pillar: Proclamation no. 7396, 66 *Federal Register* 7351 (2001). Governor's Island: Proclamation no. 7402, 66 *Federal Register* 7855 (2001).

52. Virgin Islands Coral Reef: Proclamation no. 7399, 66 *Federal Register* 7364 (2001). Buck Island Reef: Proclamation no. 7392, 66 *Federal Register* 7335 (2001). California Coastal: Proclamation no. 7264, 65 *Federal Register* 2821 (2000).

53. Proclamation no. 7295, 65 *Federal Register* 24095 (2000). As a result of two legal opinions issued in the wake of the Alaska monuments proclaimed by President Carter in 1978, NPS is required to retain some management responsibility for this monument.

54. Proclamation no. 7319, 65 *Federal Register* 37253 (2000).

55. The six new or expanded monuments that NPS has sole authority over are President Lincoln and Soldiers Home, Minidoka Internment, Virgin Islands Coral Reef, Governors Island, Buck Island Reef, and Pinnacles (enlargement, see Proclamation no. 7266, 65 *Federal Register* 2831 [2000]). For Grand Canyon–Parashant, see Proclamation no. 7265, 65 *Federal Register* 2825 (2001); for Craters of the Moon (enlargement), Proclamation no. 7373, 65 *Federal Register* 69221 (2000).

56. Utah School and Lands Exchange Act of 1998, P.L. 105-335, 112 Stat. 3139 (1998).

57. Proclamation no. 7374, 65 *Federal Register* 69227 (2000).

58. Agua Fria: Proclamation no. 7263, 65 *Federal Register* 2817 (2000). Canyon of the Ancients: Proclamation no. 7317, 65 *Federal Register* 37243 (2000). Ironwood Forest: Proclamation no. 7320, 65 *Federal Register* 37259 (2000). Sonoran Desert: Proclamation no. 7397, 66 *Federal Register* 7354 (2001). Cascade–Siskiyou: Proclamation no. 7318, 65 *Federal Register* 37249 (2000); the proclamation describes the areas as a "biological crossroads—the interface of the Cascade, Klamath, and Siskiyou ecoregions in an area of unique geology, biology, climate, and topography." Upper Missouri River Breaks: Proclamation no. 7398, 66 *Federal Register* 7359 (2001).

59. Carrizo Plain: Proclamation no. 7393, 66 *Federal Register* 7339 (2001). Kasha–Katuwe Tent Rocks: Proclamation no. 7394, 66 *Federal Register* 7343 (2001). Pompeys Pillar: Proclamation no. 7396, 66 *Federal Register* 7351 (2001). Craters of the Moon: Proclamation no. 7373, 65 *Federal Register* 69221 (2001).

60. As noted earlier, Babbitt's policy was to give local politicians the opportunity to advance legislation that would assure the protection of areas before he recommended a monument proclamation to the president.

61. For example, Babbitt refused to support legislation that would have established the Shivwits Plateau National Conservation Area because it "does not establish a management standard adequate for long term protection." Testimony of Babbitt before the House Resources Subcommittee on National Parks and Public Lands on H.R. 2795, October 19, 1999, 1999 WL 969928. This area was subsequently protected as part of Grand Canyon–Parashant National Monument.

62. For Steens Mountain, see the Steens Mountain Cooperative Management and Protection Act of 2000, P.L. 106-399, 114 Stat. 1655 (2000). The act protects about 500,000 acres of BLM land. Section 201 of the Act designates nearly 170,000 acres as the Steens Mountain Wilderness Area and provides that nearly 100,000 acres within the wilderness area be free from cattle grazing. In addition, the protected area encompasses more than a hundred miles of wild and scenic rivers. For Colorado Canyons, see the Colorado Canyons National Conservation Area and Black Ridge Canyons Wilderness Act of 2000, P.L. 106-353, 114 Stat. 1374 (2000). The national conservation area is located west of Grand Junction, Colorado, and includes 122,300 rugged acres of sandstone canyons, natural arches, spires, and alcoves carved into the Colorado Plateau along a 24-mile stretch of the Colorado River. Approximately 5,200 acres extend into eastern Utah. The Black Ridge Canyons Wilderness encompasses 75,550 acres of designated wilderness within the national conservation area. For Santa Rosa and San Jacinto Mountains, see the Santa Rosa and San Jacinto Mountains National Monument Act, P.L. 106-351, 114 Stat. 1362 (2000). For Black Rock Desert, see the act creating Black Rock Desert–High Rock Canyon Emigrant Trails National Conservation Area, P.L. 106-554, sec. 125, 114 Stat. 2763 (2000). This desert, north of Nevada's Great Basin, has remained virtually unchanged since pioneer times. It contains important relics of the Emigrant Trails to California. It also houses prehistoric Native American sites and other paleontologically significant sites. Substantial credit for protecting this area must go to Senators Harry Reid and Richard Bryan of Nevada, who persuaded their colleagues to enact this legislation on the last day of the legislative session. For Las Cienegas, see the act creating Las Cienegas National Conservation Area, P.L. 106-538, 114 Stat. 2563 (2000). Here, 42,000 acres of public lands in Arizona were designated by Congress as a conservation area. Though the land has been withdrawn from future mining claims, Las Cienegas is intended to be a multiple-use area, encompassing livestock use, recreation, and cultural preservation.

63. Northwestern Hawaiian Islands Coral Reef Ecosystem Reserve. EO 13178, 65 *Federal Register* 76903 (2000). See also the chapter by Barr and Van Dine, this volume.

64. 16 U.S.C. sec. 3213(a) (2000).

65. 16 U.S.C. secs. 3142(i), 3143 (2000). Although Babbitt was "passion-

ately opposed" to drilling in ANWR, he described the proposal to designate ANWR as a national monument a "meaningless gesture [that] adds no protection that isn't already there." H. Josef Hebert, "Babbitt Advises Clinton on Refuge," *AP Online,* January 5, 2001, available at 2001 WL 3649349.

66. 30 U.S.C. sec. 181 (2000).

67. Ten national monuments designated under the Antiquities Act have been abolished (see Appendix), but the lands encompassing at least four of these monuments were conveyed to the state or local government for use as a public park with a reverter to the United States if the lands ceased to be used as a park. See, for example, Shoshone Cavern National Monument, abolished by an act of May 17, 1954, 68 Stat. 98.

68. Congress has ratified more than half of all the designated monuments, often by expanding their boundaries, designating the lands as a national park, or both. See Appendix.

69. See, for example, S. 357, 105th Cong. (1997). Under Section 4(a)(2) of the proposed legislation the secretary would be required to "manage the resources within the Monument in accordance with the principles of multiple use and sustained yield (including recreation, range, timber, minerals, oil and gas, watershed, wildlife, fish, and natural scenic, scientific, and historical values), using principles of economic and ecologic sustainability."

70. Utah School and Lands Exchange Act of 1998, P.L. 105-335, 112 Stat. 3139 (1998).

71. P.L. 105-355, 112 Stat. 3247 (1998).

72. *Utah Ass'n of Counties v. Clinton,* 1999 U.S. Dist. LEXIS 15852 (D. Ut. 1999). In this unpublished opinion, Judge Dee Benson of the federal district court offered a lengthy analysis of the government claim of congressional ratification, ultimately concluding that the congressional action was not sufficiently clear and unequivocal to satisfy the standards for ratification established by the Supreme Court.

73. 24th Legislature of the Virgin Islands of the United States, Resolution no. 1609, Bill no. 24-0010 (2001).

74. See Cart and Shogren 2002. The Mineral Leasing Act of 1920 authorizes oil and gas leasing on federal lands, excluding, among other lands, "lands ... in national parks and monuments." 30 U.S.C. sec. 181.

75. It has been argued that the president's power under the Antiquities Act to proclaim national monuments does not necessarily include the power to amend or abolish such proclamations. This theory, however, has never been tested in the courts. See Squillace 2003, 550–568.

76. See Vincent and Baldwin (2001, 11–12), which offers a general description of the pending litigation.

77. *Mountain States Legal Foundation v. Bush,* 306 F.3d 1132 (D.C. Cir. 2002); cert. denied, 540 U.S. 812 (2003); *Tulare County v. Bush,* 306 F.3d 1138 (D.C. Cir. 2002), cert. denied, 540 U.S. 813 (2003).

78. 306 F.3d at 1136.

79. 252 U.S. 450 (1920). For more on *Cameron,* see Rothman's chapter in this volume.

80. One of the parties—the Utah Schools and Institutional Trust Lands Administration—settled their case after Congress passed legislation providing for the exchange or disposition of state lands located inside the monument's borders. See Utah School and Lands Exchange Act of 1998, P.L. 105-335, 112 Stat. 3139 (1998).

81. 316 F.Supp.2d 1172 (D. Ut. 2004).

8

Antiquities Act Monuments

The Elgin Marbles of Our Public Lands?

James R. Rasband

AS THE OTHER CHAPTERS IN THIS BOOK ATTEST, although it often escapes notice in conversations about important environmental legislation, the Antiquities Act has been one of the most powerful conservation tools of this century. Antiquities Act monuments have not only protected some of our nation's most spectacular landscapes but have paved the way for a number of our most treasured national parks. Grand Canyon, Zion, Bryce, Olympic, and Grand Teton were all monuments before they became parks. Looking back it may be hard to see how anyone could question the virtue of the Antiquities Act. Yet that is what this chapter intends, at least in part.

The problem with the Antiquities Act is not the results it has produced but the process—or, more accurately, the lack of process—by which those results have been achieved. Over and over in its 100-year history, the Antiquities Act has been wielded by presidents without any regard for the local rural communities and the state and county governments most impacted by the monument's designation. It does not need to be that way. Whether by using the withdrawal process provided in the Federal Land Policy Management Act (FLPMA), or, preferably, by amending the Antiquities Act to allow participation by state and local governments, or, at very least, by voluntarily adhering to a collaborative model under the existing Antiquities Act, largely the same preservation benefits could be achieved without disregarding affected public lands communities.

Presidential monument-making under the Antiquities Act has yielded a familiar pattern. Monument proclamations are met by a firestorm of protest in the affected community but the protest is followed by acquiescence and then acceptance. Thus, when President Roosevelt used the Antiquities Act in 1943 to set aside Jackson Hole National Monument, there was outrage in Wyoming. But, seven years later Congress added the monument lands to the Grand Teton

National Park, albeit with an amendment to the Antiquities Act prohibiting any additional monument designations in Wyoming. Likewise, when President Johnson in January of 1969, just ninety min-
utes before he was to leave office, signed Antiquities Act
proclamations adding some 264,000 acres to Arches and Capitol
Reef National Monuments, the reaction in Utah was outrage. Utah
Senator Wallace Bennett protested that the proclamations were a
"last gasp attempt to embalm a little more land in the West," and
were "unilateral . . . with no notice whatsoever, without hearing any
interested group, without prior consultation with Congress and
without consultation or discussion with state officials."[1] But when
FLPMA was debated and passed seven years later in 1976, there was
nary a word about the Antiquities Act. Indeed, although FLPMA
specifically eliminated several sources of executive withdrawal
authority, it left the Antiquities Act untouched. Likewise, when President Clinton, in 1996, set aside some 1.7 million acres of public
land in Utah's red rock country as Grand Staircase–Escalante
National Monument (Figure 8.1), Utah's congressional delegation
cried foul over the administration's failure to consult them or to
give any public notice of the proposal, and the president and
Interior Secretary Bruce Babbitt were hung in effigy in the southern
Utah counties within which the monument is located. Yet now,
nine years later, most criticism of the Grand Staircase proclamation
has faded away and Utah travel and outdoor websites are filled with
pictures and descriptions of the monument's wonders.

    Why is it that monument proclamations have so routinely
brought criticism, only to see that criticism fade over time? One part
of the answer is clear: a vast majority like the results and thus any
squeamishness about the means is rather quickly forgotten. The
public preference for preserving natural wonders is not new, but it
has increased dramatically in the last forty years. Recreation visits to
the national park system grew from 33 million in 1950 to over 277
million in 2002. Total visitor-days on BLM lands climbed from just
over 31 million in 1972 to almost 68 million in 2002. Recreation in
the national forests climbed from 27.4 million visitor-days in 1950
to 341.2 million in 1996.[2] As these numbers reveal, recreation and
preservation are rapidly becoming the dominant uses of the public
lands.

    Another reason that criticism of monuments fades is that over
time few remember the means by which lands were preserved. The
on-the-ground fact of the monument is what drives public perception, not how it was created in an ever-receding past. In assessing
the historical benefits of the Antiquities Act, it is important to avoid
falling into this trap. It is not enough to point to all of the monu-

Figure 8.1. Banded landscape at Grand Staircase–Escalante National Monument, Utah. Unattributed photograph, courtesy of Bureau of Land Management, Office of the National Landscape Conservation System.

ments and declare the Act good. Praiseworthy preservation results are not the only measure by which the Antiquities Act should be judged. Just as important is the process by which those results were achieved. In the absence of a legitimate process, Antiquities Act monuments risk becoming something like the Elgin Marbles—the sculptures taken from the Parthenon early in the nineteenth century by Lord Elgin and then sold to the British Museum. Although Elgin's preservation of the Marbles may have been wise and although they are undeniably one of Britain's treasures, the means by which they were acquired tarnishes the achievement.[3]

Ironically enough, this basic insight about the relevance of the process by which monuments are proclaimed comes from the very wilderness literature inspired by the lands that the Antiquities Act seeks to preserve. The consistent message of wilderness literature, as revealed in the philosophical writings of Henry David Thoreau, John Muir, Aldo Leopold, Joseph Sax, and other preservationists as well as in the recreational writing of anglers, mountaineers, and hunters, is that we are redeemed and ennobled by adherence to certain virtues in our interaction with wilderness.[4] Wilderness experiences are valuable because they teach us virtues like sportsmanship, restraint, deliberation, sensitivity to impact, and patient woodcraft. Yet, if these virtues govern our interaction with wilderness, should they not also govern our acquisition of wilderness, our monument-making? In the end, it is not enough merely to proclaim a monument any more than it is sufficient to simply bag a deer, net a fish, run a river, or scale a mountain; it is the manner by which the result was achieved that ultimately ennobles or devalues the activity. The irony of most national monument proclamations is that we claim to value the monument for its ability to develop within us the very virtues that we seem so quick to ignore in securing it.

If it is true that the process by which monuments are made matters, and if it is also true that the Antiquities Act has produced such beneficial outcomes, the critical question is whether the same or similar results could be achieved by a process that does not so thoroughly disregard the input and interests of rural communities and state and local governments. The answer is likely "yes." If the Antiquities Act were amended to require notice to state and local government and consideration of impacts on communities nearby the monument, or, in the absence of a change in the law, if presidents, on their own initiative, consulted with affected states and local governments prior to proclaiming a monument, it would not mean the end of monument proclamations. Nor, of course, would it likely mean the end of local community protests. But it might alleviate some of the tensions surrounding monument designations and it would surely be more in keeping with the very virtues we hope to inculcate by setting aside the land from development.

The Lessons of Wilderness Literature for Wilderness Acquisition

To identify the guideposts that should inform presidential use of the Antiquities Act, one need look no further than the principles that should inform our interaction with wild lands once they are protected. Although it would be difficult to articulate a specific catechism of wilderness values, wilderness literature identifies several basic virtues that should govern our interaction with wild places. The overarching virtue described in the literature is that "the chase, not the catching, is paramount."[5] As discussed in Joseph Sax's thought-provoking *Mountains without Handrails*, the actual result of any particular endeavor is secondary to the endeavor itself. Thus, in the recreational literature on fishing, the common message is that the joys of angling have little to do with catching fish. "Fishing is most satisfying, not when it results in accomplishment of a set task, but in refining us."[6] Climbing literature reflects the same ethos. Sax explains: "[I]n great mountaineering, the result, the reaching of a summit, is of minor importance ... the whole merit of the climb depend[s] upon the way it was done, that is the method, behavior and mental attitude of the climbers...."[7] In their book *Wilderness Ethics*, Laura Waterman and Guy Waterman ask: "A few years ago an Italian party used helicopters to help them climb Mount Everest. The mountaineering world was aghast. What was the object? Why not just build a gondola to the top? [R]isk and challenge is [sic] why climbers go to the mountains."[8] Rafting a river is likewise about more than just roaring to the take-out, led by a river guide who handles the rafts and prepares gourmet meals. At its best, river rafting involves a slower-paced exploration of the canyon where the rafter encounters the wilderness rather than simply controlling or overpowering it.[9] Hunting is the same. It is not enough to simply kill the prey. The hunt is most satisfying when it relies on subtle woodcraft and is not over-aided by technology.[10]

With respect to each wilderness venture, accomplishment is not a function of conquest but of virtuous method. Thus, wilderness literature emphasizes the principle of understanding our surroundings, as opposed to simply dominating them.[11] Similarly, the literature encourages avoiding undue impact on wild lands, and exercising self-restraint, most often self-limitation on technological advantage. As Aldo Leopold put it in *A Sand County Almanac*: "Voluntary adherence to an ethical code elevates the self-respect of the sportsman, but it should not be forgotten that voluntary disregard of the code degenerates and depraves him. Our tools for the pursuit of wildlife improve faster than we do, and sportsmanship is a voluntary limitation in the use of these armaments. It is aimed to augment the role of skill and shrink the role of gadgets in the pursuit of wild things."[12]

Leopold's use of the term "sportsmanship" is perhaps as good as any to describe the "ethical code" which should govern our interaction with wild things. His message, and the message that is pervasive in wilderness literature, is that relying on experience, patient woodcraft, and subtle comprehension of one's natural surroundings has a redeeming quality that is lacking where the result is assured by technology or gadgetry. At a broad level of abstraction, the key to virtuous interaction with wild lands is an understanding that the method employed and not the result achieved is what ennobles the participant.

Because virtue generally should not be situational or geographic, it is instructive to ask what this same principle implies for the task of monument making. Translated into the monument context, the principle that accomplishment is more a function of method than conquest suggests the necessity of a fair process. But what exactly would a fair process entail?

A fair, or, to borrow from Leopold, a sportsmanlike proclamation process would, as an initial matter, allow for public participation. Soliciting input from those connected to the land emulates the wilderness virtue of seeking understanding rather than domination. Such understanding, of course, has more than an aesthetic purpose. Allowing public comment makes it more likely that unforeseen benefits and detriments of any monument proclamation will be taken into consideration. With public participation, those opposed to the monument are more likely to accept the result if they have had an opportunity to participate in the development of the proposal. Consultation, of course, will not end opposition. Indeed, it may increase the political difficulty of presidential monument-making. Yet, by analogy to wilderness literature, undertaking the difficult task of comprehending and carefully navigating the cultural environment is what gives nobility to the venture of monument-making.

A fair or virtuous monument-making process would not only include opportunities for public input but would actually consider that input, particularly as it relates to impacts on the economy and cultural heritage of existing communities. Consider the concerns that mountaineering literature has raised about Mount Everest expeditions. In the rush to scale the world's highest peak, unqualified climbers use professional guides,[13] caution is thrown to the wind, and the mountain itself is abused, littered with empty oxygen canisters, abandoned gear, and, more and more of late, bodies.[14] Everest, mountaineering's highest achievement, has become a symbol for the "trophy recreationist" who cares nothing for method as long as he can point to achievement.[15] A monument process that focuses on the size of the withdrawal to the exclusion of the interests of local communities is little different. It is much like trophy hunting: as long as the achievement can be figuratively placed on the nation's mantle, the impact or purpose of the hunt matters little.

Considering the impact of monuments on local communities should also be understood as a manifestation of another insight of wilderness literature: that civilization is not an evil imposition on the good of wilderness. Rather, as Robert Marshall, founder of The Wilderness Society, put it, preservation decisions precipitate a conflict "between genuine values."[16] The "remedy" to that conflict, suggested Thoreau, "is to be found in the proportion which the night bears to the day, the winter to the summer, thought to experience."[17] In the end, it is civilization that makes possible the savoring of wilderness and wilderness that makes possible the appreciation of civilization.

The suggestion that the impact on local communities should be considered and balanced against the benefits of a monument should not be understood as an argument that the public lands must be managed for the benefit of local communities. Instead, the consideration of impact should be understood as a focus on how public lands deserving of protection can be preserved with the least possible negative impact on local communities. Approaches to protecting local communities have been explored by a number of writers. But the one theme common to the approaches for easing the blow suffered by local communities from public land management decisions is that the community and its interests should at the very least be included in the decision-making process.

Amending the Antiquities Act

If consultation with local communities would ennoble the monument proclamation process, why has it occurred only infrequently? The predominant reason is that the Antiquities Act does not require it. Certainly, presidents are free to seek input from state and local governments. For example, stung by the broad criticism of the process employed in the designation of Grand Staircase–Escalante National Monument,[18] during the second term of the Clinton administration Interior Secretary Bruce Babbitt actually did quite a bit of consulting with local communities about potential monument designations.[19] Nevertheless, without an amendment to the Antiquities Act, history suggests that presidents will most often ignore local concerns.

Babbitt's experience indicates that advance notice of a potential monument and consultation with local communities do not hinder monument proclamations. Following a more consultative approach, during his second term, Clinton designated 21 additional monuments.[20] Despite this record, the Clinton administration opposed amending the Act to include even the most tepid of participation obligations. For example, it threatened to veto House Bill 1487 which would have amended the Act to require the president to "solicit public participation and comment" but only "to the extent consistent with" achieving the protective purposes of the Antiquities Act and to "consult with the Governor and congressional delegation of the State ... in which the lands are located," but only "to the extent practicable."[21]

Why has there been such opposition to any amendment of the Antiquities Act, particularly when consultation has not proven an impediment to monument making? The first claim that is usually made for leaving the Antiquities Act untouched is a historical one. Supporters point to such important withdrawals as the Grand Canyon and Jackson Hole and argue that they could not have been accomplished without the Antiquities Act. However, it is not clear that an Antiquities Act amended to require notice and consultation would have failed to produce these monuments. Moreover, whatever merit this historical argument has with respect to the need for the Act in its early years, it is not particularly persuasive with respect to proclamations made after the passage of FLPMA in 1976, which created an arguably sufficient procedure for decisive executive protection of public lands.

Recall that historically the president's authority to withdraw public lands for preservation purposes has been quite broad.[22] The Antiquities Act was only one of a number of laws giving the president withdrawal authority, and the Supreme Court affirmed a variety of executive withdrawals on the premise that congressional acquiescence in the withdrawal constituted an implied delegation of authority.[23] With the passage of FLPMA, Congress attempted to limit the executive branch's withdrawal authority by repealing numerous statutory provisions giving executive withdrawal power[24] and then giving the secretary of the interior new withdrawal authority subject to congressional veto and a variety of procedural safeguards. FLPMA's withdrawal provisions require the secretary of the interior to publish notice of any proposed withdrawal, conduct public hearings, and consult with local government bodies.[25] Along with notice, the secretary must furnish Congress with a detailed report on the proposed withdrawal, a significant portion of which must address the withdrawal's impact on local communities.[26] Thus, after the passage of FLPMA, presidents committed to preservation likely could still accomplish their objectives without using the Antiquities Act, and with the added benefit of a more participatory approach to withdrawal decisions.

In light of FLPMA's withdrawal provisions, one could conclude that the Antiquities Act is superfluous, that instead of amendment to include a participation requirement, the Act should simply be repealed. While this view is not without merit, repealing the Antiquities Act before testing the limits of FLPMA's withdrawal provisions seems unwise. Before explaining why that is the case, however, it is useful to explore more fully whether it at least makes sense to consider FLPMA, rather than an unamended Antiquities Act, as the preferred preservation tool.

Supporters of the Antiquities Act often argue that it is critical because it allows the president to respond rapidly to emergency situations where public lands are threatened with irreparable harm. Yet most monument proclamations have not arisen as a result of emergencies. Moreover, FLPMA's withdrawal provisions specifically allow the secretary of the interior to make an emergency withdrawal of any amount of lands for a period not to exceed three years.[27] Thus, in a real emergency, FLPMA already allows circumvention of public participation to protect critical resources.

Supporters have also argued that the Antiquities Act is critical to accomplish preservation because it allows the president rather than Congress to decide whether particular lands should be protected. Given that the Constitution's Property Clause charges Congress with the obligation of managing the public lands,[28] the Act's supporters do not often make the blunt argument that they do not want Congress to make the decision because Congress might not favor the withdrawal. They make a subtler point. They assert that the public and a majority in Congress would indeed support preservation legislation but that the majority's will is often thwarted by filibusters and sharp legislative maneuvering, particularly the ability of long-standing committee chairmen from public lands states to bottle up protective legislation in committee.[29] This frustration is legitimate and reflects historical reality. That is precisely what led President Eisenhower to declare Chesapeake & Ohio Canal National Monument and President Franklin D. Roosevelt to declare Jackson Hole National Monument.[30] Moreover, given the increasing public preference for recreation and preservation of the public lands, it does indeed appear that a current and growing majority in Congress would support greater preservation.

Nevertheless, this legitimate concern is not a persuasive argument for the necessity of using the Antiquities Act because FLPMA was again designed to answer this concern. FLPMA allows the secretary of the interior to make withdrawals of any acreage for a period of up to twenty years unless Congress within ninety days rejects it by a concurrent resolution.[31] Moreover, FLPMA specifically prohibits the committee to which the withdrawal is referred from bottling up the vote on the resolution if any proponent demands a discharge of the withdrawal issue.[32] Thus, FLPMA provides a mechanism to circumvent committee roadblocks and actually test Congress' support for the withdrawal.

These same veto provisions, however, present the greatest risk in relying exclusively on FLPMA and simply repealing the Antiquities Act. Given the United States Supreme Court's decision in *Immigration and Naturalization Service v. Chadha*,[33] finding a similar legislative veto provision unconstitutional, there are serious questions about whether FLPMA's legislative veto provisions would survive constitutional challenge. Although the secretary's FLPMA withdrawal authority could even be strengthened if FLPMA's veto provisions were held to be unconstitutional yet severable from the rest of the withdrawal process, it is also possible that a court could strike down the secretary's entire withdrawal authority.

The *Chadha* precedent presents a threat to the FLPMA withdrawal process, but not enough of one to justify wholesale rejection of FLPMA's more inclusive and deliberative process. It would still be possible, for instance, to simultaneously withdraw a monument under both FLPMA and the Antiquities Act. If FLPMA's withdrawal provisions proved unconstitutional, the monument would still survive, and the process would have been more collaborative. If FLPMA's veto provisions survived legal challenge, the argument for using the Antiquities Act would be further diminished. Admittedly, the FLPMA approach might be a bit more arduous, time-consuming, or politically difficult, but that is not a sufficient justification for completely excluding affected communities from the decision.

Even if FLPMA's veto provisions survived judicial scrutiny, some might be reluctant to use it as a substitute for the Antiquities Act. Under FLPMA, Congress can veto presidential action and a secretarial withdrawal assures only twenty years of protection, whereas under the Antiquities Act the president may act unilaterally and monuments have no expiration date. Neither of these arguments is overwhelming. Antiquities Act withdrawals can themselves be overturned by Congress, albeit only after clearing more procedural hurdles than with the FLPMA veto process. Moreover, if Antiquities Act supporters are correct, and they surely are, that locally disputed monuments have broad public support and quickly become national treasures, it is extremely unlikely that Congress would initially veto a withdrawal, and even more unlikely that, after twenty years, Congress would not finally ratify the withdrawal.

Nevertheless, it is true that FLPMA's twenty-year limit on the withdrawal and its potential to be vetoed by Congress do pose some additional risks to monument-making. But that conclusion is not an argument for leaving the Antiquities Act unamended. The notification, consultation, and impact study requirements contained in FLPMA could be grafted onto the Antiquities Act without significant harm to preservation efforts. On balance, for those concerned about both preservation and a more ennobling process, this appears the best course for now. Although FLPMA's withdrawal process is preferable to an unamended Antiquities Act, amending the Act to include process protections would retain the benefit of decisive presidential action while diminishing any risk of losing a monument at the end of twenty years.

The political reality, of course, is that amendment of the Antiquities Act is as unlikely now as it has been historically. Nevertheless, nothing prevents the president from voluntarily engaging in a worthier monument withdrawal process. In fact, noncompulsory adherence to a virtuous process may ultimately enhance the nobility of the preservationist project more than obligated adherence to codified virtue. To quote Leopold again: "Voluntary adherence to an ethical code elevates the self-respect of the sportsman, but it should not be forgotten that voluntary disregard of the code degenerates and depraves him."[34] An ethical code of sorts should guide the president in the withdrawal process and preservationist advocacy more generally, just like an ethical code informs the voluntary activities of the sportsman.

Conclusion

In his book *Fire on the Plateau*, Charles Wilkinson concludes that the history of the American West has been one of "conquest by certitude." He contends that many of the harms suffered by the Indian peoples and the lands of the Colorado Plateau have been the result of decisions by government officials "who knew to an absolute certainty what was right for the Colorado Plateau."[35] Wilkinson's "conquest by certitude" thesis seems a largely accurate characterization of public lands policy in the nineteenth century. Confident in the moral, economic, and scientific wisdom of Manifest Destiny, Americans were sure about what was the best use of the public lands and what was best for the Indian tribes who dwelled there. Means were not particularly important because the ends were so plainly correct.

The more interesting question is whether Wilkinson's thesis remains applicable today. Specifically, is aggressive use of the Antiquities Act a repetition of this historical pattern of conquest by certitude? Should we be so certain about the altruism and correctness of our preservation preference that we eschew any obligation to consult with those rural communities that have developed real and lasting attachments to the public lands, at least in part because of their reliance on public policies that encouraged that attachment? If so, we are forgetting that our nineteenth-century predecessors believed with just as much conviction that settling and developing those lands was the right thing to do.

If our current public lands agenda runs the same risk of conquest by certitude, what is the answer? Must monument-making take a back seat to natural resource extraction? Not necessarily. The solution is not to abandon the preservation preference but to exhibit more skepticism about its achievement. At a minimum, skepticism implies a willingness constantly to question the necessary scope of our public lands aspirations and our means for achieving them. In the monument context, some of that questioning should be directed at rural communities in the form of requiring public participation and impact studies prior to a monument proclamation. The idea of public participation and impact studies is neither novel nor earth-shattering in natural resources law, except, apparently, in the case of the Antiquities Act.

Ultimately, the test for those of us who favor the increasingly dominant public land uses of preservation and recreation is whether this time we can exhibit less certitude about our public lands preference by recognizing the interests of the communities who are a part of the fabric of those lands. Amending the Antiquities Act to include minimal notification and public participation requirements would be a good beginning.

Editors' note: Portions of this chapter were published previously in two articles by the author: "Utah's Grand Staircase: The Right Path to Wilderness Preservation?", University of Colorado Law Review 70 (1999), *and "The Future of the Antiquities Act,"* Journal of Land Resources and Environmental Law 21 (2001).

Notes

1. "Bennett Blasts LBJ 'Land Grab' to Expand 2 Monuments in Utah." *Salt Lake Tribune,* January 22, 1969, sec. 2, 17.

2. Rasband, Salzman, and Squillace 2004, 557.

3. For a review of the dispute over whether the Elgin Marbles should be repatriated to Greece, see Merryman 1985, 1881.

4. Sax 1980, 103.

5. Nash 1967, 247.

6. Sax 1980, 28.

7. Sax 1980, quoting Rowell 1977, 37; and quoting English alpinist Geoffrey Winthrop Young, 147.

8. Waterman and Waterman 1993, 208.

9. Sax 1980, 94–96.

10. Sax 1980, 32–33.

11. Muir 1992, 593. "Nearly all my mountaineering has been done on foot, carrying as little as possible, depending on camp-fires for warmth, that so I might be light and free to go wherever my studies might lead."

12. Leopold 1949 [1970], 212.

13. Nordland 1997, 44, describing the guided tours up Everest and a base camp "cushier than ever, supplied by daily chopper flights, with video movies and propane heaters in some of the tents. The Malaysians even had Coca-Cola packed in by Sherpas, while camp caterers cranked out bagels, pizza and sushi."

14. Rana 1998, quoting Nepal officials that one clean-up expedition brought back two tons of rubbish and that "[w]e will probably have to mount two expeditions to clear the mountain of empty oxygen cylinders, human bodies and even [the] remains of a crashed Italian helicopter"; Krakauer 1997, describing the 1996 Mount Everest disaster in which a number of climbers on professionally guided trips died when caught in a storm near the summit.

15. Leopold described the "trophy-recreationist" as a person who "must possess, invade, appropriate" (1949 [1970], 294).

16. Nash 1967, 205, quoting Marshall 1937, 240.

17. Nash 1967, 92, quoting "Walking," in *The Writings of Henry David Thoreau* (1893 ed.), 9:258.

18. See DiMeglio 2000, quoting Babbitt: "What I've said to everybody in the West after Escalante is that it won't happen again on my watch."

19. Squillace 2003, 539–540.

20. Squillace 2003, 473.

21. H.R. 1487, 106th Cong. sec. B (1999). *Inside Energy/with Federal Lands,* "Senate Energy Committee Approves Weaker Version of Monument Bill," October 25, 1999, 14 (reporting the veto threat).

22. The Property Clause of the United States Constitution allocates primary control over the public lands to Congress, giving it the power to "dispose of and make all needful Rules and Regulations respecting the Territory or other Property belonging to the United States." United States Constitution, article IV, sec. 3, cl. 2. In theory, therefore, it is Congress, and not the executive branch, that makes withdrawal decisions. Thus, Congress may exercise its constitutional power to make withdrawals by statute (for example, by creating a national park), or Congress may pass legislation delegating that authority to the executive branch.

23. *United States v. Midwest Oil Co.,* 236 U.S. 459 (1915). Quite a bit has been written on the withdrawal authority of the executive branch. The most comprehensive review of executive withdrawal authority is the 1970 report of the Public Land Law Review Commission (PLLRC 1970). The PLLRC recommended that large-scale withdrawals "be accomplished only by act of Congress" in part because of its finding that "areas set aside by executive action ... have not had adequate study and there has not been proper consultation with people affected or with the units of local government in the vicinity, particularly as to precise boundaries" (PLLRC 1970, 54, 1). Much of this recommendation was enacted in FLPMA six years later, although the Antiquities Act was not repealed.

24. In FLPMA, Congress repealed 29 statutory provisions granting withdrawal authority to the executive branch. See P.L. 94-579, sec. 704(a), 90 Stat. 2744, 2792 (1976).

25. 43 U.S.C. sec. 1714.

26. 43 U.S.C. sec. 1714(c)(2).

27. 43 U.S.C. sec. 1714(e).

28. United States Constitution, article IV, sec 3, cl. 2.

29. Leshy 1998, 86.

30. Leshy 1998, 86.

31. 43 U.S.C. sec. 1714(c)(1).

32. 43 U.S.C. sec. 1714(c)(1).

33. 462 U.S. 919 (1983).

34. Leopold 1949 [1970], 212.

35. Wilkinson 1999, 309.

Part 3

More than Monuments

The Act's Impact on Archaeology,
Historic Preservation, and Nature Conservation

9

The Foundation for American Public Archaeology

Section 3 of the Antiquities Act of 1906

Francis P. McManamon

THE ANTIQUITIES ACT OF 1906 IS NOT WIDELY KNOWN, yet it is among the most important of American laws for archaeological and historical preservation, as well as for natural resource conservation. To the extent that the law is known, it is most commonly understood to be the authority by which the president can establish national monuments on public lands. In this chapter, I shall focus on another important aspect of the law: its position as the foundation for public archaeological and historic preservation policies in the United States. Specifically, the three aspects of this policy foundation are: (1) archaeological resources are public resources and their uses should be regulated publicly and for a public benefit rather than for private commercial or personal gain; (2) the primary values of archaeological resources are educational and commemorative; and (3) archaeological resources should be investigated and interpreted by qualified professionals using the best historical and scientific methods and techniques. Section 3 of the Antiquities Act established these policies regarding archaeological sites. Later in the twentieth century, the Historic Sites Act (1935) and the National Historic Preservation Act (1966) extended these same fundamental policies to a wider range of historic and cultural resources, including those located on other-than-public lands.

Two Generations' Efforts

Enactment of the Antiquities Act required 25 years of politically oriented effort by individuals and organizations concerned about the preservation of American archaeological sites. These efforts are well described in the chapters by Lee and Thompson in this book. Interest in the archaeological remains of the United States began in the eighteenth century. Interest expanded both socially and geographically through the nineteenth century as the substantial and visible remains of ancient earthen architecture in the Mississippi and Ohio valleys and in the southeastern states were encountered by settlers pushing West.[1] As the final quarter of the 1800s began, much of the interest in American archaeological sites was focused on the Southwest; during this period the effort to protect archaeological sites through government means began.[2]

Some of the interested parties were those who plundered the prehistoric ruins, removing ancient artifacts for personal use or commercial sale. At some ancient sites, building stone and roof beams were removed for contemporary uses. Other people, some of them explorers from newly established natural history museums or archaeological organizations, wanted to examine and study ancient sites, as well as make collections for their institutions and the public they served. Investigators who began to visit and report on the condition of prominent ruins noted the destruction that was occurring. Adolph Bandelier's 1881 report on the looting and destruction of the ruins and archaeological deposits at the site of Pecos in New Mexico was used during discussions and debate in the United States Senate when the issue of government action to protect archaeological sites was raised.[3] Such descriptions motivated early advocates of government action to protect archaeological sites. One notable success along the path to the Antiquities Act was the setting aside in 1892 of Casa Grande Ruin as the first national archaeological reservation.[4]

Beginning in the 1870s, major public exhibitions, two of the best known being the World's Columbian Exposition in Chicago (1893) and the Louisiana Purchase Exposition in St. Louis (1904), exposed more of the American public to United States antiquities. Municipal and university museums in large cities throughout the country featured American Indian antiquities in their displays. Investigators of the southwestern ruins and archaeological sites in other parts of the country and hemisphere published popular accounts of their adventures and the sites they visited. The growing popular appeal of American archaeology was accompanied by a commercial demand for authentic prehistoric antiquities. The unsystematic removal of artifacts from archaeological sites for private use expanded, especially in the increasingly accessible Southwest.[5]

The legislative and political history of the Antiquities Act shows that the issue was first raised in the Senate by Senator George F. Hoar of Massachusetts in 1882.[6] At that time and subsequently, debates between those who favored conservation or preservation and those who favored commercial uses of public lands laced the issue. Interestingly, objections to government protection of archaeological sites did not deny that the problem existed. It was generally acknowledged that looting of archaeological sites was occurring and descriptions of such activities were found with increasing frequency. Detractors of the effort to provide protection and preservation first argued that the government couldn't possibly protect all of these resources. Some were alarmed by the creation of federal forest reserves, which by 1901 totaled 46 million acres. These legislators objected to creating another means by which the president could set aside large areas of the public domain for conservation or preservation, further reducing the land available for private development and economic activity. Eventually, these objections were overcome by public sentiment, expressed by advocates from archaeological organizations, museums, and universities, to remedy the increasing destruction of archaeological sites in the Southwest and the wholesale removal of artifacts that was occurring (Figure 9.1). Efforts to protect specific archaeological sites, such as Mesa Verde and Chaco Canyon, became more frequent and widespread. Finally, these efforts culminated in the Antiquities Act, which enabled the protection of specific important archaeological areas and regulated how such sites on public land would be preserved and protected and how they would be used.[7]

The Department of the Interior and Archaeological Site Protection

Historical accounts of the long effort to devise a means of protecting archaeological sites from looting and vandalism during the last quarter of the nineteenth century and the first decade of the twentieth have emphasized the roles of scholars, scientists, and their supporters. The activities of Edgar Lee Hewett, Frederic W. Putnam, W. H. Holmes, and Francis W. Kelsey, for example, have been a focus of

Figure 9.1. Protection of southwestern archaeological sites was a principal reason for the passage of the Antiquities Act. Clockwise from upper left: Hovenweep National Monument, Colorado; Montezuma Castle National Monument, Arizona; Aztec Ruins National Monument, New Mexico; Gila Cliff Dwellings National Monument, New Mexico. Photo of Hovenweep: NPS / Fred E. Mang, Jr., courtesy of National Park Service Historic Photo Collection, Harpers Ferry Center; all others: National Park Service Digital Image Archives.

these studies.[8] The role of congressional leaders, most notably John F. Lacey, a Republican representative from Iowa and chairman of the House Committee on Public Lands also is well recognized. Beginning in 1900, Lacey worked on legislation that led to the Antiquities Act and introduced it as a bill in 1906, shepherding it safely through hearings and votes in Congress.[9] Officials of the Department of the Interior (DOI), in particular the General Land Office (GLO), also played important roles and actively shaped and promoted the archaeological preservation and protection legislation.[10] In the American Southwest, where the results of archaeological site looting could be observed regularly, GLO field agents had important roles in emphasizing the need to protect the sites.

Perhaps the earliest activity of the DOI related specifically to antiquities was the care of Casa Grande Ruin in Arizona following the establishment of a federal reservation to protect the ancient structure and its immediately surrounding area by executive order on June 20, 1892.[11] Subsequent appropriations to the DOI were provided for the repair and protection of the site.[12] Conservation and documentation of the ancient structures were carried out by experts from the Smithsonian Institution: in 1891 and 1892 by Cosmos Mindeleff, in 1895 by W J McGee, and in 1906 and 1908 by Jesse Fewkes.[13]

Setting Basic Archaeological Preservation Policy: Section 3 of the Antiquities Act

In 1900, efforts to preserve archaeological sites on public lands took a more practical tack. Advocates for archaeological preservation and protection began producing draft bills that would accomplish their aims and working directly with legislators on submitting these drafts for consideration in Congress. The ardent, but diffuse earlier approach, such as the 1882 petition calling upon Congress to save ancient ruins and sites, which was prepared by antiquities advocates in the Boston area and introduced by Senator Hoar, was replaced by direct work with members of Congress and officials in the DOI on specific legislative bills.[14] It was in the bureaucratic arena of review and recommendations regarding bills that DOI officials had the most impact on the outcome of the Antiquities Act.

Between February and April 1900, four bills providing for the protection of archaeological sites on public lands were introduced in Congress, one by Representative Jonathan P. Dolliver of Iowa and three by Representative John F. Shafroth of Colorado.[15] Representative Lacey, as chair of the House committee that would consider these bills, asked the secretary of the interior to review them and offer advice or suggestions. From this point onwards until the passage of the Antiquities Act in 1906, officials at the DOI were active in evaluating proposed laws, drafting substitutes, and providing information on this topic.

Binger Hermann, then commissioner of the GLO, responded for the secretary to Representative Lacey's request. The commissioner's report on the bills endorsed the notion of enacting a law to protect archaeological sites and other objects of scientific interest on public lands. He criticized some of the means by which the bills sent for review would accomplish this, and offered a substitute bill.

The text of Hermann's substitute bill contains a Section 3 that is remarkably similar to the Section 3 ultimately included in the Antiquities Act itself. The DOI substitute bill's Section 3 followed closely a portion of the text of Section 1 of the Dolliver bill, which is likely to have been the prototype for the final text.[16] The language of this section describes the permitting authority assigned to the land managing department—in 1900 it was assumed that this would be the DOI—and provides general guidance for how permits are to be used to regulate archaeological investigations. In a middling-size paragraph the DOI substitute bill includes an important set of policies that established the approach public agencies would take in their treatment of archaeological resources from 1906 onwards.

The text of Section 3 in the 1900 DOI substitute bill reads:

> Sec. 3. That the Secretary of the Interior be, and is hereby, authorized to permit examinations, excavations, and the gathering of objects of interest within such parks by any person or persons who he may deem properly qualified to conduct such examinations, excavations, or gatherings, subject to such rules and regulations as he may prescribe: Provided, always, That the examinations, excavations, and gatherings are undertaken for the benefit of the Smithsonian Institution or of some reputable museum, university, college, or other recognized scientific or educational institution, with the view to increasing the knowledge of such objects and aiding the general advancement of archaeological science.[17]

Section 3 of the substitute bill provided by Hermann establishes three important policies about how the government regards and treats archaeological sites. This version of Section 3 is short, consisting of only one long sentence. Most importantly, the first part of the sentence establishes as a matter of public interest that government officials shall regulate the treatment of archaeological sites on public lands. The text identifies archaeological sites as important to the American public and the secretary of the interior is authorized to use a system of permits to direct and oversee how they are used. The first part of the sentence also establishes the second important policy. It requires that only persons who are "properly qualified" will be permitted to conduct archaeological investigations. In this phrase, there is an immediate assertion that those who seek permits must show that they possess special capability, expertise, experience, and commitment to conduct archaeological investigations on public lands. The third policy is equally important and is explained in the second part of the sentence. This part of the sentence describes the intent of the permitted investigations. It is established that the objective of the investigations—"examinations, excavations, and gatherings"—is to advance knowledge; the goal is to improve understanding of the past using archaeological methods. The objective is not commercial or personal gain; it is not the collection of objects for public or personal display. Rather, investigations must have as their objective improving the understanding of the past.

The text of this early version of Section 3 limits the permitting to archaeological investigations "within such parks." This phrase relates to Sections 1 and 2 of the DOI substitute bill which would have authorized the president to establish "national parks" on public lands. This language would have limited the requirement for archaeological permits to those areas designated as national parks. As such, this version of Section 3 would have been more limited in scope than the ultimate version, which applies to all public land. In other aspects, Section 3 of the original DOI draft and that of the Antiquities Act are remarkably congruent. Congressman Lacey introduced the DOI substitute bill late in April 1900, but Congress took no action on any of the 1900 bills.

Between 1900 and final passage of the Antiquities Act in 1906, other bills and versions of bills were presented and debated. Disagreements about whether or not to give the president authority to create national parks or set aside public lands as national monuments, and if so, how large these designated units should be, were major topics. Another matter of concern was the role of the Smithsonian Institution: whether it should be the agency that managed archaeological sites that would be protected by the Act, or whether the protector and manager should be the DOI. These matters eventually were resolved and the outcomes articulated in the final version of the Act.[18]

The fundamental policies embedded in the text of Hermann's Section 3 seem not to have been contested and in the final version of the Act a Section 3—still only one long sentence—again appears. The final version of Section 3 reads:

Permits for the examination of ruins, the excavation of archaeological sites and the gathering of objects of antiquity upon the
lands under their respective jurisdictions may be granted by the
Secretaries of the Interior, Agriculture, and Army to institutions
which they may deem properly qualified to conduct such examination, excavation, or gathering, subject to such rules and regulation as they may prescribe: *Provided,* That the examinations,
excavations, and gatherings are undertaken for the benefit of
reputable museums, universities, colleges, or other recognized
scientific or education institutions, with a view to increasing the
knowledge of such objects, and that the gatherings shall be
made for permanent preservation in public museums.

The final version of Section 3 of the Antiquities Act is very similar to the version in the 1900 DOI substitute bill, although it contains three important additions. Most important, the final version
requires permits for archaeological investigations on all public
lands, not only within the boundaries of national monuments or
parks. In addition, after the first part of the sentence asserts the public's interest in how archaeological sites on public lands are treated,
two additional cabinet secretaries are assigned responsibilities
because their duties include management of public lands upon
which archaeological sites are found. The final text also requires
that applicants be properly qualified, but identifies them as "institutions" rather than "person or persons." This is an improvement to
the original, perhaps recognizing that archaeological investigations
require institutional support to be successful, and that the results of
many investigations will include collections and records that
require long-term care and curation, normally impossible without
institutional support.

Significantly, the goal of archaeological investigations remains
as described in the original version—increasing knowledge. The
final text adds a requirement that collections made as part of the
permitted investigations be kept "for permanent preservation in
public museums." This important addition recognizes the critical
need for long-term care and curation of archaeological collections, a
challenge we still face a hundred years after passage of the Antiquities Act.[19]

The quarter-century struggle to provide for public protection of
archaeological sites overlaps with the related development of private and public preservation of historic structures and places—for
example, Civil War battlefields. Examining these developments,

Richard West Sellars points out that early preservation efforts led to the gradual recognition of the need for group or joint or public ownership devoted to the preservation of important historic properties.[20] Such a recognition of public interest in archaeological resource preservation is found in the Antiquities Act.

Today, a century after they were promulgated, the basic policies of a public interest in archaeological sites, the need for well-qualified individuals with sufficient institutional support to conduct archaeological investigations, and the fundamental commemorative, educational, and scientific values of archaeological resources are well established. In contrast, one can consider what might have been. What if, for example, the purpose of these permitted excavations and gatherings had been to collect items for sale to the highest bidder, with some portion of the proceeds going into the government's coffers? What if the permits had been based on which institution could provide the largest commercial return from the excavations or gatherings? What if the main purpose of the excavations had remained the collection of objects with little concern about context, archaeological recording, analysis, or interpretation? Fortunately, such commercial initiatives and values were opposed by the advocates for public protection of archaeological sites, and their views were supported by administration and congressional leaders. Section 3 of the Antiquities Act makes this very clear.

The DOI Demonstrates Competence in Archaeological Protection

After the initial flurry of bills in 1900 was not acted on by Congress, the debate about how to protect archaeological sites on public lands continued. One aspect was which government agency should be given responsibilities regarding archaeological sites if federal legal protections were enacted. The two obvious candidates were the DOI, which managed most of the public lands, and the Smithsonian, which employed archaeologists and carried out research on American archaeological sites.

Officials at DOI acted to show the department's competence on the topic and used existing federal authorities to protect specific sites and sensitive areas. One particular activity undertaken by DOI officials in the development of antiquities legislation was the collection and distribution of information about archaeological sites in the Southwest and the need for their protection. In 1904, GLO Commissioner W. A. Richards, who had succeeded Binger Hermann, moved to provide an official report on the overall situation regarding archaeological sites in the Southwest. Sizing up the contested situation in Congress, and presented with another request for the DOI's opinion on the bills being considered, Richards took the opportunity to submit a detailed description of the archaeological sites in the Southwest that were endangered by looting and vandalism.[21]

For information on the situation, Richards turned to Edgar Lee Hewett.[22] Hewett submitted the report requested by Richards in September 1904. Hewett's text provided a clear summary of the state of knowledge about archaeological sites in the territories of Arizona and New Mexico in particular, but also those in the southeastern corner of Utah and the southwestern corner of Colorado. The report grouped sites into a series of districts, generally organized around river drainages, and provided an apparently comprehensive list of manuscript and published sources. The report "for the first time ... provided the General Land Office and eventually Congress with a comprehensive review of all the Indian antiquities located on federal lands.... Better than any other single document, Hewett's memorandum clearly foreshadowed, in remarkable detail, the system of archaeological national monuments established in the Southwest following passage of the Antiquities Act."[23]

Richards took Hewett's report and made it the GLO's. Before the end of the year, he had it printed as an official GLO report, entitled *Circular Relating to Historic and Prehistoric Ruins of the Southwest and Their Preservation*.[24] In addition to Hewett's text and map, the circular includes an interesting set of excerpts from letters and GLO documents as addenda. Hewett's introductory paragraph in the addenda summarizes clearly their purpose:

> Since the ... [preparation] of the foregoing I have had the opportunity to inform myself fully as to the care which the Interior Department has exercised, and is prepared to exercise when properly informed, over the ruins in the Southwest. Much more has been accomplished than is known to the general public. It will be helpful to all who have the subject under consideration to know that a vigorous policy has been developed and is in operation, which accomplishes the main object to be desired.[25]

The various letters and documents, apparently supplied by Richards, describe the activities by DOI bureaus related to the preservation of antiquities.[26] By publishing the information, DOI officials showed that the department had expertise on the topic of American antiquities and laid out the steps that were being taken for their protection and preservation. The report indicated that the DOI was able to carry out archaeological preservation and protection. Richards' intention in having the report prepared and published may well have been to emphasize to congressional supporters that the DOI was the proper government agency—as opposed to, for example, the Smithsonian Institution—to be assigned this responsibility in any legislation considered by Congress.

DOI leaders also took specific steps through administrative means to restrict legal access to archaeological sites, making looting more difficult. Following the setting aside of the Casa Grande ruins in 1892, the GLO used administrative actions to protect other archaeological sites by removing them from lands available for homesteading or other kinds of private uses. The following list includes archaeological sites or areas identified in 1904 as having been set aside and made unavailable for homesteading claims:

- In New Mexico, the Pajarito cliff dwellers' region, the Jemez cliff dwellers' region, and the tract known as El Morro, or Inscription Rock, and critical parts of Chaco Canyon;
- In Colorado, the Mesa Verde cliff dwellers' region;
- In Arizona, the tract containing the petrified forest and the greater portion of the Rio Verde region, containing among other sites Montezuma Castle.[27]

It is interesting to note that among the sites listed are three of the four national monuments proclaimed by President Roosevelt in 1906: El Morro, Petrified Forest, and Montezuma Castle. Also on this list are Mesa Verde, a portion of which was established as a national park by statute in June 1906, shortly after the enactment of the Antiquities Act, and Chaco Canyon, which was made a national monument in 1907.

The Antiquities Act and the Progressive Agenda

Government and private efforts to protect archaeological sites on public lands coincided with the rise of scientific resource management, a part of the Progressive political agenda. Support for Progressive ideas and methods was boosted substantially when Theodore Roosevelt rose to the presidency following the death of William

McKinley in September 1901. In his detailed history of the early years of conservation during the Progressive era, Samuel Hays presents a wealth of information about how political leaders and civil servants developed and applied scientific information and methods for the management of a wide range of natural resources.[28]

Scientific and hydrographic recording in the West by U.S. government expeditions and survey parties since the 1880s extended into a variety of kinds of natural resource management. First irrigation, then forest management, then grazing were incorporated into a coherent policy. Eventually, a number of public agency leaders who espoused scientific management of resources combined all of these management schemes into an overall approach to federal land management. "These leaders were especially enthusiastic about the possibilities of vast economic growth in the West if the federal government planned the development of its resources on a large scale," Hays writes. "By 1906, Pinchot [Gifford Pinchot, chief of the U.S. Forest Service], Newell [Frederick H. Newell, commissioner of the U.S. Reclamation Service] and other officials had formulated comprehensive land management concepts which during the remainder of Roosevelt's presidency they tried to apply to the public domain."[29]

The elements of scientific land management involved a revision of the standard way in which the public lands had been dealt with under the laws passed by Congress up to that point. These earlier laws were modeled on homesteading. They focused mainly on distributing public land to private individuals who would develop the land according to the requirements of the land laws. In the fall of 1903, President Roosevelt appointed a Public Lands Commission that reflected the desire for a more orderly and planned approach to use of the public lands.

Hays summarizes four aspects of the new orderly, rational, and scientific approach to public land management as it developed in the early years of the Roosevelt administration. The authorities embodied in the Antiquities Act, and the activities by DOI officials as they demonstrated their competence to protect archaeological sites in anticipation of the Act, display all of the characteristics of this new approach to resource management.

First, scientific land management required that federal agencies would have control over the resources and could regulate their use. Requiring permits by resource users provided a means of control. By issuing permits of limited duration, the government could control use. By setting conditions with the permits, limits of use and scientific management principles could be enforced. For example, grazing should not exceed the carrying capacity of the vegetation.[30] As we have seen, Section 3 of the Antiquities Act, and the archaeological protection bills dating back to 1900 from which it derived, assert a federal interest in the control of American antiquities and include such a permitting requirement.

Second, scientific management required that the appropriate uses of resources be determined and applied objectively. Decisions had to be made consistently about who would be allowed to use the public resources. For example, regarding uses in the forest reserves,

> the administration never set down a definite code but did assume a rough system of priorities in attempting to resolve specific use conflicts. In the national forests Pinchot granted top priority to domestic use of water, followed by irrigation and power.... On agricultural lands homesteading should precede grazing.... The conflict between recreation and commercial use Pinchot found to be extremely hazardous to resolve, but he firmly argued that commercial uses of the public lands should precede their use for recreation. Reservoirs for municipal supply of water, for example, should be permitted in national parks.[31]

Regarding archaeological sites, Section 3 of the Antiquities Act directs that permits are to be used to carefully examine and record sites and provides that the information and items collected will be cared for and interpreted in public museums.

Third, scientific management required expertise in handling resources. "The new land management entailed administrative innovations. Experts rather than politically appointed officials, for example, should take charge of the program."[32] Pinchot, for example, had long stressed the need for properly trained foresters and the use of civil service exams to select them. "The Roosevelt administration constantly increased the number of trained foresters, range specialists, and geologists in its public lands program."[33] Again, Section 3 of the Antiquities Act requires that permits be given only to qualified institutions that can carry out the proper kind of examination and subsequent duration and public interpretation.

Finally, scientific land management involved understanding the resource. Information about the resource was gathered, classified, summarized, and used in making decisions about how the resource should be used. By the early 1900s, the Forest Service was classifying areas within the forest reserves according to their best function. Richards' use of Hewett's 1904 report on the archaeological areas and sites of the Southwest represents an attempt to show that the GLO had a systematic understanding of these public resources. The inclusion in the report addenda of a series of DOI documents and letters describing activities the agency already had taken for the protection of archaeological sites was intended to show that the department and its field offices had the expertise and knowledge to take responsibility for them on public lands in the West.

Hays does not mention the preservation of antiquities or the creation of national monuments in his history. The Antiquities Act is mentioned only once in the index and national parks only a few times in the book. Yet Section 3 of the Act calls for three of the four components of the scientific land management approach recognized as part of Progressive conservation. The increased role of the federal government envisioned by the Antiquities Act is characteristic of many laws and programs established in the decades immediately before and following the turn of the twentieth century through the influence of the Progressive political movement. Progressive politicians asserted new ways of looking after the public good within a federal system staffed by professional civil servants able to provide technical assistance to the public and for public resources. The Antiquities Act seems to have been influenced by this national movement.

The Antiquities Act and
Later Historic Preservation Statutes

The Antiquities Act is recognized widely as the first general statute addressing archaeological and historic preservation needs in the United States.[34] It established basic public policies concerning protection, proper treatment, and value of archaeological sites on the public lands of the United States. During the twentieth century, other statutes broadened the geographic scope of policies to cover archaeological sites located on other kinds of lands. These subsequent statutes also extended the policies to encompass other kinds of cultural resources and historic properties.

Section 3 of the Antiquities Act recognizes that archaeological sites and the artifacts recovered from them are most valuable as sources of historic and scientific information about the past. Archaeological sites are both a means of understanding the past through proper study and exist as places where this past can be commemorated. Careful archaeological excavation, analysis, and interpretation reveal ancient events and long-term cultural, economic, and social developments. Archaeological remains tell stories of people and places not mentioned in historical documents. The general policy embodied in the Act recognized that it is improper and wasteful to dig archaeological sites for the few commercially valuable artifacts they might contain. The information gained from proper archaeological study provides the major public benefit derived from archaeological sites and objects, a benefit that must be shared through schools, parks, museums, public programs, books, articles, videos, and other means of interpretation.

Proponents of the Antiquities Act succeeded in having their perspective—that archaeological resources are mainly valuable as sources of information about the past—embedded in the law. Relatively few archaeological remains have any inherent monetary value. Retrieval of artifacts that do have such monetary value for commercial purposes is not the primary benefit to be derived from archaeological investigation. Rather, the information gained from the careful investigation and analysis of archaeological sites is most properly shared, along with the artifacts collected, as public resources. The law established that archaeological resources, at least those on public land, were to be considered as common resources from which all Americans could benefit. Defining archaeological resources as non-commercial and public is the most basic public policy established by the Antiquities Act.

The second aspect of national preservation policy initiated by the Antiquities Act is nearly as fundamental. By placing special requirements on who may excavate or remove archaeological remains, how the excavation or removal will be accomplished, and what will happen to the objects excavated or removed, the statute acknowledges that archaeological sites have a sufficiently important public value to be dealt with in a special way. They merit special consideration and protection. That is, like clean water and air, the preservation of these kinds of resources and learning from the information they contain contribute to the public good.

These basic policies of the Antiquities Act regarding protection and preservation of archaeological resources apply on lands owned or controlled by the United States government. During the twentieth century, these policies of non-commercial and public values have been extended to additional types of historic properties and cultural resources and to non-federal land in certain circumstances. The broadening of application of the policies came in two increments. Nearly thirty years after the Antiquities Act, the Historic Sites Act of 1935 asserted concerns of the national government and a responsibility for recognizing and providing technical assistance to historic American sites, buildings, objects, and antiquities of national significance, no matter what their land status. In testifying on the bill that served as the basis for the Historic Sites Act, Secretary of the Interior Harold L. Ickes noted that the Antiquities Act provided protection for archaeological and historic resources on publicly owned land, but that "we have never faced squarely the whole great problem of a definite governmental policy or the preservation of historic sites and buildings of transcendent national significance.... [T]he need for governmental action along these lines is urgent and immediate...."[35] This first expansion of coverage extended to additional kinds of historic properties if they were nationally significant, whether or not they were on land owned or controlled by the United States government.

The policy expressed in the 1935 statute follows from the non-commercial and public value policies established by the Antiquities Act. Section 1 of the Historic Sites Act states "[t]hat is hereby declared that it is a national policy to preserve for public use historic sites, buildings, and objects of national significance for the inspiration and benefit of the people of the United States." A more direct commitment to a policy asserting the non-commercial and public value of these resources would be hard to construct.

The second expansion of the basic policy of the Antiquities Act came 60 years after its enactment in the National Historic Preservation Act (NHPA) of 1966. The NHPA is a very broadly written statute, and has been expanded in many ways through substantial amendments in 1980 and 1992. It embraces a wider range of historic property types than both the Antiquities Act and the Historic Sites Act. It is more inclusive as well in providing consideration to historic properties that are of local or state significance, a much wider context than the national significance focused on by the Historic Sites Act.

Like the Antiquities Act and the Historic Sites Act, the NHPA adheres to the public policy that historic properties have a value to all of the public. Section 1(a)(4) states that "the preservation of this irreplaceable heritage is in the public interest so that its vital legacy of cultural, educational, aesthetic, inspirational, economic, and energy benefits will be maintained and enriched for future generations of Americans." The non-commercial value of historic properties also is recognized, and the need to raise its profile in decision-making about the way in which these resources are treated is recognized in the purposes of the statute, as described in Section 1(a)(5): "[I]n the face of ever-increasing extensions of urban centers, highways, and residential, commercial, and industrial developments, the present governmental and nongovernmental historic preservation programs and activities are inadequate to insure future generations a genuine opportunity to appreciate and enjoy the rich heritage of our Nation." Like the earlier statutes, the NHPA has as a central policy focus the public and noncommercial values of historic properties. The ways in which historic properties are treated is of public concern.

The policy espoused by the NHPA calls for considering historic properties within the context of the United States' modern development and economy. In fact, many examples exist of the preservation of historic properties leading to economic, as well as aesthetic, associative, and historical benefits. This is especially so regarding historic structures successfully rehabilitated for modern commercial uses. The preservation of such historic properties may have the additional economic benefit of enhancing the likelihood of their preservation within the context of modern economic conditions. The NHPA has broader application than either of the earlier laws. The extent to which it applies varies according to ownership of specific resources and whether or not there is any federal involvement in an undertaking that may affect them.

Preserving Specific Archaeological Sites as National Monuments

Prior to the Antiquities Act, specific areas had been set aside as parks or reserves; for example, Hot Springs (1832), Yellowstone National Park (1872), Sequoia National Park (1890), Yosemite National Park (1890), and Casa Grande Ruin (1892). A number of national military parks centered on the areas where important Civil War battles had been fought were established during the last decade of the nineteenth century.[36] However, each of these parks or reserves required an act of Congress as well as presidential approval. Section 2 of the Antiquities Act made the establishment of national monuments administrative actions that were quicker and far easier to execute.[37]

Section 2 of the statute gives the president the authority to set aside for protection "historic landmarks, historic and prehistoric structures, and other objects of historic or scientific interest that are situated upon the lands owned or controlled by the Government of the United States...." These protected areas were then designated as "national monuments" and the federal agencies assigned to oversee them were required to afford proper care and management of their resources. This section of the statute provided an additional tool for Progressive politicians and their supporters to determine the uses of public lands and resources in the rational, conservation-oriented manner they favored.[38]

During his presidency, Teddy Roosevelt proclaimed the national monuments of Devils Tower, El Morro, Montezuma Castle, Petrified Forest, Chaco Canyon, Cinder Cone, Lassen Peak, Gila Cliff Dwellings, Tonto, Muir Woods, Grand Canyon, Pinnacles, Jewel Cave, Natural Bridges, Lewis and Clark Cavern, Tumacacori, Wheeler, and Mount Olympus. Since then, this provision of the Act has been used to protect many other places of outstanding archaeological, historical, natural, or scientific importance. Dozens of important archaeological sites, and areas with concentrations of them, are among the areas preserved by being proclaimed and set aside for special protection as national monuments (Figure 9.2). Many of these national monuments are now units of our national park system or are specially cared for by other land-managing agencies. Presidents Taft, Wilson, Harding, Coolidge, Hoover, Franklin D. Roosevelt, Truman, Eisenhower, Kennedy, Johnson, Carter, and Clinton all established national monuments by executive proclamation.

Support for Professional and Scientific Methods and Techniques

The final broad policy of lasting and widespread importance that was established by the Antiquities Act is the requirement that investigations of and removal of artifacts and other material from archaeological sites must be conducted by appropriately qualified and trained experts using the best contemporary methods and tech-

Figure 9.2. Earthworks at Mound City Group National Monument, Ohio, 1960. Proclaimed in 1923 by President Warren G. Harding, the monument is an example of the Antiquities Act being applied to an important archaeological site in the Midwest. In 1992 Mound City was redesignated as Hopewell Culture National Historical Park. Unattributed photograph, courtesy of National Park Service Historic Photo Collection, Harpers Ferry Center.

niques. The use of professional and scientific approaches in the examination and treatment of other kinds of cultural resources, including historic structures, museum objects, cultural landscapes, etc., is accepted and valued, at least in part, due to this policy. Section 3 of the Antiquities Act established such approaches as a basic aspect of public policy in dealing with archaeological sites, historical structures, and other cultural resources.

The law prohibited individuals from digging haphazardly into ancient or historic sites, disturbing whatever caught their fancy, and removing artifacts for personal use or commerce. As described above, Section 3 of the Antiquities Act required that investigations be done under permit by qualified professionals with proper institutional support. By emphasizing these requirements, the federal government supported the professionalization of the young discipline of archaeology. The careful excavation and removal of artifacts required by Antiquities Act permits were necessary for the development of typological and stratigraphic description and analysis that would become methodological and technical standards for professional archaeology in the United States.[39]

Furthermore, these permitted activities were to be carried out "for the benefit of reputable museums, universities, colleges, or other recognized scientific or educational institutions, with a view to increasing the knowledge of such objects." The Act required that approved investigations would result in public education and bene- fit. As one means of ensuring these public benefits, Section 3 also required that the collections of materials from these investigations be placed in public museums.

Improving the Protection of Archaeological Sites

In the century since the Antiquities Act became law, the means of preserving and interpreting America's archaeology has expanded and improved, in particular through the Historic Sites Act and the National Historic Preservation Act. The enforcement and protection aspects of the Antiquities Act also have been improved upon. Although the Antiquities Act proved to be a means of overseeing and coordinating educational and scientific archaeological investi- gations on federal and Indian lands, it did not effectively prevent or deter deliberate, criminal looting of archaeological sites on those lands. Problematic for many years, this situation became critical in the 1970s when several attempts by federal land-managing agencies and prosecutors in the Southwest to convict looters using the Anti- quities Act resulted in adverse court decisions. In two cases judges ruled that the terms of the Act were unconstitutionally vague and therefore unenforceable.[40] This situation led to a concerted effort by archaeologists and preservationists, their allies in the law enforce- ment community, and several essential supporters in Congress, in particular Senators Jeff Bingaman (D-NM) and Pete Domenici (R-NM) and Representative Morris Udall (D-AZ), to strengthen the legal protection of archaeological resources. The eventual outcome was a new statute, the Archaeological Resources Protection Act of 1979, which was amended in 1988 to improve its effectiveness.[41]

Conclusion

The Antiquities Act is important for many reasons, both specific and general. Specifically, it asserted broad public interest in and control over archaeological resources on federal and Indian lands. This assertion of public interest and concern continues to the present and is the basis for public agency efforts to protect archaeological sites from looting and vandalism and to manage them for public benefit. The Act also permitted the protection and preservation of specific areas important for their archaeological, historical, and scientific resources. The Act also stands as an important achievement in the progress of conservation and preservation efforts in the United States. Ronald Lee has written eloquently about the creation of the law, which involved

> a whole generation of dedicated effort by scholars, citizens, and members of Congress.... More important, this generation, through its explorations, publications, exhibits, and other activities, awakened the American people to a lasting consciousness of the value of American antiquities, prehistoric and historic. This public understanding, achieved only after persistent effort in the face of much ignorance, vandalism, and indifference, was a necessary foundation for many subsequent conservation achievements. Among them were several of great importance to the future National Park Service, including the establishment of many national monuments, development of a substantial educational program for visitors, and eventually the execution of a far-reaching nationwide program to salvage irreplaceable archaeological objects threatened with inundation or destruction by dams and other public works and their preservation for the American people.[42]

Many public agencies, such as the National Park Service, Bureau of Land Management, Bureau of Reclamation, U.S. Fish and Wildlife Service, U.S. Forest Service, state historic preservation officers, state archaeologists, universities, museums, Indian tribes, and local governments play important roles in contemporary archaeological and historic preservation. State programs exist that provide models, such as the especially noteworthy public–private partnership between the Arkansas Archaeological Survey and Arkansas Archaeological Society. Private, professional, and advocacy organizations, such as the American Cultural Resources Association, the Archaeological Conservancy, the Archaeological Institute of America, the National Conference of State Historic Preservation Officers, the National Trust for Historic Preservation, the Society for American Archaeology, and the Society for Historical Archaeology, also are important partners. Widespread support for archaeological preservation and interpretation is essential for better understanding the depth and variety of American history and prehistory.

The world is more complicated than it was in 1906. There now exist contemporary perspectives regarding the treatment of archaeological resources that were not envisioned by the promoters and supporters of the Antiquities Act. Those who work at archaeological protection, preservation, and interpretation seek to accomplish goals and to develop consensus about appropriate treatments that take into account the multitude of perspectives. We also have recognized the legitimate claims to traditional uses of other kinds of cultural and natural resources and the value of ethnographic approaches to develop appropriate consultation and treatment in these contexts. The goals of modern archaeological protection, preservation, and interpretation must be accomplished while also taking account of a range of legitimate perspectives. Traditional uses and views of American Indians, Native Alaskans, Native Hawaiians and other Pacific Islanders, as well as other ethnic groups with close associations to particular archaeological sites, must be taken into account through appropriate consultation and treatment.

Indeed, these days many more individuals and distinct groups have expressed opinions about archaeological sites. Some have made claims of unique or sole authority regarding how archaeological resources are to be treated. Worse, some individuals have taken actions to destroy sites for personal or commercial gain, thereby excluding the possibility of any public benefit deriving from the resources. We continue to reject, as the supporters of the Antiquities Act did in 1906, those who pillage archaeological sites for personal or commercial gain. Such behavior destroys the public benefit that can be derived from careful study of archaeological sites and objects.

This chapter has been prepared and is presented as a private work of scholarship. It is not an official statement of the National Park Service or the Department of the Interior. It does not necessarily represent the views of the National Park Service or the Department of the Interior.

Notes

1. Silverberg 1968; Kennedy 1994; Squier and Davis 1998; Milner 2004.
2. Clemensen 1992, chapter 2; Fowler 2000, 79–202.
3. Bandelier 1881; Lee 2000, 198–205.
4. Clemensen 1992, chapter 3; Lee 2000, 205–209.
5. Rothman 1994, chapters 1 and 2; Fowler 2000, 203–219; Lee 2000, 213–219.

6. Lee 2000, 202–205.

7. Thompson 2000, 284–314.

8. For example, Rothman 1994, chapter 3; Fowler 1999; Snead 2001, 76–82.

9. Thompson 2000, 301–303; and Conard's chapter in this volume.

10. Lee 2000, 223–242; Thompson 2000, 289–293.

11. Lee 2000, 205–209.

12. Claus 1945, 1.

13. Matero 1999.

14. Lee 2000, 202–205, 223–242; Thompson 2000, 284–286.

15. Rogers 1958, 1–2; Lee 2000, 223–230.

16. "A Bill for the Preservation of Prehistoric Monuments, Ruins, and Objects, and to Prevent their Counterfeiting," H.R. 8066, 56th Cong., 1st Sess., cited in Rogers 1958.

17. DOI 1900; "A Bill to Establish and Administer National Parks, and for Other Purposes," H.R. 11021, 56th Cong., 1st Sess., cited in Rogers 1958.

18. Rothman 1994; Lee 2000, 223–242; Thompson 2000, 284–318.

19. Childs and Corcoran 2000; Sullivan and Childs 2003.

20. Sellars 2005, 27–29.

21. Thompson 2000, 291–293.

22. Thompson 2000, 289–293; see also his chapter in this volume.

23. Lee 2000, 237; see also his chapter in this volume.

24. DOI 1904.

25. DOI 1904.

26. DOI 1904; for the addenda, see 12–17.

27. DOI 1904, 12–13; Lee 2000, 220; Thompson 2000, 290.

28. Hays 1999.

29. Hays 1999, 66.

30. Hays 1999, 71.

31. Hays 1999, 71.

32. Hays 1999, 71.

33. Hays 1999, 71.

34. For example, McGimsey 1972, 111; Fowler 1974, 1473–1474; Fowler 1986, 140–143; Lee 2000, 198; and the chapter by Rogers in this volume.

35. Ickes 1935, 4.

36. Sellars 2005.

37. Rothman 1994; Lee 2000, 247–265; Squillace 2003.

38. See Rothman 1994, 52–71.

39. Trigger 1989, 127–129, 186–195; Willey and Sabloff 1993, 38–95; Fowler 2000, 247–320.

40. Collins and Michel 1985.

41. McManamon 1991; McManamon 2001, 248–249, 265–268.

42. Lee 2000, 246–247.

10

The Antiquities Act
and Historic Preservation

Jerry L. Rogers

"ABOUT ONCE IN EACH GENERATION, it seems, the United States Congress enacts major legislation to preserve the nation's historical heritage." Ernest Allen Connally used these words in 1967 to open a series of conferences around the country to explain the newly enacted National Historic Preservation Act. He went on to cite the Antiquities Act of 1906, followed a generation later by the Historic Sites Act of 1935, and a second generation later by the 1966 act. In so doing, he correctly identified the Antiquities Act as the primary wellspring of the two later laws and also, therefore, of the now enormous array of federal, state, local, tribal, and private-sector activities that are linked to or inspired by them.[1] Connally was followed on the podium by William J. Murtagh, the first keeper of the National Register of Historic Places, who described the local origins of historic preservation at Hasbrouck House, New York; Mount Vernon, Virginia; and in districts like Charleston, South Carolina; Savannah, Georgia; and New Orleans, Louisiana. The comprehensive history of historic preservation, yet to be written, will show that the field had many points of origin beyond those cited by Murtagh, with an especially greater role for Civil War battlefields.[2] It will also reveal a number of earlier federal laws focused upon specific individual places, but it will certainly show that the three basic federal laws, two generations apart, have launched a national idea of historic preservation. These laws consolidated federal leadership of the field in the National Park Service, and spread their effects throughout an amazingly extensive and effective network in the United States.[3]

The connection that was clear to Connally was not at all predictable six decades before. After a century and a quarter of experience in managing an enormous public estate, the United States was still shaping policies of the most fundamental nature about national heritage. The basic policy governing public lands and the valuable resources they contained had been to get them into private owner- ship and the capitalist economy as quickly and completely as possi- ble. At various times lands had been sold at market rates, given to veterans as a bounty for military service, given to corporations as subsidies for railroad construction, and finally given to homestead- ers just for living on them, developing them, and making them eco- nomically productive. Publicly owned minerals had been, and still are today, sold for nominal fees in order to facilitate their extraction and use. By the beginning of the twentieth century, pre-Columbian ruins on the public domain were coming to popular attention. These places and the artifacts they contained had important scien- tific value but also had significant potential economic value. Uni- versities, museums, and scientists competed with private entrepre- neurs, thieves, and looters to lay claim to them. Although a few places had been reserved from sale or disposition for the public ben- efit, most of the precedent lay in the direction of disposition and development, and there was absolutely no reason to expect that large numbers of places would be preserved.[4]

The Antiquities Act of 1906 is best known for authorizing the president to create from the public domain national monuments of historic or scientific interest, but more fundamentally, as noted in the chapter by McManamon, it established three basic principles that are still important in historic preservation. First, archaeological places and the information they contain are valuable primarily for what can be learned from them with proper study rather than for whatever passing value they might bring on a collectors' market. Second, archaeological sites and objects on public lands are public resources, and any removal of them should be for continued public benefit rather than for the private benefit of the person who removes them. Third, archaeological resources require the attention of qualified professionals who would research sites under federal permits rather than being available for exploitative excavation tan- tamount to mining. McManamon has argued persuasively that not only the policy of preserving cultural resources for the public bene- fit but also the policy of doing so according to professional stan- dards—now widely applied under a number of contemporary laws— is traceable to the Antiquities Act.[5]

National monuments created under the Antiquities Act joined a growing and motley array of more than two dozen national parks and other special places set aside by law or presidential proclamation.[6] It was not until August 25, 1916, forty-four years after the first national park had been created, that the National Park Service came into being under Stephen T. Mather's direction in order to provide consistent and coordinated management of areas that were already being recognized as national treasures. Seventeen more years passed before Mather's successor as National Park Service director, Horace M. Albright, persuaded President Franklin D. Roosevelt to reassign the monuments and battlefields that were under the Agriculture and War Departments to his bureau.[7]

In 1933, when the reassignment occurred, the National Park Service was a busy bureau. In addition to a lead role for the service in the Civilian Conservation Corps, the Historic American Buildings Survey had been created by administrative action within the service to provide work for unemployed architects. Other ideas were bubbling for using emergency employment to preserve the nation's history, but statutory authority was needed to back up administrative creativity. The result was the Historic Sites Act of 1935, which explicitly declared for the first time "a national policy to preserve for public use historic sites, buildings, and objects of national significance for the inspiration and benefit of the people of the United States." Wonderfully broad, from an administrator's point of view, the act authorized a wide range of contracts, cooperative agreements, and direct action to research, document, mark, acquire, preserve, and maintain nationally significant places. Formalizing Roosevelt's solution to what had been a patchwork of federal administrative arrangements for historic places, it put the National Park Service firmly in the lead.

What the Antiquities Act had begun a generation before for the public domain, the Historic Sites Act took to all of America. National historic sites and other "cultural resource" units could now be created and *added to* the public domain under National Park Service management. Part of Albright's earlier brilliant vision of a national park system no longer confined to a few western states, this development, together with acquisition of the battlefields and national monuments, enabled the young bureau to become national in scope as well as in name. In order for the service to have the support of people throughout the United States, it was necessary to be present, visible, and valued throughout the nation. Albright's successor, Arno B. Cammerer, used the new authority to secure creation of numerous new national historic sites, generally in states that had previously lacked national park system units. The trend they started continues to this day with the result that the system now encompasses almost 400 units in 49 of the 50 states. A significant majority of these are primarily focused on historical, architectural, archaeological, ethnographic, or curatorial resources, which in composite have come to be called "cultural resources."

But the Historic Sites Act also introduced another concept of perhaps ultimately greater importance. The act made it clear that while all nationally significant places ought to be preserved, not all needed to be brought into federal ownership. Even while clearly authorizing and encouraging creation of new units to be owned and managed by the National Park Service, the act also provided sweeping new authority to work with state and local governments and willing private owners to identify and preserve nationally significant places without changing their ownership, use, or management. Broad language on contracts and cooperative agreements actually provides an authority—seldom and thus far not very successfully used but still pregnant with possibility—for some national historic sites to be owned and operated by others under the guidance of the National Park Service. This authority has generally been seen by national park advocates as a threat to the ability of the service to provide strong and cohesive management to the select few places that ought to be national historic sites. The reluctance to use the authority has probably been wise during the 70 years it has been on the books and may still be wise into the near future, but the world is rapidly changing. As population grows, empty lands fill up, and land values increase by orders of magnitude, it becomes more and more difficult to obtain the public support necessary for creating new national historic sites and placing them under federal management. As historic preservation philosophies and practices evolve, it becomes clearer that some places, even of national significance, need to be preserved in active social and economic use rather than set aside. The time may come when these unusual authorities prove to be valuable.

The idea of preserving certain nationally significant places outside the national park system has been most significantly advanced through identification and designation of national historic landmarks. Because the service focused so energetically for the first 25 years after the Historic Sites Act's passage on the authority to expand the system, the first national historic landmarks were not designated until 1960,[8] but once the program began, it flourished. Broad themes of American history were studied, the results published, and landmarks of generally high quality were designated in large numbers. By the time the National Historic Preservation Act came under serious consideration by the Congress, over 600 landmarks had been designated. This proved fortuitous, for as Congress considered which agency should administer the proposed "new" National Register of Historic Places, Park Service Director George B. Hartzog was able to claim that the approximately 200 historic units of the national park system and over 600 national historic landmarks already constituted the beginning of a National Register.[9] He was, in essence, citing the cumulative accomplishments of the Antiquities Act and the Historic Sites Act in order to win leadership of the National Historic Preservation Act. He succeeded.

In yet another innovation, the Historic Sites Act allowed the first tentative move beyond the restraint of preserving only places of national significance. The authority to "secure, collate, and preserve drawings, plans, photographs, and other data of historic and archaeologic sites, buildings, and objects" gave statutory legitimacy to the two-year-old Historic American Buildings Survey. Later, the same clause would spawn the Historic American Engineering Record, the Historic American Landscapes Survey, and the Historic American Maritime Survey. These programs, similar in method and different primarily in subject matter, make or collect documentary records such as measured drawings, photographs, and written studies of historic buildings, structures, landscapes, and objects. Called "preservation through documentation," the products of these programs have a reputation for extraordinary quality and are very popular among researchers and preservationists. The innovation important to this account, however, is that the programs never limited themselves to documenting resources of national significance. Whether or not Congress consciously intended this, the practice was afoot. By 1966, the Historic American Building Survey had documented some 17,000 resources of various degrees of significance.

The Historic Sites Act's recognition that not all historic preservation needs could be met by action within the federal government led the National Park Service to propose and Congress to create the National Trust for Historic Preservation in 1949. This non-profit corporation was intended to accomplish more in the private sector than could be done entirely within government. The original intention was for the trust to supplement National Park Service work primarily by acquiring and preserving historic properties but, wisely it turns out, the trust acquired only a few properties and instead placed its priority upon developing, promoting, and leading a budding historic preservation movement beyond the federal government.

Ironically, the federal government itself soon became the primary threat to historic places. The two decades following the end of World War II brought an unprecedented boom of demolition and redevelopment. With a "brave new world" attitude, the United States decided to renew its cities and to create an infrastructure that would carry it into the twenty-first century. "Urban renewal" programs cleared "slums," consolidated inner-city property parcels, and sold them to people who would build sparkling modern structures of vastly greater size. Army Corps of Engineers skills, proven during the war, were turned to remaking waterways. An interstate highway program was launched to upgrade the slow and congested network of highways into a nationwide system of high-speed freeways. Unfortunately, many of the places where it seemed most sensible to carry out all these presumed improvements were the very places most likely to contain historic and archaeological resources. Here and there, citizens attempted to stand up for local heritage, but the combined power of a booming economy, private entrepreneurship, and backing by the national government produced an unstoppable "federal bulldozer." In response, preservationists, with significant leadership from the National Trust and encouragement from the National Park Service, mounted the initiative that became the National Historic Preservation Act of 1966.[10]

This act, still the keystone to most historic preservation in America, went beyond its 1935 and 1906 predecessors in four significant ways. First, it emphasized that its goals included preservation far beyond that which could be accomplished by setting aside a few national historic sites. Instead, a far greater number of resources were to be preserved "as a living part of our community life and development." This clearly indicated approaches that would include, but go beyond, public ownership and operation. Second, the act implicitly established that a vastly greater number of resources were to be included in the National Register of Historic Places. Third, federal agencies were required to take the significance of historic places into account, and to obtain the comment of the Advisory Council on Historic Preservation when their projects affected historic places. Fourth, consistent with President Lyndon B. Johnson's "New Federalism" policy of federal/state cooperation, the act made the states important partners in the program.

Even though the new law was strong and clear, it would be impossible to overestimate the roles of a few specific individuals in launching the programs it authorized. In the National Park Service, Robert M. Utley pulled together the heretofore separate and disparate cultural resource programs into a single Office of Archeology and Historic Preservation to provide the necessary professional and managerial focus. Heading that office, Ernest Allen Connally provided depth and vision. Seeing the new organization as the potential equivalent to the "historic monuments" offices of major European nations,[11] Connally observed that the National Register and its associated grants program had the potential to become "a humane form of urban renewal": in other words, to have a positive effect upon historic places equivalent to the negative effect then being produced by the biggest "federal bulldozer."[12] Keeper of the National Register William J. Murtagh tutored Americans on determining what qualified for the National Register, espousing a broad and encompassing interpretation that would help local people everywhere protect what they thought was important to their communities. Robert R. Garvey led the Advisory Council on Historic Preservation the way John Marshall had led the Supreme Court, choosing cases carefully and arranging outcomes that steadily strengthened the effect of the council's "comment."

Perhaps the single most important choice made by these leaders, however, was the decision to treat historic preservation as a citizen movement as well as a government program. This was done by decentralizing the program as much as possible to the state historic preservation officers, by encouraging them to further decentralize their own programs within each state, and by consciously developing program guidelines that enabled creative and flexible action by others rather than prescribing and directing details. Soon the national historic preservation program was virtually indistinguishable from the national historic preservation movement. Like a net, its individual strands were weak, but they were everywhere and together they were strong.

This net has only grown with the passage of time. President Richard Nixon's 1971 executive order titled "Protection and

Enhancement of the Cultural Environment" brought other federal agencies into the partnership to a far greater degree. Several new historic preservation laws, mostly amendments to the National Historic Preservation Act, expanded the partnership to include local governments and Native American tribes and organizations, put the basic provisions of the executive order into law, and extended authorities similar to those in the Historic Sites Act to federal agencies in general. They even provided for a permanent Historic Preservation Fund of hundreds of millions of dollars to finance the activities. Getting money appropriated out of the fund was a different matter, however; and money available annually from these sources has never exceeded the "bare bones" level.

As it happened, major financial support did come, but from an unexpected source and only for part of the overall historic preservation program. The internal revenue code of the United States had long discriminated against historic preservation by providing incentives for the new construction that often involved demolition of historic buildings or destruction of archaeological sites. Along with the 1971 executive order, Nixon had proposed a provision to correct this flaw in the tax laws. Not enacted until 1976, this provision had little effect until modified in 1981 at President Ronald Reagan's initiative to provide a 25% investment tax credit to private investors who rehabilitated historic buildings in a manner that preserved their historic character. This measure took the funding decisions out of the hands of congressional appropriators and placed them in the hands of individuals who wanted to rehabilitate buildings. The preservation and financial effect has been that more than 32,000 historic buildings have been rehabilitated to date with a cumulative private-sector investment of over $33 billion. This was not what Connally had envisioned, and there have been negative effects along with the positive, but the tax incentive approach brought the nation closer in a practical sense to "a humane form of urban renewal" than grants could ever have done.

Above all, the move toward tax incentives forced yet more expansion of the National Park Service's "enabling" approach to leadership of the historic preservation programs. Local government, state historic preservation offices, and Park Service staffs were flooded with rehabilitation proposals that had to be reviewed promptly, professionally, and with a defendable degree of consistency. In response to this demand, the service turned to a hierarchy of statutes, standards, guidelines, and technical information that enabled a small number of people to exercise responsible leadership and provide guidance to a potentially infinite preservation movement and its work.[13] Furthermore, with the ability to capture lessons from its own experience, this system produced practices and behaviors consistent with the most advanced management concepts of its time.[14]

This brief chapter has not covered every aspect of historic preservation, which in a more comprehensive statement would not only include much more about archaeology, but also about a group of professional programs that guide cultural resource management within the units of the national park system as well. The park-oriented programs have pioneered ethnographic approaches that, combined with the tribal programs authorized under amendments to the National Historic Preservation Act, are making important progress in the area of intangible cultural heritage.[15] Similarly, park innovations in the field of cultural landscapes, spread beyond the parks via the historic preservation programs, are gradually erasing the conceptual boundaries that have separated cultural resource management from natural resource management.[16] As the conceptual differences are reconciled, it becomes possible also to reconcile the wasteful differences in the ways natural and cultural resources are managed in the parks and beyond park boundaries.[17]

The 1990s, one more generation after Connally's observation, were not marked by a major act of Congress equal to those of 1906, 1935, and 1966, but developments in the Executive branch of government may prove to be the equivalent. During the nineties the Antiquities Act began to be used in ways that some saw as a retreat to the pre-1935 chaos, and others saw as the opening to a greater future. President Bill Clinton used the Antiquities Act to proclaim several new national monuments, but rather than adding them to the national park system for cohesive management he left them under the bureaus, especially the Forest Service and the Bureau of Land Management, that controlled the areas before proclamation. In some cases the National Park Service was given a cooperative or consultative role, but in other cases not. This development can be viewed from polar-opposite perspectives. Those who believe the national interest in preservation and conservation lies in expanding the national park system and strengthening the National Park Service are appalled at the apparent dissolution of the center of authority and expertise carefully built since 1916 and solidified by the Historic Sites Act of 1935. Others who believe the national interest lies in converting all land-managing agencies into more careful stewards of natural and cultural resources see it as a bold gamble that the agencies will rise to the challenge of managing national monuments. Either could be correct. The answer may depend upon whether the presidential administration in power wishes there to be more conservation and preservation or wishes to diminish what exists already. Aside from this, however, the answer is likely to depend substantially on how the National Park Service itself behaves. If the service "hunkers down" and defends its prerogatives against further erosion, the agencies with new national monument responsibilities are apt to go their own ways and to follow their own standards and practices without concern for National Park Service opinions. Ironically, then, a defensive posture is likely to exacerbate the service's perceived loss into a genuine loss. If, on the other hand, the service perceives these developments as opportunities for exporting its standards and philosophies and for recruiting other agencies to the cause, it will become a willing and active leader, sharing the expertise the other agencies need and helping them to succeed. A bold leadership posture by the National Park Service, risking the security of past gains for the possibility of greater future gains, holds the potential of creating a new paradigm in public land management. The National Park Service stands at a visionary moment equal to those captured by Mather, Albright, and Hartzog. It remains to be seen whether a leader will arise whose vision is equal to the opportunity.[18]

In the course of a century, what the Antiquities Act *began* the Historic Sites Act *advanced,* and the National Historic Preservation Act and other laws keyed to the National Register have *matured* into a model that other parts of the national agenda would do well to imitate. In this interactive system of federal, state, local, tribal, and private-sector partners the greater part of initiative begins locally and in the private sector, where maximum flexibility is encouraged within generally applicable standards. Each successive "higher" level consciously attempts to limit itself to doing what the other levels cannot do for themselves. Within the federal government there are few if any programs that reach as far; that as successfully meld the interests of federal, state, local, tribal, and private entities; and that do so with a generally high degree of professional quality.

As the Antiquities Act turns one hundred, there are great national debates over values and priorities, including what should be preserved, how, and by whom. The rhetoric of these debates tends to run to generalization and oversimplification about the virtues or evils, the qualities and the shortcomings, of public versus private action and of federal versus state versus local versus tribal actions. The experience that has grown from the Antiquities Act and its successor laws demonstrates that each of these possibilities individually has strengths, and each individually has weaknesses, but that none of them individually is enough. Let us hope that the debate will result in a reinvigorated national partnership and yet more innovation in aligning federal law and policy with the wishes of citizen movements. New generations await their chance to contribute.

Notes

1. Glass 1990, 31–33; Mackintosh 1986, 33–34.

2. Sellars 2005, 22–52. For a general treatment of historic preservation, see Stamm and Peatross 1983.

3. This chapter does not attempt to cover a number of federal laws that, either by statutory language or by administrative decision, are linked to the National Register of Historic Places and thereby to the National Historic Preservation Act.

4. Francis P. McManamon, personal communication, February 28, 2005.

5. McManamon 1996b, 17; 1996a, 18–23.

6. Mackintosh 1991, 13.

7. Albright and Cahn 1985, 297; Mackintosh 1991, 24.

8. Mackintosh 1985, 45.

9. Connally 1986a; 1986b. See also Rogers 1987.

10. Rogers 1986. See also Hodel 1986; NPS [1991].

11. Utley 2004, 104–108.

12. Personal conversation with Connally, 1969.

13. Rogers 1984.

14. Senge 1990.

15. Rogers 2004, 7–11.

16. Webb 1987, 77.

17. Rogers 1988, 10.

18. For two recent examples of strategic thinking as it relates to the National Park Service, see NPS [1993] and National Park System Advisory Board 2001.

The Antiquities Act at One Hundred Years

A Native American Perspective

Joe E. Watkins

THE ANTIQUITIES ACT OF 1906 has been heralded as the foundation of America's program of historic preservation,[1] yet its passage was an attempt to save the material remnants of a particular past—that of American Indian people—as representative of a particular "idea" of the past—that of Americans of European descent. Not only was this Euroamerican idea of the past very different from the way American Indians conceived of their own history, it was an idea completely disconnected from the reality that all Americans faced at the turn of the twentieth century. Archaeologists who view the formulation and passage of the Antiquities Act as an act of a benevolent government view it in isolation from the social and cultural milieu that led to the formulation and passage of the Act. The Act has been beneficial to archaeology and its study of the material remnants of America's past cultures, but it has also prevented American Indians from having an exclusive control of their past.

The last two decades of the nineteenth century—the period during which the Antiquities Act was being formulated—was a time of government action aimed at integrating (at times forcibly) American Indians into the "American" mainstream. The decade started with the last organized physical assault of the Indian Wars (Wounded Knee) and ended with an organized legal one (the Curtis Act) with the Jerome and Dawes Commissions in between.

December 29, 1890, was the date of the last "battle" of the Indian Wars, when, according to the official government account, "eighty-four men and boys, forty-four women, and eighteen children"[2] of the Lakota were killed alongside Wounded Knee Creek in

South Dakota by members of the Seventh Cavalry under the command of Major S. M. Whitside and Major George A. Forsyth. Started by an accidental discharge of a rifle, the "battle" between the Indians and the soldiers of the Seventh Cavalry marked the end of the Indian Wars. Another estimate gives 346 Lakota people killed, 150 of whose bodies were dumped in a mass grave;[3] Prucha gives a count of 146 Indians killed, with 25 soldiers also killed and 39 more wounded.[4]

While the United States military thought its way was the only way to finalize the "Indian problem," others were working to find more peaceful (though equally as drastic) ways of forcing the Indian to disappear. The Lake Mohonk Conferences of Friends of the Indian, meeting from 1883 to 1916, marked the beginning of serious, organized attempts at the assimilation of American Indians.

The Lake Mohonk Conferences were initiated by Quaker schoolteacher Albert K. Smiley as a means of expanding discussions begun in meetings of the Board of Indian Commissioners between board members and representatives of missionary societies. Because of the religious orientation of many of the attendees, the meetings were a mixture of formal papers given by a variety of experts and informal discussions centered on the papers. According to Prucha, "[T]he Lake Mohonk Conference of the Friends of the Indian had no official status" but used its considerable influence for "the deliberate focusing of public opinion behind specific measures of Indian policy and aggressive propagandizing of these measures in the press and in the halls of government."[5] Thus, it became "a dominant force in the formulation of Indian policy in the last decade and a half of the nineteenth century, when the formulations for solving the 'Indian problem' were finally set."[6]

Of the goals and aims of the Indian reform movements of this time, one of the most important was a plan for allotment in severalty: the abolition of the reservations and distribution of tribal lands to individual Indians as a means of "promoting White standards of civilization and education, in the hopes the Indians would be absorbed into the general stream of White society."[7] The Jerome Commission (1889–1893) and the Dawes Commission (1893–1907) turned millions of acres of American Indian tribally owned land into small allotments owned by individual Indians, with the "excess" land made available to homesteaders and non-Indian settlers. In this way, Congress helped American Indians to "disappear," at least from the government's view, whether they actually disappeared or not. The opening years of the 20th century were part of the continuation of the grand experiment to "de-Indianize" American Indians by turning them into farmers and "owners" of land.

On June 28, 1898, President William McKinley signed the Curtis Act into law. The act basically annulled the previous United States policy that recognized the idea of Indian sovereignty; instead, it pushed to forcibly integrate American Indians into the dominant, American society. The Curtis Act legislated the Dawes Commission to proceed with the allotment of tribal lands, abolished tribal courts, and declared Indian laws unenforceable in federal courts. It also ordered tribal governments dissolved after allotment.[8] An amendment to the law passed in 1906 made the chiefs of the Five Civilized Tribes (in what was then called Indian Territory—now Oklahoma) removable by the president, and provided for the sale of buildings owned by the Indian governments. This law almost completely destroyed the Indian governments of the Five Civilized Tribes and appeared to resolve the "Indian problem" by essentially doing away with anything "Indian"—Indian governments, Indian lands, Indian individuals, and the Indian Territory.

Thus, in the cultural milieu within which America was operating at the turn of the twentieth century, reformers took it on good faith that these policies of assimilation would lead to the melting of Indian populations into the dominant society so that they would cease to be visible. Throughout this period, anthropologists struggled to keep up with the onslaught and to collect data on the American Indian tribes before they disappeared. As one contemporary anthropologist has noted, "anthropologists fanned out into many reservation communities at a time when White officialdom was losing patience with the Indian's curious unwillingness to understand they were supposed to vanish."[9]

With the establishment of the Bureau of Ethnology (later renamed the Bureau of American Ethnology) within the Smithsonian Institution in 1879, anthropologists and historians began operations to "salvage" the cultures of American Indians before they "disappeared." These anthropologists thought it was their duty to record the traditional culture before it died by conducting field research to record information on the tribal groups. As Bieder notes, anthropologists and archaeologists of the time were scrambling to gather information before "[t]he changing life-styles in many Indian tribes and the decline in Indian population resulted in cultural disintegration," and, ultimately, the possibility of "a whole race disappearing before its history was discovered."[10] Anthropologists took to the field, returning with more examples of objects made by these exotic cultures, more information on the cultures themselves, and more concern for the information being lost. As anthropologists gathered and published comparative data on America's tribal groups, they became the "experts" and the tribal people almost superfluous.

Anthropologists, by virtue of their positions in museums and universities, influenced the public perception of American Indians either directly by promoting and affirming the dominant picture of the Indian as a primitive savage, destined to die (or be killed) off, or influencing the public indirectly by subordinating or rejecting alternative views.[11] It is this role as a producer of public image that has contributed to American Indian discontent with anthropologists and museums.

The legislative acts passed in the last two decades of the 19th century were overt attempts at forcing American Indians into giving up their tribal cultures and assimilating into the dominant culture. The Dawes Commission and the Curtis Act were meant to remake Indians into "white people" and force them to assimilate. In some ways, the Antiquities Act of 1906 can be viewed to be an "assimilationist" policy as well.

On June 8, 1906, President Theodore Roosevelt signed the Antiquities Act (P.L. 59-209). As the first legislative attempt to protect cultural resources, the four short paragraphs of the Act provided for the protection of historic and prehistoric remains on public lands through the establishment of criminal sanctions for the unauthorized destruction or appropriation of antiquities owned or controlled by the federal government, established a process whereby the president could set aside areas of "importance" for national monuments, and authorized a permit system for the scientific investigation of antiquities on federal land. It basically established the principle that cultural resources, regardless of origin, were important to the cultural history of the United States and worthy of protection.

The period during which the Antiquities Act was passed is described by Lee[12] and will not be discussed in detail here. The perspective of the Archaeological Institute of America regarding the study of American Indians helped formulate a perspective that is prevalent today: that the history of the human race and a "legitimate curiosity concerning the condition of man on this continent previous to its discovery"[13] is somehow a justification for co-opting the heritage of another culture. Inherent also in this quote is the idea that the continent was unknown until its "discovery" by European (read "civilized") cultures.

Lee's analysis of the attempts to legislate the protection of the "remnants of very ancient races in North America"[14] provides a glimpse into the political and social problems met by legislators who tried to pass the first laws aimed at protecting the material heritage within the southwestern United States. The passage of legislation aimed at protecting Casa Grande near Phoenix, Arizona, in 1889 (followed three years later by an executive order permanently protecting it) was the first such action taken by the federal government to protect the material remnants of an area of antiquity from depredation by people and destruction by the elements.

At the time, the "public interest in the history and art of the Southwestern Indians in the 1890s was accompanied by a swelling demand for authentic prehistoric objects."[15] Much of this demand was met through the "discoveries" and depredations that accompanied the spread of prospecting and ranching in the Four Corners area of Colorado, New Mexico, Arizona, and Utah during the 1880s and 1890s.[16] By the time of the passage of the Antiquities Act in 1906, Gustav Erik Adolf Nordenskjöld had carried off a "large and valuable collection" of artifacts from Mesa Verde (with the help of Richard and Alfred Wetherill—and needing no one's permission) to Stockholm.[17]

Archaeologist Jesse Fewkes' call for legislation to protect American antiquities was a call to arms, so to speak. He wrote that "unless laws are enacted ... at the close of the twentieth century many of the most interesting monuments of the prehistoric peoples of our Southwest will be little more than mounds of debris at the bases of the cliffs."[18] And yet, "[t]he principal demand for authentic prehistoric objects came from private collectors, exhibitors, and museum curators in the East and in Europe."[19] Museums were not exempt from contributing to the destruction of archaeological sites: the Hyde Exploring Expedition to Chaco Canyon from 1896–1899 led to the "excavation" of "198 rooms and kivas ... and most of the artifacts, including several complete rooms, were donated by the Hydes to the American Museum of Natural History."[20]

While the depredations and destruction of the material remains of America's indigenous populations continued in the American Southwest, Edgar Lee Hewett worked to influence the passage of legislation to protect that material culture. Hewett's role in the passage of the Antiquities Act is discussed in great detail by Thompson[21] and should help the reader to understand the situation that finally resulted in the passage of legislation aimed at protecting the material heritage of America's non-European populations from being destroyed.

But the passage of the Antiquities Act carried with it (perhaps?) an unintended complication: the permit system that supposedly was established to benefit all Americans was organized so that "examinations, excavations, and gatherings are undertaken for the benefit of reputable museums, universities, colleges, or other recognized scientific or educational institutions, with a view to increasing the knowledge of such objects, and that the gatherings [are] made for permanent preservation in public museums."[22] The law acted to reduce the amount of illegal digging conducted by non-professional archaeologists and furthered "the interests of professional archaeologists in having access to the sites unimpeded by amateur pot hunters and looters."[23] This action placed the information available from, and the material remains of, the past squarely within the purview (and control) of the scientist, further placing the control of "America's heritage" in the hands of those "qualified" to "protect" it.

Additionally, by failing to take into consideration any interests American Indians might have had in protecting their own unwritten history and material culture from appropriation by "reputable museums, universities, colleges, or other recognized scientific or educational institutions," the law bypassed Indians as well. While it was deemed important to protect the evidence of the cultures that had gone before, the Act "legally transferred the Indian past to the American public domain ... without Indian involvement and with no suggestion that Indian people might have legitimate affiliations with the past."[24] Congress' actions, whether by accident or by design, benefited the scientific community more than it benefited the cultures whose heritage it was supposed to protect.

Walter Echo-Hawk, an attorney for the Native American Rights Fund of Boulder, Colorado, speaks about the consequences of the Antiquities Act in this manner: "At the turn of the century ... Congress enacted the Antiquities Act of 1906. And this act was intended to protect the nation's cultural resources—archaeological resources. However, what that act did was to convert native dead who were interred on public lands into federal property, and called these human beings federal property and archaeological resources. And the Antiquities Act said that you could dig up these resources for permanent preservation in a public museum with a federal permit."[25]

For more than 60 years, the Antiquities Act served as the primary legislative protection against the illegal taking of objects of antiquity by unqualified individuals. However, in 1974 the Ninth Circuit Court of Appeals held the law to be unconstitutionally vague in regard to its definition of "object of antiquity," based on the case of *U.S. v. Diaz*.[26] The case of *U.S. v. Smyer*[27] in the neighboring Tenth Circuit Court of Appeals had no such problem in identifying the material illegally excavated and taken by the defendants as that taken from a prehistoric archaeological site obviously attributable to a time of "antiquity" (being more than 900 years old).[28]

Nonetheless, the protection of archaeological resources under the Antiquities Act was dealt a nearly fatal blow in this period due to the Ninth Circuit's determination that the term "object of antiquity" was too vague. The Act is still in effect, of course, and its criminal prosecution capabilities are still used as a means of helping deter illegal excavations on federal lands. However, most of the permits issued for scientific archaeological excavations are now handled through the Archaeological Resources Protection Act of 1979 (ARPA).

Because of inconsistent rulings in the prosecution of violators of the Antiquities Act, ARPA was proposed, passed, and basically took the place of the older law as the primary legislative remedy for illegal excavation of "objects of antiquity." The primary purposes of ARPA are "to secure, for the present and future benefit of the American people, the protection of archaeological resources and sites which are on public lands and Indian lands" and to "foster increased cooperation and exchange of information between governmental authorities, the professional archaeological community, and private individuals having collections of archaeological resources and data which were obtained before the date of the enactment of this act."[29]

Two points of ARPA are notable: firstly, it defines an "archaeological resource" as "material remains of past human life or activities which are of archaeological interest ... [which] shall include but not be limited to ... human skeletal remains";[30] secondly, it requires that the wishes and consent of the Indians or Indian tribes owning or having jurisdiction over the land upon which an archaeological resource is situated be obtained before it can be excavated and removed.[31]

While the second aspect of ARPA is notable in that American Indian tribes (and their wishes) are explicitly mentioned regarding the issuance of excavation permits, the first aspect of the law, in defining Native American human remains as an "archaeological resource," is a continuation of the scientific perspective on human remains and continues to be largely at odds with American Indian perspectives in relation to such material.

The inter-relationships between archaeologists intent on the scientific excavation of archaeological sites and human remains and the wishes of American Indian groups in these areas have been variable over the years, with some archaeologists working beyond the law to meet the concerns of such groups,[32] while other archaeologists and biological anthropologists have worked to try to convince American Indians of the utility of the scientific study of such material.[33] Throughout this time, American Indian perspectives have been presented by American Indian academicians in a rather straightforward and caustic manner.[34]

While the protection of "objects of antiquity" within the Antiquities Act has largely been negated by the Ninth Circuit Court ruling and taken over by ARPA, the second aspect of the Antiquities Act—the right of the president to declare areas of importance as national monuments—has also impacted American Indian groups. Many of the monuments declared by presidents as areas of natural importance were held to be more than places of natural beauty by American Indians.

Devils Tower rises 1,267 feet above the Belle Fourche River in northeastern Wyoming. Proclaimed a national monument on September 24, 1906, by President Theodore Roosevelt, Devils Tower is the nation's oldest national monument and represents the first time the Antiquities Act of 1906 was used to preserve some of the remarkable resources found throughout the United States.[35] Since that autumn day in Wyoming, American presidents have used the Antiquities Act to preserve icons of the American landscape.

Devils Tower is an imposing sight. A granite plug rising more than 860 feet from its base to its top, Devils Tower was given worldwide notoriety by the 1977 science fiction movie *Close Encounters of the Third Kind* as an otherworldly apparition in the middle of nowhere. It is a place where recreational rock climbers challenge their skill and strength against some rock climbing routes, but it is also a place that is sacred to more than twenty American Indian tribes, including the Kiowa Tribe of Oklahoma.[36] The site was named "Devils Tower" by a scientific team in 1875, but the Kiowa call it "Bear Lodge" and have a special story that describes its creation. Thus, while the tower is considered a favorite place of recreation for climbers, it has special significance and sacred meaning to the Kiowa. Even the name creates a conflict between American Indians and the non-Indian majority: its very name equates a native sacred site with the personification of evil, Christianity's "Devil."

More recently, of course, American Indians have regained a place within the monument proclamation process as a result of the Antiquities Act. Section 2 of the Act authorizes the president "to declare by public proclamation historic landmarks, historic and pre-historic structures, and other objects of historic or scientific interest that are situated upon the lands owned or controlled by the Government of the United States to be national monuments...." A recent example of American Indian involvement is in the creation of Grand Staircase–Escalante National Monument, covering approximately 1.9 million acres of land in south-central Utah.

Grand Staircase–Escalante was established by presidential proclamation in September 1996, and tribal groups were involved early on in the consultation process as a means of trying to utilize, as much as possible, the tribal perspective in managing the monument. Eaton provides a glimpse of the involvement of tribal groups in the management of the monument.[37] The Hopi, Zuni, Paiute, Southern Paiute, Kaibab Paiute, Ute, and Navajo Nations participated in the consultation held by the Bureau of Land Management as part of the development of the Grand Staircase–Escalante management plan. There has been mixed success, but the tribal members seem to be glad to have been allowed at least the opportunity to be involved in the process.

But the establishment of the monument was not without controversy.[38] Western legislators saw the establishment as contrary to Utah's interests and an attempt to curry favor with environmentalists. In October 1996, H.R. 1127, "The National Monument Fairness Act," introduced by Utah legislator Jim Hansen (R-UT), would have prevented the president from proclaiming monuments more than 50,000 acres in size in one state in a single year. Additionally, for any monuments more than 50,000 acres in size, the president would have to consult with governors and state legislatures, and receive prior congressional approval. Any monument declared by the president would be abolished if it were not approved by a joint resolution of Congress.[39] The move, according to the proponents of the bills, was to force the government to get back to the original purpose of the Antiquities Act: to protect environments and objects of historic or scientific interest that are under imminent threat, rather than acting as a mechanism for "proactive" protection.

Although this and subsequent similar legislative proposals failed, the attack on the Antiquities Act from this area is strong and well funded, something that American Indian issues seem not to be. American Indians and anti-Act politicians might be seen to be strange bedfellows in this regard, but it is unlikely that the two groups will band together to mount a concerted effort to have the law repealed.

While the Antiquities Act was the initial law that set the American historic preservation program in motion, it has been lately pushed to the side as a means of protecting items of antiquity and objects of historic and scientific interest. Contemporary Indian involvement in historic preservation is primarily through the National Historic Preservation Act of 1966,[40] especially growing out of the 1992 amendments to that law.[41] Those amendments authorize Indian tribes to develop tribal historic preservation offices and assume the historic preservation functions regarding projects on tribal land that were formerly the responsibility of a state historic preservation office. Twelve American Indian tribes took over a portion of the historic preservation duties in July 1996; as of February 1999, 17 had tribal historic preservation officers in place; by October 2003, 38 had appointed tribal historic preservation officers; as of February 2005, there were 52 tribes listed by the National Association of Tribal Historic Preservation Officers as having taken over the functions of the state historic preservation officer.[42]

It is obvious that American Indians are getting more involved in all aspects of historic preservation issues. The Antiquities Act is part of the reason for that involvement, but the Act is also part of the reason why American Indian involvement in historic preservation issues has taken so long to reach the point that it currently has. In some ways the Antiquities Act of 1906 can be seen to be a continuation of government policies that were aimed at erasing the image of the contemporary American Indian from the landscape in favor of the "dead and disappearing culture" destined to exist only in museums or to be engulfed in mainstream America. As noted before, the "past" was protected for its scientific value as a means of understanding the "soon-to-have-disappeared Indian" and not because of its value to a living, vibrant culture. This is something that the scientific community has had to come to grips with in recent years, and something that some scientists are reluctant even to admit might exist.

Is there a future for the past? Yes, I think there is. The Antiquities Act is not as strong as it was when it was first passed, but it still forms the basis for the federal historic preservation system that protects America's past for *all* Americans, not just for specific groups. It is the cornerstone of our historic preservation system, and without it, the system would not be nearly as strong. As we celebrate this law, it is important that we be aware of the social structure that was in place at the time of its passage, and to realize the unintended impacts it has had on American Indians throughout the last century.

Acknowledgments

An incipient kernel of this paper was presented as part of the "Common Ground, AAM, and the Antiquities Act: 1906–2006 and Beyond" session of the 2005 American Association of Museums meeting in Indianapolis, Indiana, but it has been fleshed out with the help of, and through earnest discussion with, Dorothy Lippert and Desirée Martinez. As usual, Carol Ellick also has participated in discussions that allowed me to examine issues I might have missed otherwise; for that and much more I thank her. Any errors are definitely my own.

Notes

1. See the chapters by McManamon and Rogers in this volume, and also McManamon 1996a.
2. Prucha 1976, 363.
3. Fine-Dare 2002, 48.
4. Prucha 1976, 363.
5. Prucha 1976, 144.
6. Prucha 1976, 145.
7. Prucha 1988, 40.
8. Prucha 1990, 197–198. See Higham 1955, especially chapter 9, for an account of similar assimilationist pressures on newly arriving immigrants.
9. Lurie 1988, 549.

10. Bieder 1989, 248.

11. See Ames 1992, 49–58, for a detailed discussion.

12. Lee 2000, 198–269; and the abridgment published as chapter 1 of this volume.

13. Norton et al. 1885, 32, as quoted in Lee 2000, 200.

14. Lee 2000, 203.

15. Lee 2000, 213.

16. Lee 2000, 213–219.

17. Lee 2000, 214.

18. Fewkes 1896, 269–270, as quoted in Lee 2000, 215.

19. Lee 2000, 217.

20. Pierson 1956, as quoted in Lee 2000, 218.

21. Thompson 2000, 271–318; and the abridgment published as chapter 2 of this volume.

22. Antiquities Act of 1906, sec. 3.

23. Tsosie 1997, 68.

24. Thomas 2000, xxxv.

25. Echo-Hawk from the Public Broadcasting System television show *Who Owns the Past?* On-line at www.pbs.org/wotp/nagpra/.

26. 368 F.Supp. 856, (D. Ariz. 19730); reversed, 499 F.2d 113, 9th Cir. (1974).

27. 596 F.2d 939 (10th Cir.); cert. denied, 444 U.S. 843 (1979).

28. See Hutt, Jones, and McAllister 1992, 23–25.

29. 16 U.S.C. 470 sec. 2(b).

30. 16 U.S.C. 470 sec. 3(1).

31. 16 U.S.C. 470 sec. 4(g)(1) and (2).

32. Cf. Sprague and Birkby1970.

33. Cf. Landau and Steele 1996; Rose, Green, and Green 1996; Ubelaker and Grant 1989.

34. Cf. Mihesuah 1996; Riding In 1992; Trope and Echo-Hawk 1992.

35. The Wilderness Society 2001, 1.

36. Gulliford 2000.

37. Eaton 2001.

38. Anonymous 1998, 4–6. See also the chapters by Squillace and Rasband in this volume.

39. Anonymous 1998, 5.

40. Public Law 89-665.

41. Public Law 102575, also known as the Fowler Bill.

42. National Association of Tribal Historic Preservation Officers 2005, on-line at www.nathpo.org/THPO_Members/state_list.htm.

12

The Antiquities Act
and Nature Conservation

David Harmon

IN 1917, just over a decade after the Antiquities Act was passed, a packed auditorium at the fourth National Parks Conference in Washington, D.C., listened to an impassioned plea from a thin, bespectacled government wildlife biologist named T. S. Palmer. He was talking about newly minted, remote national monuments, and he must have sounded half-crazy to many of his listeners—a proverbial mad scientist. Palmer was seriously arguing that places few had ever heard of, such as Pinnacles National Monument, tucked into a corner of the Coast Range of California far off the beaten path, were critically important parts of the embryonic national park system. Not because this spot was ever likely to be attractive to the emerging tourism industry that was being counted on by the new National Park Service director, Stephen T. Mather, in his quest to make the parks a powerhouse public institution. Instead, Pinnacles was important because it was "one of the last strongholds and breeding places of the California condor, the largest and one of the most characteristic birds of the State."[1] The highest and best use of this national monument, and several others equally obscure, was as a preserved habitat complex that could support all the native biota, both plants and animals, found there. Much could be done to make these places more accessible to travelers, but regardless of whether people would ever much visit them, Palmer was saying, these small national monuments should be maintained by the federal government —and not just at one notch above starvation—fundamentally because they were a kind of "natural outdoor laboratory or observatory."[2]

Reading Palmer's remarks nearly 90 years later, one has the sense of being in the presence of someone who, if not exactly a visionary, certainly was a pioneer. He was propounding an essentially biocentric reason for these new natural-area monuments: they should be preserved as examples of naturally functioning ecosystems. At the same time, he was indirectly justifying the liberal construction of the Antiquities Act that so many have found so dubious: its use to protect "objects" of "scientific interest" that, far from being discrete "natural wonders," are diffuse systems of not-easily-defined ecological interactions. Others in this book cover the controversies that have sprung from that broad interpretation of the Act. This chapter sets those aside and looks at results: namely, the Act's record of achievement in protecting ecosystems and noteworthy natural features. With all the acrimonious debate surrounding the law, it is easy to lose sight of the central fact that the Act has been responsible for the creation of some of the most important protected natural areas in the United States. Among these are iconic parks such as Grand Canyon, Olympic, Death Valley, and Carlsbad Caverns, as well as a host of less storied but—as Palmer knew—no less significant protected areas that began as presidentially declared national monuments.

To some, the ecological accomplishments of the Antiquities Act are vitiated by their having been more opportunistic than systematic. This criticism carried more weight thirty years ago and earlier than it does today. The Carter monument proclamations in 1978, which put over 50 million acres in Alaska into protected status, were the largest strategic conservation acquisition in American history. While there is no doubt that political considerations played a key role in the proclamations, they were backed by extensive scientific studies on subjects ranging from anthropology to zoology: between 1972 and 1978, 176 research reports on proposed Alaska additions were prepared by the National Park Service. According to historian G. Frank Williss, "The magnitude and variety of research carried out, or sponsored by the Park Service, in Alaska during [this] period was unprecedented in the Service's history."[3] This approach was reprised in the Clinton administration, when science-based monument proposals were carefully prepared by the Department of the Interior under Bruce Babbitt.[4]

The ratio of politics to science in national monument proclamations can be endlessly debated. What is beyond dispute is this: the Antiquities Act has been the indispensable means for achieving critical protections of America's natural heritage. The national monuments (hereafter this term refers to all areas, no matter what their current designation, that were created under the Act) embody three of the characteristics that contribute to ecological significance:

- Rarity, the quality of uniqueness, and the closely related concept of superlativeness—that is, being considered one of the best examples of its kind;
- Representivity, the quality of covering as many different kinds of ecosystems as possible; and
- Integrity, the quality of protecting enough of a particular kind of ecosystem so that its main features and functions remain substantially unimpaired.

Sometimes these characteristics overlap in a given monument, sometimes not, but taken cumulatively, across all the monuments, they signify an impressive measure of ecological protection.

To assess the monuments' contribution to rarity and superlativeness, I will discuss their protection of unique geological features as a contribution to geodiversity, followed by a profile of monuments that are World Heritage sites, which are the most superlative protected areas of all. To assess representivity, I will look at how much ecoregional coverage the national monuments provide. Finally, to assess integrity I will consider how national monuments are contributing to the monitoring of "Vital Signs" indicators in the U.S. national park system. These assessments do not exhaust the possibilities, of course, nor are the three characteristics of ecological significance considered here an all-inclusive list. But even the following partial evaluation of the monuments is enough to show how important they have been, and continue to be, to nature conservation in America.

The Geological Portal to Ecological Significance

The first national monument, Devils Tower in Wyoming, is one of the most recognizable geological features in the world. The visual outlines of the monolith itself, so impressive in its mass, the way it thrusts into the sky, and the repetition of its columnar jointing, overwhelm the remainder of the park, which in any case is a relatively small area whose boundaries enclose, in a classically unecological manner, a nearly square polygon. There are many other national monuments that were created primarily to protect what, in the old days, would have been called natural "curiosities" but which today are recognized as geological features of special scientific interest (Figure 12.1). Among these are Bryce Canyon, where erosion has formed thousands of spires, fins, pinnacles, and mazes in the limestone, sandstone, and mudstone; Capulin Volcano, a nearly perfectly shaped cinder cone; Cedar Breaks, site of a huge natural amphitheater; Devils Postpile, one of the world's finest examples of columnar basalt; Kasha-Katuwe Tent Rocks, with cone-shaped volcanic rock formations, many of which are capped by boulders; Pompeys Pillar, a prominent sandstone butte that figured in the Lewis and Clark Expedition; and Rainbow Bridge, the world's largest natural bridge.

Even these small monuments have ecological significance. There is a growing awareness of *geodiversity* as a parallel concept to *biodiversity*. One of the key ideas in the definition of geodiversity is that abiotic, or non-living, variety (landforms, minerals, soils, geological processes, etc.) is a central part of the structure of ecosystems. Geodiversity acknowledges that all ecosystems are composed of living and non-living components, and the diversity of both is valuable.[5] In this broadened perspective, even very small national monuments such as those named above have ecological value because they protect geological features that are important contributors to global geodiversity, either by virtue of their rarity or superlativeness.

Caves are another class of monuments that have ecological significance because of their geology. Here too we find several examples of superlativeness in small parks. These include Jewel Cave, the third-longest in the world; Oregon Caves, one of the most biologically and geologically diverse; Lehman Caves (now incorporated into Great Basin National Park), one of the best places to see rare shield formations; and Timpanogos Cave, uniquely known for its high abundance of helictites and the coloration of its formations. (On an entirely different scale altogether is Carlsbad Caverns, whose more than 100 known caves make it one of the world's premier protected cave ecosystems, and whose World Heritage status is discussed below.) It is now recognized that all these caves depend upon above-ground processes and hydrological regimes that go well beyond the park borders. In some cases, such as at Carlsbad and Jewel, they are important hibernation areas for bat species.

In addition, there are numerous other monuments proclaimed in reference to geological features but which are extensive enough to afford significant nature protection: among them are Arches, Black Canyon of the Gunnison, Chiracahua, Cinder Cone and Lassen Peak (now Lassen Volcanic National Park), Craters of the Moon,

Figure 12.1. Smaller national monuments proclaimed primarily for their geological features have played an important part in the history of the Antiquities Act. Clockwise from upper left: Capulin Volcano National Monument, New Mexico; Jewel Cave National Monument, South Dakota; White Sands National Monument, New Mexico; Devils Postpile National Monument, California. Unattributed photographs, courtesy of National Park Service Digital Image Archives.

Grand Canyon, Grand Staircase–Escalante, Lava Beds, Mount Olympus (now Olympic National Park), Mukuntuweap (the original basis for today's Zion National Park), Petrified Forest, Vermillion Cliffs, and White Sands.

Superlativeness: The World Heritage Monuments

The Convention Concerning the Protection of the World Cultural and Natural Heritage, commonly known as the World Heritage Convention, is an international treaty under which natural and cultural sites "of outstanding universal value" are recognized by the United

Nations and accorded special status by being inscribed on the World Heritage List, which is managed by UNESCO (the U.N. Educational, Scientific, and Cultural Organization). "Outstanding universal value" means "cultural and/or natural significance which is so exceptional as to transcend national boundaries and to be of common importance for present and future generations of all humanity. As such, the permanent protection of this heritage is of the highest importance to the international community as a whole."[6] Each nation holds in trust for the rest of humankind those World Heritage sites found within its borders, and agrees to allow other signatories the right to assess the degree to which its treaty obligations are being met.[7]

World Heritage sites are meant to be the *crème de la crème* of protected areas. Under the convention, sites may be inscribed for their natural properties, for their cultural significance, or for a mixture of the two. The convention defines "natural heritage" as:

- Natural features consisting of physical and biological formations or groups of such formations, which are of outstanding universal value from the aesthetic or scientific point of view;
- Geological and physiographical formations and precisely delineated areas which constitute the habitat of threatened species of animals and plants of outstanding universal value from the point of view of science or conservation; and
- Natural sites or precisely delineated natural areas of outstanding universal value from the point of view of science, conservation, or natural beauty.[8]

After going through a nomination and evaluation process (which, for natural sites, is overseen by IUCN–The World Conservation Union), sites accepted for the World Heritage List have a "statement of outstanding universal value" recorded by the World Heritage Committee. This statement is a qualitative benchmark against which the future protection and management of the site is measured.[9]

To be entered as a natural World Heritage site, the area being nominated has to meet at least one of four criteria. It must contain:

- Superlative natural phenomena or areas of exceptional natural beauty and aesthetic importance;
- Outstanding examples representing major stages of Earth's history, including the record of life, significant on-going geological

processes in the development of landforms, or significant geomorphic or physiographic features;

- Outstanding examples representing significant on-going ecological and biological processes in the evolution and development of terrestrial, freshwater, coastal, and marine ecosystems and communities of plants and animals; or
- The most important and significant natural habitats for *in situ* conservation of biological diversity, including those containing threatened species of outstanding universal value from the point of view of science or conservation.[10]

Needless to say, these are high standards. Out of the 812 total sites on the World Heritage List as of 2005, only 160 had been inscribed exclusively for their natural values, along with 24 more listed as "mixed" sites for both natural and cultural values.

Of the United States' 20 World Heritage sites, 12 have been inscribed in recognition of their natural heritage, and of these, four originated as national monuments:[11] Grand Canyon, Olympic, Carlsbad Caverns, and Wrangell–St. Elias/Glacier Bay, which, together with two protected areas in Canada, form a huge complex that counts as a single World Heritage site (Figure 12.2).

Grand Canyon National Park originated in 1893 as a forest reserve, but first received protected status in 1908 when Theodore Roosevelt used the Antiquities Act to proclaim Grand Canyon National Monument.[12] Today's national park became a World Heritage site in 1979. At the time of nomination, there was no doubt whatsoever about its worthiness. The IUCN review of the park's nomination form was emphatic in its endorsement: "Within the walls of the canyon we have a view of geologic time that covers two billion years. The canyon is a vast biological museum stretching through five different life zones.... The characteristics of the Grand Canyon are so exceptional that they meet all four of the [natural] criteria" used by the convention. The reviewers went on to cite accolades that call the canyon "the world's most moving geographical wonder" and "the biggest living lesson in geological history in the world," as well as the words of Theodore Roosevelt himself: "In the Grand Canyon, Arizona has a natural wonder which, as far as I know, is in kind absolutely unparalleled throughout the rest of the world."[13] Very few people would disagree.

In 1923, President Calvin Coolidge used the Act to proclaim Carlsbad Cave National Monument, which was redesignated as

Figure 12.2. Four of the United States' twelve natural-area World Heritage sites originated as national monuments under the Antiquities Act. (Glacier Bay and Wrangell–St. Elias have been incorporated into a single transboundary World Heritage site.) Clockwise from upper left: Olympic National Park, Washington; Glacier Bay National Park and Preserve, Alaska; Grand Canyon National Park, Arizona; Carlsbad Caverns National Park, New Mexico. Unattributed photographs, courtesy of National Park Service Digital Image Archives.

Carlsbad Caverns National Park in 1930. The over 100 caves in the park are, according to the UNESCO, "outstanding not only for their size but also for the profusion, diversity and beauty of their mineral formations." The recently discovered Lechuguilla Cave "stands out from the others, providing an underground laboratory where geological and biological processes can be studied in a pristine setting."[14]

The park was designated a World Heritage site in 1995, meeting two of the four natural heritage criteria. The IUCN review of the nomination noted the park's Capitan Reef complex as an example of the major stages of the Earth's history. Dating back to the Permian period, the exposed sections of the Capitan lying within the park "are among the best preserved in the world accessible for scientific study," both in the caves and above ground, with numerous fossils in evidence. "On-going geological processes are most apparent in the active portions of caves where rare speleothems continue to form," the reviewers noted, especially in Lechuguilla, "where helictites are forming underwater, a process which has never been described from any other cave in the world.[15] Carlsbad also meets the "superlative natural phenomena or natural beauty" criterion with its large underground rooms, the world's largest and most extensive accumulations of gypsum chandelier speleothems, and the abundance of other calcite and gypsum formations.[16] In sum, "of the many thousands of caves occurring in North America . . . the caves within the park are among the most outstanding. They are also notable worldwide because of the size, their mode of origin and the abundance, diversity and beauty of the decorative rock formations (speleothems) they contain. The Lechuguilla cave is particularly noteworthy as an underground laboratory where geological processes can be studied in a virtually undisturbed environment."[17]

The Kluane/Wrangell–St. Elias/Glacier Bay/Tatshenshini–Alsek World Heritage site covers a vast area in southeastern Alaska and adjacent areas of Canada. Kluane National Park is in Yukon Territory, while Tatshenshini–Alsek Provincial Park is in northern British Columbia. The two American components of the complex, Wrangell–St. Elias National Park and Preserve and Glacier Bay National Park and Preserve, each originated as a national monument proclaimed under the Act. The Kluane/Wrangell–St. Elias World Heritage site was declared in 1979. It was extended in 1992 with the addition of Glacier Bay and again in 1994, when Tatshenshini–Alsek was added.

The original nomination was justified by Kluane and Wrangell's meeting three of the four criteria. On-going geological processes are represented by active glaciation (the area hosts the world's largest non-polar glacier fields), areas of exceptional natural beauty are found throughout both parks, and the habitats of several rare or endangered species are present within an environment of relatively undisturbed ecological processes.[18] When the Glacier Bay extension was proposed in 1992, the IUCN evaluation team noted that the park had much in common with other similar areas in Alaska and elsewhere, but unlike them it is "one integral component of a natural continuum that extends from the Pacific Ocean, up over the coast mountains and down into the Yukon Territory." "In sum," the evaluators wrote, "the qualities that distinguish Glacier Bay and its associated Alaska/Yukon World Heritage site are: the breadth of the display of active natural processes (tectonic, volcanic, glacial, fluvial, aeolian, mass wasting, soil formation, plant succession, animal migration); the combination of spectacular marine, coastal, wild river, and high mountain scenery; the diversity and abundance of habitat for wildlife and fisheries (resident and migratory, marine and terrestrial); the minimal extent of human modification, paucity of permanent human settlement, and pristine wilderness qualities; and the quality and amount of research that has been conducted on both the Alaska and Yukon sides."[19]

Added to the World Heritage List in 1981, Olympic National Park began its existence as one of Theodore Roosevelt's most distinguished Antiquities Act proclamations, second only to Grand Canyon. He proclaimed Mount Olympus National Monument in 1909 and it became a national park in 1938, five years after being transferred to the jurisdiction of the National Park Service. The qualities of Olympic that make it worthy of World Heritage status are readily apparent:

> Olympic National Park is renowned for the diversity of its ecosystems. Glacier-clad peaks interspersed with extensive alpine meadows are surrounded by an extensive old growth forest, among which is the best example of intact and protected temperate rainforest in the Pacific Northwest. Eleven major river systems drain the Olympic mountains, offering some of the best habitat for anadromous fish species in the country. The park also includes 100 km of wilderness coastline, the longest undeveloped coast in the contiguous United States, and is rich in native and endemic animal and plant species, including critical populations of the endangered northern spotted owl, marbled murrelet and bull trout.[20]

By virtue of these characteristics, as well as the presence of low-latitude glaciers and a rainforest whose remarkably dense, diverse biomass rivals any other in the world, the park was judged eminently worthy of becoming a World Heritage site. IUCN's evaluation of the nomination flatly declared that the park's "outstanding examples of on-going evolution and superlative natural phenomena" make Olympic "unmatched in the world."[21]

So we can say that the national monuments created under the Antiquities Act encompass rare geological formations that are important in their own right as well as, in some cases, being a portal to protection being afforded for a wider ecosystem. In addition, a small number of monuments have been judged to be of global ecological significance. But as important as the protection of the rare and the superlative is, in recent years protected area planning has taken a marked turn toward a systems approach. It is that to which we turn next.

Representivity:
The Monuments' Ecoregional Coverage

In conservation planning for protected natural areas, much more emphasis is now being given to protecting representative samples of different ecosystems, and to integrating the management of individual protected areas with that of the surrounding "matrix" of other land uses. All of this comes under the rubric of *ecosystem management.* This approach has been bolstered by the emergence of scientifically credible systems that classify ecological regions, or *ecoregions,* in a hierarchical manner. Ecoregional schemes have a practical as well as scientific rationale, as they are intended to meet the need for a common geographic framework that allows environmental management to be conducted according to ecological rather than political boundaries.[22]

In the United States, two ecoregional classifications have gained broad currency; one was put forward by the Environmental Protection Agency,[23] and the other by the U.S. Forest Service in the Department of Agriculture, compiled under the direction of Robert G. Bailey.[24] Bailey's classification is widely used within the National Park Service, and, because most national monuments are under NPS jurisdiction, it is the one used here to discuss their ecoregional representivity.

In Bailey's classification, four large *domains* are divided into 14 *divisions,* based on ecological climate zones. These are further subdivided into 52 *provinces* that express more refined climatic differences and fairly contiguous vegetation types (and, in mountainous areas, distinct altitudinal zonation). The province level is a medium scale of refinement convenient to our purpose; the classification also has more fine-grained levels that we will not consider here.

As it happens, the national monuments provide a rather robust coverage of the 52 provinces. Table 12.1 lists the provinces along with the national monuments located within them. It will be seen that the monuments provide coverage in 27 of the 52 provinces. Coverage in Alaska is especially good, with 12 of the state's 15 provinces represented by monuments, most of which were proclaimed by President Carter. Not surprisingly, coverage is sparsest in the East, where only a handful of large natural-area monuments have been proclaimed. Even so, these figures understate the ecoregional coverage of the monuments: because of a lack of comparably mapped data, those under the jurisdiction of the Bureau of Land Management, U.S. Forest Service, and U.S. Fish and Wildlife Service are not included in the two figures and the table. If they were, coverage of a few additional provinces probably would be obtained.

Does representivity enhance (let alone ensure) the ecological protection of a particular natural area? Not by any means, but that is not really the salient question. Rather, one should ask whether representivity increases the resilience of natural areas—across entire landscapes—to pervasive human-caused changes. On this, there is an emerging scientific consensus: ecoregional representivity is a buffer against the effects of global environmental change, such as climate change.[25]

Integrity: National Monuments and "Vital Signs" Monitoring

Turning to our third characteristic, ecological integrity, it is important to understand that the concept operates on two levels with respect to parks. The park itself has integrity if it is in "a condition that is determined to be characteristic of its natural region" and if that condition is "likely to persist, including abiotic components and the composition and abundance of native species and biological communities, rates of change, and supporting processes."[26] However, no park is large enough to encompass all the ecosystems found within its ecoregion, so the second level of integrity takes into account how the park relates to stresses coming from the surrounding area (and beyond).

Parks Canada is the leader in applying the concept of ecological integrity to parks and other protected areas, and the definition given above is enshrined in the Canada National Parks Act of 2000, the country's keystone parks law. In the U.S. national park system, the approach to measuring ecological integrity is made through the National Park Service's Vital Signs monitoring program. In this context, "park vital signs are selected physical, chemical, and biological elements and processes of park ecosystems that represent the overall health or condition of the park, known or hypothesized effect of stressors, or elements that have important human values." Monitoring these indicators is important because "understanding the dynamic nature of park ecosystems and the consequences of human activities is essential for management decision-making aimed to maintain, enhance, or restore the ecological integrity of park ecosystems and to avoid, minimize, or mitigate ecological threats to these systems."[27] Thus, the Vital Signs monitoring program is directly linked to the ecological integrity of the U.S. national park system.

Vital Signs is divided into 32 regional networks, each of which contains anywhere from three to nineteen parks. In all, 270 out of the more than 380 national park system units are part of Vital Signs. Parks that originated as (or absorbed) national monuments created under the Antiquities Act play a key role in these networks. Of the 270 Vital Signs parks, 84 (31%) are Antiquities Act monuments, and at least one monument is included in 26 of the 32 networks. All five of the parks in the Arctic Network and all three in the Central Alaska Network originated as national monuments, while in seven other networks at least half of the parks did (Sonoran Desert, Northern Colorado Plateau, Mediterranean Coast, Southwest Alaska, Southern Colorado Plateau, Klamath, and Mojave Desert).

Some Vital Signs parks, including several national monuments, have prototype long-term monitoring programs. As one example, scientists at Buck Island Reef National Monument, Dry Tortugas National Park (formerly Fort Jefferson National Monument), and Virgin Islands National Park have developed protocols for monitoring coral reefs and reef fishes with digital video cameras. Scientists are testing an underwater positioning system which will allow a statistically rigorous sampling design for the coral monitoring. In addition, protocols have been completed for monitoring water quality and populations of sea turtles. The overall monitoring program in this cluster of parks is designed to address effects of development and increased visitation on terrestrial and marine ecosystems; effects of hurricanes, droughts, and other natural stresses on marine and terrestrial resources; effects of fishing on fish assemblages and associated reef systems; effects of soil erosion; and the status of rare, endangered, and endemic species.[28]

Table 12.1. Ecoregional coverage of national park system units that originated as, or absorbed, national monuments proclaimed under the Antiquities Act. Only areas of more than 1,000 acres are considered. Province names are preceded by Bailey's key designator.

	Province	Park name
124	Arctic Tundra	—
125	Bering Tundra (Northern)	Bering Land Bridge, Cape Krusenstern, Kobuk Valley
126	Bering Tundra (Southern)	Katmai
M121	Brooks Range Tundra–Polar Desertv	Cape Krusenstern, Gates of the Arctic, Kobuk Valley
M125	Seward Peninsula Tundra–Meadow	Bering Land Bridge
M126	Ahklun Mountains Tundra–Meadow	—
M127	Aleutian Oceanic Meadow–Heath	Aniakchak, Katmai
131	Yukon Intermontane Plateaus Tayga–Meadow	Denali, Gates of the Arctic
135	Coastal Trough Humid Tayga	Wrangell–St. Elias
139	Upper Yukon Tayga	—
M131	Yukon Intermontane Plateaus Tayga–Meadow	Denali, Lake Clark
M135	Alaska Range Humid Tayga–Tundra–Meadow	Denali, Lake Clark, Wrangell–St. Elias
M139	Upper Yukon Tayga–Meadow	Yukon–Charley Rivers
212	Laurentian Mixed Forest	—
M212	Adirondack–New England Mixed Forest–Coniferous Forest–Alpine Meadow	Acadia
221	Eastern Broadleaf Forest (Oceanic)	—
222	Eastern Broadleaf Forest (Continental)	Effigy Mounds
M221	Central Appalachian Broadleaf Forest–Coniferous Forest–Meadow	—
M222	Ozark Broadleaf Forest–Meadow	—
231	Southeastern Mixed Forest	—
232	Outer Coastal Plain Mixed Forest	—
234	Lower Mississippi Riverine Forest	—
M231	Ouachita Mixed Forest–Meadow	—
242	Pacific Lowland Mixed Forest	—
M242	Cascade Mixed Forest–Coniferous Forest–Alpine Meadow	Olympic
M244	Pacific Coastal Mountains Forest–Meadow	Glacier Bay, Kenai Fjords, Wrangell–St. Elias
M245	Pacific Gulf Coastal Forest–Meadow	Wrangell–St. Elias
251	Prairie Parkland (Temperate)	—
255	Prairie Parkland (Subtropical)	—
261	California Coastal Chapparal Forest and Shrub	Channel Islands

Table 12.1 (continued)

	Province	Park name
262	California Dry Steppe	—
263	California Coastal Steppe, Mixed Forest, and Redwood Forest	—
M261	Sierran Steppe–Mixed Forest–Coniferous Forest–Alpine Meadow	Death Valley
M262	California Coastal Range Open Woodland–Shrub–Coniferous Forest–Meadow	Pinnacles
311	Great Plains Steppe and Shrub	—
313	Colorado Plateau Semidesert	Grand Canyon
315	Southwest Plateau and Plains Dry Steppe and Shrub	—
M313	Arizona–New Mexico Mountains Semidesert–Open Woodland–Coniferous Forest–Alpine Meadow	—
321	Chihuahuan Desert	Chiricahua
322	American Semidesert and Desert	Death Valley, Joshua Tree, Organ Pipe Cactus
331	Great Plains–Palouse Dry Steppe	Scotts Bluff
332	Great Plains Steppe	—
M331	Southern Rocky Mountain Steppe–Open Woodland–Coniferous Forest–Alpine Meadow	Black Canyon of the Gunnison, Grand Teton
M332	Middle Rocky Mountain Steppe–Coniferous Forest–Alpine Meadow	—
M333	Northern Rocky Mountain Forest-Steppe–Coniferous Forest–Alpine Meadow	—
M334	Black Hills Coniferous Forest	Devils Tower, Jewel Cave
341	Intermountain Semidesert and Desert	Death Valley, Great Basin
342	Intermountain Semidesert	Lava Beds
M341	Nevada–Utah Mountains Semidesert–Coniferous Forest–Alpine Meadow	—
411	Everglades	Dry Tortugas
M411	Puerto Rico	—
M423	Hawaiian Islands	—

A Century of Accomplishments

On the basis of the three characteristics of ecological significance considered here—rarity/superlativeness, representivity, and integrity—we can say that the national monuments created under the Antiquities Act have made a strong and lasting contribution to nature conservation in America. They are responsible for preserving numerous examples of geodiversity, the importance of which often belies the small size of the area being protected. They form the basis of a third of the country's natural-area World Heritage sites, and so again are making a large contribution to the protection of these areas of outstanding universal significance. They represent more than half of the country's ecoregional provinces. Finally, they are a critical part of the National Park Service's ecological integrity monitoring program. Perhaps nothing on this scale was envisioned by the creators of the law, not even by someone as bold as Theodore Roosevelt. But from our vantage point a century later, speculations such as these fade into insignificance. What remain are the ecological accomplishments of the Antiquities Act, and they only grow more and more important as the years go by.

Acknowledgments

I thank Jim Omernik (U.S. Environmental Protection Agency, retired) and Ed Wiken (Canadian Council on Ecological Areas) for helping me get information about interpreting ecoregional classifications. I am especially indebted to Mark Romanski (Isle Royale National Park) for preparing maps showing the relationship of the ecoregions and the national monuments, from which the information in Table 12.1 is derived.

Notes

1. Palmer 1917, 218–219.
2. Palmer 1917, 225. This paragraph owes much to the description in Rothman 1989, 94–97.
3. Williss 1985; quotation on-line at www.cr.nps.gov/history/online_books/williss/adhi5b.htm.
4. Squillace 2003, 473–610, and his chapter in this volume.
5. See the pioneering analysis in Gray 2004.
6. UNESCO 2005, 14.

7. Hales 1984, 744–745. For further historical background on the convention, see Thorsell 1992.

8. UNESCO 2005, 13.

9. UNESCO 2005, 14, 37–38.

10. UNESCO 2005, 19.

11. Two other U.S. World Heritage sites, inscribed for their cultural heritage, originated as national monuments: Chaco Culture National Historical Park and Statue of Liberty National Monument.

12. The monument was redesignated a national park in 1919. Herbert Hoover used the Antiquities Act in 1932 to declare a second Grand Canyon National Monument, and Lyndon Johnson used the Act to proclaim Marble Canyon National Monument in 1969; both were merged into the present national park.

13. IUCN 1979a, 1–2.

14. Statement on UNESCO website at whc.unesco.org/pg.cfm?-cid=31&id_site=721.

15. Speleothems are cave structures formed by mineral deposition from water, such as stalactites and stalagmites. A helictite is a distorted form of a stalactite resembling a twig.

16. IUCN 1995, 46.

17. IUCN 1995, 52.

18. IUCN 1979b, 2.

19. IUCN 1992, 148.

20. Statement on UNESCO website at whc.unesco.org/pg.cfm?-cid=31&id_site=151.

21. IUCN 1981, 2.

22. Omernik 2004.

23. Omernik 1995.

24. Bailey 1995; Bailey 1998.

25. Welch 2005.

26. Canada National Parks Act 2000, Section 2. On-line at laws.justice.gc.ca/en/N-14.01/19348.html.

27. National Park Service, "An Overview of Vital Signs Monitoring and Its Central Role in Natural Resource Stewardship and Performance Management." Undated report on-line at science.nature.nps.gov/im/monitor/docs/Vital_Signs_Overview.doc.

28. Statement on NPS website at science.nature.nps.gov/im/monitor/vsmAdmin.htm.

Part 4

New Horizons for the Act

13

The Antiquities Act Meets the Federal Land Policy and Management Act

Elena Daly and Geoffrey B. Middaugh

WHETHER THROUGH TREATY OR PURCHASE, the fledgling nation of the United States of America added vast expanses of land during its first one hundred years. The challenge of putting these land additions to the best national interest seemed clear to the nation's founding fathers, who left numerous writings about their vision for this vast western landscape. They saw everything west of the Potomac as a potential source of income for the national coffers. As early as 1788 James Madison wrote in the *Federalist Papers* that "the western Territory is a mine of vast wealth to the United States ... and under proper management, it could be used to effect a gradual discharge of the domestic debt."[1] Jefferson's charge to Lewis and Clark at the outset of their expedition in 1803 was to explore and catalogue the resources of the western territories for commercial as well as educational purposes. The canvas of the American West, already marked with peoples, landscapes, and resources, was about to experience further modification.[2] That canvas would eventually be filled in with cities, ranches, farms, logging camps, mining operations, national parks, and national monuments. Those eventualities went far beyond the vision of the founding fathers. Indeed, if the founding fathers had any vision at all of national parks or monuments— of landscapes set aside for other than commercial purposes—that vision is poorly documented. The canvas of the American West continues to change today, adapting to new circumstances.[3]

When the West was formally opened up to exploration and settlement, challenges of ownership and revenue generation previously not seen began to emerge. Habitation by native peoples, random explorations by European nations, and overlying claims to land made for a complex and often convoluted history. Documenting the ownership of and generating revenue from western lands required skills that are necessary components of democratic government in developing countries to this day. Creating mechanisms for public land surveys, documenting ownership of the land as private property (land patents), transferring ownership of lands as a matter of record (land titles), and instituting a legal system that supported both the private and public interests in land (courts)—all of these needed to be designed. The era of exploration and settlement became an era of innovation and experimentation as well.

The beginning steps for democratization and documentation of the land were awkward. Congress originally set up a system of selling land in 1788. The effectiveness of the process was mixed. Some historians point out that the first years of administration of the public domain by Congress (between 1788 and 1812) generated more embarrassment than cash to the federal treasury.[4] Early failures led Congress to decide quickly that an agency dedicated to land disposal and revenue management was necessary. In 1812 the General Land Office (GLO) was created with a single purpose: generate revenue for the federal treasury through the disposal of the public domain.[5]

Over the nineteenth century, Congress approached the task with great zeal as new laws were drafted and passed to assist with public land disposal. Disposal of these western lands was often complicated by their inhospitable nature. Aridity made some of the lands useless for farming or difficult for ranching. Rocky, steep slopes impeded development and the plow. Grass for grazing was scarce on lands with less than eight inches of annual precipitation. Few lands yielded up valuable minerals like gold or silver. Technology had not yet made fossil fuels easily identified or located. Conservation of the land was an idea not yet considered. At the conclusion of the nineteenth century, the canvas of the West had been painted in with towns, cities, emigrant trails, roads, railroads, Indian reservations, logging camps, and mining camps. Relatively few lands were retained for purposes of parks or conservation.

It was not until the beginning of the twentieth century that conservation of western lands was seriously discussed. That discussion became a part of the Progressive-era idea about expansion of presidential power. At the forefront of this discussion was Theodore Roosevelt.

Using the premise of federal control of the public lands, and with the federal government retaining ownership of the public domain as a condition of statehood,[6] the competing ideas of generating revenues and providing a conservation element began to emerge with Roosevelt's assumption of the presidency in 1901. By 1906, when the Antiquities Act was passed, the concept of conservation was just beginning to expand beyond the earlier successful prototype experiments in protection at Yellowstone, Yosemite, and a few other national parks, and the beginnings of the wildlife refuge and forest reserve systems. A hallmark of Progressive-era legislation, the Antiquities Act was well suited to the aims of President Roosevelt, who was not afraid to use the law's far-reaching power in the name of the public interest—a novel concept in 1906. Theodore Roosevelt's vision of the public interest was a new aspect of the presidency. He understood the uniqueness of the western lands—their drama and their beauty—from personal experience. In 1903 Roosevelt took a whirlwind trip by railroad across the country. The Southwest and California were new landscapes for him to see, and he was awed by the spectacular vistas.[7] His vision for the western lands began to come into focus. He peered over the edge of the Grand Canyon and camped in the backcountry with John Muir at Yosemite. Upon his return to the White House, his concept of conservation continued to take form. Roosevelt would add to his new system of conservation areas with his new tool: the Antiquities Act. He acted with a clear vision and no fear of political controversy, creating national monuments to go alongside the existing national parks, wildlife refuges, and forest reserves. An expanded policy of conservation was growing as a public interest value.[8]

At about the same time, Gifford Pinchot convinced the president that many of these lands also had conservation value for more utilitarian reasons, such as timber harvest, livestock grazing, or mineral development. As Roosevelt and Pinchot looked at the survey maps of the vast mountain ranges in the West, and drew bold black lines around them as forest reserves, the notion that the General Land Office, created for the disposal of land, could manage these lands for this new form of conservation was quickly discounted. A new organization and mission statement would be needed to address the new utilitarian conservation concept. Thus the Forest Service was created in 1905, with Pinchot as its chief.

By World War I, two unique models for conservation management were evolving together: the national park system and the national forest system. The National Park Service (created in 1916) would manage one set of lands as parks and monuments, a unique concept that expanded land management far beyond survey, sale, disposal, or the occasional out-and-out fraud. In its administration of national forests, the Forest Service would manage and "use these lands wisely for the present and future generations."[9] The national parks were charged with preservation; the national forests, with conservation and wise use. What was novel about the concepts of parks and forest reserves, as many historians have pointed out, is that they embodied the paradox of development versus preservation—a paradox still present in federal land management to this day. There were other federal lands, such as the wildlife refuges under the Bureau of Biological Survey, and archaeological sites under the watch of GLO special agents. Beyond these, the rest of the federal lands, administered by the General Land Office—the lands that no one wanted—were left to be managed under a litany of evolving and emerging land disposal policies defined by Congress to generate revenue and encourage their disposal to state or private hands. These were the General Land Office's two primary purposes, and the GLO wasn't seriously considered as a manager of lands in perpetuity, whether as parks, forest reserves, or wildlife refuges. Yet as the decades passed it was recognized that these GLO lands were far from valueless, and, as we will see, in 1946 a third agency, the Bureau of Land Management (BLM), was created to manage what remained of the public domain.

The rest of this chapter outlines the context of protected area management within BLM's multiple-use mandate as defined by its guiding legislation, the Federal Land Policy and Management Act (FLPMA), passed in 1976. With its National Landscape Conservation System (NLCS), BLM has embarked on a new paradigm of protected area management. That paradigm continues to evolve today within the framework of multiple-use resource management, the legacy of the General Land Office, and the expanding role of landscape-scale management. At the dawn of the twenty-first century, the western canvas, already filled with twentieth-century additions of parks, forest reserves, and refuges, is about to be altered again.

 ## The Status of the GLO under Theodore Roosevelt

When Theodore Roosevelt signed the proclamation that created the boundary to Grand Canyon National Monument in 1908, the lands from which it came were part of the public domain. There was no public discussion of the value of Grand Canyon National Monument. Roosevelt just created it. He put in place a marker that defined a new mandate for the federal lands and further challenged the pure disposal policies of the nineteenth century.

The lands from which Grand Canyon National Monument was created came under the administration of the General Land Office in the Department of the Interior. At this time, the GLO remained focused on its orders from Congress to dispose of the public domain even though many people began to see the limits to the vast land resources on the North American continent. Whether this disposal was wise or short-sighted is a debate best left to another time. What remains is the historical fact that disposal of the public domain has influenced the history of the United States and public land law as much after 1900 as before.

It is no surprise that in Roosevelt's time the General Land Office would play no management role in either the new parks or forest reserves. The GLO's predisposition towards land disposal and sales, and—unfortunately—incidents of graft and corruption, meant that it was never seriously considered for the role of protecting the public conservation interest. In fact, when Roosevelt transferred over 46 million acres to the Department of Agriculture by signing the Transfer Act on February 1, 1905, it was specifically to keep these lands "safely out of the hands of the General Land Office."[10] Likewise, as new units were added to the national park system or the national wildlife refuge system, the notion that the General Land Office might be made the manager of these treasures was not seriously considered.

The Closing of the Public Domain: The End of the Era of Disposals

The vast acreage under the administration of the General Land Office slowly began to draw interest both from those interested in the new concept of conservation as well as the old concept of resource development. Disposal was still national policy, but in 1908, the end of the Roosevelt administration, national policy turned the corner, and the outright theft of nationally valued lands began to come to an end with the repeal of certain legislation.[11] New public interest values began to influence policy, and Congress began to respond.

No constituency in 1908 pressured Congress to create another land management agency; one new agency, the Forest Service, had just begun and within a decade another, the National Park Service, would join it. The estimated 500 million acres still in federal owner-ship were by and large the lands that no one wanted to buy, develop, homestead, farm, put in a national forest reserve, or make into a park. The unknown, leftover lands in the public domain had no major external support from Congress or the American people. If lands under the jurisdiction of the General Land Office were deemed to have conservation or recreation values, they were given to another entity to manage. To Congress and to too many Ameri-cans, these lands would remain unknown and unwanted until 1976, when FLPMA was passed.[12]

In 1934, Congress determined that what was left of the public domain had value for livestock grazing. Before this value could be realized, the lands needed an arbitrator between sheep and cattle grazers. The Dust Bowl years of the Depression resulted in conflicts between users of the public lands and produced competition for valuable forage.[13] In the Public Land Law Review Commission's pri-mary analysis, *The History of Public Land Law Development*, an entire chapter is focused on the detailed history of "The Administration of Public Grazing Lands."[14] By the 1930s another Roosevelt was in the White House, but the conservation battles were still familiar. The congressional response to this was the creation of the Grazing Ser-vice, established under the authority of the Taylor Grazing Act of 1934.[15]

From 1934 to 1946, the Taylor Grazing Service and the General Land Office co-existed. Livestock grazing use was being managed, and the disposal of federal lands and minerals continued. In 1946, President Truman merged the Taylor Grazing Service and the Gen-eral Land Office to create the Bureau of Land Management.[16]

From 1946 to 1976 the newly created BLM held public lands for management under a multiple-use formula, with the caveat that this management was an interim step pending ultimate disposal. Disposal meant transfer to private ownership, state government, or some other federal agency. At the same time, BLM generated rev-enue through its grazing and minerals programs and made attempts at multiple-use management. Recreation as a use began to emerge, but only if it did not interfere with livestock grazing, disposal, or minerals development.

The passage of the Federal Land Policy and Management Act of 1976 (43 U.S.C. 1701), with amendments, resulted in BLM finally having an organic act. Almost two hundred years after the founding fathers declared the West open for settlement and commercialization, FLPMA defined a broader role for the public lands. In Section 102(a), Congress stated in the opening declaration of policy "that the public lands be retained in federal ownership."[17] FLPMA went on to repeal 2,500 individual public land laws,[18] such as the various Homestead Acts, and focused on the concept of conservation and land use planning in order to provide for the multiple-use management of the public lands. The mandate was clear and statutory: the public lands had values beyond disposal values, and those lands were to be managed "in a manner that will protect the quality of scientific, scenic, historical, ecological, environmental, air and atmospheric, water resource and archeological values; that where appropriate, will preserve and protect certain public lands in their natural condition; that will provide food and habitat for fish and wildlife and domestic animals; and that will provide for outdoor recreation and human occupancy and use."[19]

After FLPMA passed, the idea that the BLM would or could manage protected areas was still not taken seriously. FLPMA did not provide for any BLM management of traditional conservation units, such as national monuments. BLM had authority to recommend and manage wilderness areas, wild and scenic rivers, and, on a case-by-case basis, national historic or scenic trails. The concept of a conservation unit, such as a reserve, park, or monument, was not a role considered under the mandates of FLPMA. BLM could create and manage administratively designated units such as recreation areas or areas of critical environmental concern. BLM had authority to manage other types of land systems that Congress chose to designate, most notably national conservation areas. For example, FLPMA identified two national conservation areas: the California Desert Conservation Area and the previously designated King Range National Conservation Area. The only mention FLPMA makes of the Antiquities Act is to assure that under the withdrawal review provisions that national monuments are not decreased in size or protection level by administrative action.[20] Other than this affirmation of Antiquities Act authorities, FLPMA remained silent on agency responsibility for management of national monuments.

Conservation System Development
After the Passage of FLPMA

BLM underwent a period of rapid growth after the passage of FLPMA. New mandates, new authorities, and heightened public awareness led to growing budgets and evolving programs. Evolving case law stemming from the National Environmental Policy Act of 1969 (NEPA; 42 U.S.C. 4321 et seq.) increased conflict and litigation. BLM faced new and diverse challenges to its management of the public lands as both the agency and the public attempted to understand FLPMA and NEPA. The challenges were the classic battles of preservation versus development, similar to what had been debated in conservation management since Theodore Roosevelt's time. Some argued that BLM was managing for too much preservation, e.g., in its identification and study of public lands for wilderness values. Others argued that BLM was managing for too much use, e.g., through its continuing emphasis on exploring the public lands for oil and gas resources.

The West was changing, again. The frontier had long since closed. Lands were becoming more valuable for reasons not related to development. The public was beginning to discover that the left-over federal lands had valuable resources and increased potential for public benefit and recreation. BLM's new challenge would be to determine how to manage landscape resources for an increasing panoply of uses. The image of the western canvas, once seemingly so clear-cut, was beginning to get even more muddled.

National Monuments in the Context of FLPMA

As the frustrations of providing for protected area management in a multiple-use context played out, several interests began to look for creative ways to meet resource protection objectives and accommodate the complexities of multiple uses. Part of this equation was determining how to manage mixed land ownership and how to address the demands of local governments.

Multiple-use management is difficult. In 1972, "the legislative cousin of the national monuments,"[21] the national conservation area, was inaugurated by the creation of King Range along the California coast. Many observers were not sure what designation as a national conservation area meant. It had a protection emphasis, but other uses could continue. The correlation in terms of management actions or restrictions was not clear. The King Range had wild, undeveloped coastal beaches, large trees (redwoods), steep hillsides, and sweeping ocean vistas. But it also had challenging problems of mining claims management, potential sloughing of steep slopes from logging, intermixed inholdings of state and private lands, people living illegally on the public lands, and a variety of difficulties associated with public lands prior to the passage of FLPMA.

Congress had identified conservation objectives for BLM lands before President Clinton used the presidential authority under the Antiquities Act in 1996 to assign the bureau its first national monument. In 1988, congressional designation of the San Pedro National Conservation Area in Arizona added depth to the western canvas. The picture sharpened with the addition of other national conservation areas such as Red Rocks in Nevada and Birds of Prey in Idaho. These designations recognized the landscape, ecological, social, and economic values of the lands under BLM management. Nevertheless, there simply was not an easy way to meet protection objectives and manage within the confines of multiple use and complex public land law.

The National Landscape Conservation System, established in 2000 and managed by BLM under a framework of FLPMA-based multiple use, was designed to meet these challenges. National monuments created under the authorities of the Antiquities Act would prove to be the catalyst for such a system. The proclamation of Grand Staircase–Escalante National Monument in 1996 moved BLM forward toward achieving the full resource-oriented, multiple-use vision of the agency's organic act.

The National Landscape Conservation System Focus

Grand Staircase–Escalante was the first national monument to be administered by the BLM. The proclamation that created the monument was a detailed explanation of the complexities of multiple use, and its wording addressed the balancing act between development and protection.[22] The establishment of the monument, the creation of a detailed land management plan, and implementation of that plan have all been controversial. Much of the controversy has focused on the lack of state and community involvement prior to monument designation. Courts have upheld presidential authority under the Antiquities Act several times, but even at this writing litigation continues. The lack of local involvement in the proclamation process remains a point of contention.[23] Critics assert that the creation of the monument violated Utah's state sovereignty. These arguments were not new assaults upon the Antiquities Act; BLM had simply never had to deal with them.

In a March 24, 2000, speech announcing the creation of the National Landscape Conservation System for BLM, Secretary of the Interior Bruce Babbitt stated: "In the twenty-first century ... BLM ... can become the greatest modern American land management agency, the one that sets the standard for protecting landscapes, applying evolving knowledge and social standards, and bringing people together to live in harmony with the land."[24] Babbitt pointed out that over the previous half-century a pattern had developed regarding BLM lands. Whenever a local movement sprang up to protect a piece of the BLM landscape, the newly discovered area was carved out of the BLM land base and given to the National Park Service to manage. From 1946 to 1996, Babbitt asserted, every single large new national monument established under the Antiquities Act was taken away from the Bureau of Land Management.[25] Babbitt saw the designation of Grand Staircase–Escalante as a dramatic opportunity for the BLM to manage a new kind of national monument, one rooted in the landscape, responsive to evolving science, and in harmony with long-standing community use (Figure 13.1). Babbitt's vision was a new monument system, managed by the BLM in partnership with surrounding communities. The BLM would not provide food, lodging, or other visitor services within the monument. Instead, visitors would be encouraged to see the landscape in the context of the history and tradition of the entire region.

The challenge of managing natural resources within the context of use and demand is increasingly important in the West. Western populations, including many rural communities, are currently experiencing phenomenal growth. The need to conserve resources, cultures, and economic viability is growing along with population density. Technology, principally in the realm of recreation, offers experiences never before imagined. Protective management in this rapid-growth environment means focusing on landscape integrity to ensure sustainability of monument resources.

Figure 13.1. National monuments are a central part of the BLM's new National Landscape Conservation System. Clockwise from upper left: Cascade–Siskiyou National Monument, Oregon; Canyons of the Ancients National Monument, Colorado; Carrizo Plain National Monument, California; California Coastal National Monument. Unattributed photographs, courtesy of Bureau of Land Management, Office of the National Landscape Conservation System.

The importance of BLM monuments designated for conservation values in a multiple-use context has been endorsed by both Democratic and Republican administrations. The NLCS was formally established under the Clinton administration in June 2000. When George W. Bush assumed the presidency in 2001, he named Gale Norton as secretary of the interior. Secretary Norton reviewed the goals and policies of the new NLCS in the spring of 2001. As a result of that review, the Bush administration endorsed the philosophy of recognizing unique landscapes on the public lands and expanded the mandate to focus on working with communities of place and interest in the spirit of cooperative conservation.

In April 2002, Norton announced her plans to develop strong, locally based land use plans for the 15 national monuments managed by BLM. She challenged "the Bureau of Land Management and the National Park Service to make the planning process a model of how to involve the people who live and work closest to these monuments." BLM Director Kathleen Clarke added: "If the planning and management process for the monuments is to be effective, we must make sure it is citizen centered. We must ensure that local communities have a true stake in these national monuments to guarantee that generations of future Americans can enjoy them too."[26] The emphasis was on meeting conservation objectives and listening to local communities. In practice, these two goals can be compatible.

In Executive Order 13352, dated August 26, 2004, President Bush committed his administration to the concept of "cooperative conservation." Cooperative conservation means that communities join with the federal government to identify the vision and goals for public land management and stewardship.[27] The public engages at the outset of the discussions, not at the conclusion of the process. Cooperative conservation sets in place all subsequent avenues of participation and partnership.

The twenty-first century requires a system of protected areas on the public lands that allows for meeting conservation objectives as well as addressing the complexities of multiple uses and the needs of local communities. Adrian Phillips has described what has become known as the "new paradigm" for protected areas: the evolution of management from the traditional concepts of national parks and reserves to more complex systems of landscape management. He proposes a paradigm for protected area management that depends heavily on community-conserved areas.[28] In the American context, complex patterns of private, state, local, tribal, indigenous, and federal lands all contribute toward meeting a conservation objective. This new paradigm has utility primarily because it addresses the diverse levels of interest in both conservation and development of the federal lands. It also has great utility because there simply aren't big blocks of public land left (outside of Alaska—which is another unique story) that can be easily made into large, landscape-level parks or reserves. Phillips also speaks to the interest of citizens to determine and work toward commonly shared goals for integrated land systems.

Cooperative conservation is the next generation in collaborative management of public lands. For BLM, cooperative conservation uses full participation and open engagement of communities in (1) setting public land goals, (2) integrating those goals with community goals, (3) problem-solving keyed to planning processes and the daily operation of public lands, and (4) implementing management plans. Cooperative conservation addresses the growing public interest in federal land management. This movement represents a marked departure from the traditional designation and management of monuments, and is in keeping with Phillips' new paradigm for protected areas.

BLM policies for management of monuments include guidance for assuring a close partnership with local communities and wider interests. The importance of local interest in monument status has been a lesson learned through experience. When the San Rafael Swell region of central Utah was recommended to be added to the NLCS, Emery County (where the Swell is located) held a referendum to gauge the degree of local support. Local residents voted down the suggestion. The decision by the BLM to honor state and local community wishes is consistent with the Phillips' paradigm for protected areas and rooted in the concept of collaborative conservation. Now and in the future, community support and endorsement is a necessary component of protected area management.

As the concepts of NLCS and cooperative conservation have evolved, differences from traditional monument management have become apparent. At some visitor contact stations local volunteers provide glimpses of history and culture. Minimal dependence on infrastructure means that new roads, new campgrounds and other facilities are not constructed in the monument but are instead located in surrounding communities.

Another difference between BLM-managed monuments and those of other federal agencies is BLM's mission to make multiple use work when it is consistent with the conservation objectives and the proclamations that created the monument. BLM monuments may have grazing, hunting, oil and gas development (leaseable minerals), and a host of other existing uses.[29] The existing uses are managed to a standard of best management practices so that they do not conflict with the values for which the monument was proclaimed. The monuments under BLM jurisdiction offer opportunities to provide the products and services the American public wants from its public lands while maintaining the ecological integrity and economic viability of those lands. NLCS monuments offer models of balancing resource demand with resource sustainability in a variety of settings.

The NLCS monuments recognize the need to address conservation in the context of surrounding state and private lands. The NLCS policy acknowledges that "nature and culture are often linked and that healthy landscapes are shaped by human culture as well as by the forces of nature; rich biological diversity often coincides with cultural diversity; and conservation cannot be undertaken without the involvement of those people closest to the resources."[30]

With cooperative conservation as the governing principle, NLCS offers opportunities for BLM, local communities, and wider interests to work together in managing large blocks of public lands that contribute to landscape protection and restoration while providing goods and services, providing wildland recreation, working to diversify local economic bases while preserving local customs and culture, applying emerging science to address resource issues, and expanding opportunities for advances in resource management.

Conclusion

The Antiquities Act provided the opportunity for an enhanced conservation role within BLM that both balances the protection of national-level resources and addresses the complexities of modern resource management. Much is left to be done, however. The ideas of working with local communities and embracing historic uses of the lands across a region are ones that Teddy Roosevelt would have found useful from a pragmatic political point of view. From a resource protection and a common-sense political perspective, agency staffers need to work toward gaining the support of local communities to protect lands. In the future, the American public, through their elected officials, will likely add to the National Landscape Conservation System. These new pictures on the majestic western canvas will include more landscapes that focus on conservation. In all likelihood, they will be managed through cooperative conservation.

Notes

1. Watkins 1992, 305.

2. James Ronda, address to the Lewis and Clark First Bicentennial Signature Event, Monticello, Virginia, January 18, 2003.

3. Ronda, address.

4. Watkins 1992, 305.

5. For the purposes of this paper, we use the term "public domain" to refer to all the public lands that have not been withdrawn, reserved, or purchased for some purpose other than management under the mandates of FLPMA. In past times, "public domain" referred to all the federal lands, but currently they refer more specifically to the lands managed by the BLM. See Foss 1987.

6. The requirement that vacant and unclaimed land within a territory was to remain a federal asset as a condition of statehood was a unique aspect of American federalism that has sparked protests such as the "sagebrush rebellion" to this day.

7. Morris 2001, 231. Roosevelt became president in 1901 after William McKinley was assassinated, and won the office in the 1904 elections.

8. Roosevelt's personal interest in the Antiquities Act in particular is open to historical speculation. The concept of the Antiquities Act as a tool of presidential power, as is discussed elsewhere in this book, was evolving before Roosevelt used the Act in 1906. Roosevelt's expansion of presidential power, his Progressive view of conservation as a federal public interest value, and his expansion of a system of parks, refuges and forest reserves is, however, beyond question.

9. Watkins 1992, 312.

10. Watkins 1992, 312.

11. Watkins 1992, 312. The date considered by historians as that which marks the closing of the public domain varies greatly. For this paper, we are using 1908 because the first steps at ending the abuses of the settlement laws were taken at the end of the Roosevelt administration. For more information, see Gates 1968, 490–492. Clawson (1983, 31) cites the passage of FLPMA in 1976 as the point where Congress changed the preamble to the Taylor Grazing Act (1934), which refers to management of the public domain "pending final disposal."

12. Watkins and Watson 1975, chap. 8.

13. Gates 1968, 607.

14. Gates 1968, 620.

15. 43 U.S.C. 315, as amended by the Act of August 28, 1937, 43 U.S.C. 1181d.

16. Reorganization Plan no. 3 of 1946, Section 403. The authority to merge the General Land Office and the Grazing Service was a function of the

reorganization plan submitted by the secretary of the interior and affirmed by the president. It did not result from an executive order, but rather from the approval of the secretary's plan.

17. 43 U.S.C. 1701, sec. 102(a).

18. D. Michael Harvey, "Use and Limits of the Federal Lands Today—Who Cares and How Should the Current Law Work," as quoted in Brubaker 1984, 116.

19. 43 U.S.C. 1701.

20. 43 U.S.C. 1714.

21. Bruce Babbitt, remarks to the BLM Town Hall Meeting, Phoenix, Arizona, March 24, 2000 (transcript).

22. Presidential Proclamation no. 6920, September 18, 1996.

23. Squillace (2003, 570–581) discusses in great detail the advantages and disadvantages of a democratic process in the creation of a National Monument. See also the chapters by Squillace and Rasband in this volume.

24. Babbitt, remarks to the BLM Town Hall Meeting, 1.

25. Babbitt, remarks to the BLM Town Hall Meeting, 2.

26. "Interior Secretary Makes Plans to Manage National Monuments," Department of the Interior press release, April 24, 2002.

27. Executive Order 13352, "Executive Order on Facilitation of Cooperative Conservation," August 26, 2004.

28. Phillips 2003.

29. The presidential proclamations that established the monuments sometimes specify the parameters by which future uses are managed. For example, while no new mineral or oil and gas leasing is allowed in monuments because the managing agency's discretion is withdrawn by the proclamations, usually existing leases can continue. Of BLM's national monuments, for example, four have producing oil and gas leases that continue (Grand Staircase–Escalante, Upper Missouri River Breaks, Canyon of the Ancients, and Carrizo Plain). As Squillace states, "Monuments are like snowflakes, each one with a character of its own" (2003, 519). Multiple use is complex.

30. Brown and Mitchell 2000, as quoted in Phillips 2003.

14

Co-Managed Monuments
A Field Report on the First Years of
Grand Canyon–Parashant National Monument

Darla Sidles and Dennis Curtis

GRAND CANYON–PARASHANT NATIONAL MONUMENT was established by presidential proclamation on January 11, 2000. This marked the first national monument in history for which joint management responsibilities were given to the National Park Service (NPS) and the Bureau of Land Management (BLM). Bruce Babbitt, secretary of the interior at that time, was originally interested in ensuring protection of the Colorado River and Grand Canyon watershed. There was also interest in establishing a jointly managed monument so that each agency could learn from the other's strengths. Over months of deliberations leading up to the proclamation, the proposed boundaries changed several times to reflect different political and environmental interests. The final area encompassed by the presidential proclamation included federal land and interests in land of 1,014,000 acres, which was declared to be the smallest area compatible with the proper care and management of the objects to be protected.

Grand Canyon–Parashant National Monument ("Parashant," for short) is located in the northwest corner of Arizona in an area known as the "Arizona Strip." The Strip is the northern portion of Arizona that is separated from the remainder of the state by the Grand Canyon. The monument is bounded on the south by Grand Canyon National Park, on the west by the Nevada boundary, and juts northward nearly to the Utah border. It is a vast land of open, undeveloped spaces and engaging scenery (Figure 14.1). Encompassing an incredible biological diversity, the area spans four ecoregions, ranging from the Mohave desert at 1,200 feet above sea level to old-growth ponderosa pine forests at over 8,000 feet. Parashant is a geological treasure dating back almost 2 billion years, and displays a rich human history spanning more than 11,000 years (Figure 14.2). Because of the remoteness and lack of easy access to this area, the natural and cultural resources in the monument are relatively undisturbed. This same remoteness presents a significant challenge for land managers, since access to the monument is two hours away from headquarters in St. George, Utah, on rough, unpaved roads. There are no paved roads or visitor services within Parashant's million-plus acres, so visitors need to be self-sufficient and prepared by traveling with an appropriate high-clearance vehicle equipped with extra spare tires, water, and food to last several days.

Prior to the monument's creation, approximately 800,000 acres of the area was managed by the Arizona Strip District of the Bureau of Land Management, while about 200,000 acres was managed by Lake Mead National Recreation Area of the National Park Service. The proclamation did not change these land allocations—the area remains under the previous Arizona Strip BLM and Lake Mead NPS

Figure 14.1. The landscape of Grand Canyon–Parashant National Monument is largely undeveloped. BLM/NPS photograph, courtesy of Grand Canyon–Parashant National Monument.

Figure 14.2. The monument's human history includes Native American and Euroamerican influences. Left: rock art at Nampaweap; right: remains of the Grand Gulch Mine. BLM/NPS photographs, courtesy of Grand Canyon–Parashant National Monument.

management and authorities. The monument designation is essentially an additional layer of protection, subject to the overriding purpose of protecting the scientific and historic objects described in the proclamation.

Original Organizational Alignment

One of the first charges to the monument was to establish the organization. The leadership and staffs of both the BLM Arizona Strip and the NPS Lake Mead National Recreation Area met regularly both before and after the monument proclamation to chart a course of "seamless management" for Parashant. The mission was to create

238 / Sidles & Curtis

and understand a "new model" of management, whereby both agencies would have a highly visible opportunity to demonstrate their stewardship and government effectiveness. The concept was to ensure protection of the area, while not eliminating the traditional and historic uses such as hunting and grazing. The monument's management was to serve as a model of efficient interagency coordination and co-operation, incorporating the strengths of each agency.

Many different organizational structures were prepared and considered. In the end, it was determined that the most efficient structure was to create an "executive council," chaired by the BLM Arizona Strip field office manager and the NPS Lake Mead superintendent. Under their shared leadership, a single monument manager (from the BLM) was proposed, with two assistant managers, one from the BLM and the other from the NPS. The BLM assistant manager would supervise biological and earth sciences, and the NPS assistant manager would supervise cultural resources, recreation/wilderness, and visitor services. Each assistant manager would supervise both BLM and NPS staff members who were responsible for their field of expertise across the entire monument, such that, for example, an NPS botanist would serve both agencies and acreage, and a BLM range conservationist would serve both agencies and acreage.

Monument staffers were hired, with the majority of the fourteen BLM staff coming from the existing BLM Arizona Strip Field Office, while most of the seven NPS staff came from other parks or agencies. Establishment of a separate monument office, apart from the Arizona Strip Field Office and Lake Mead National Recreation Area, was one of the most important aspects of defining the jointly managed monument. The staff of twenty-one operated under the original organizational structure for approximately three and a half years.

Changes in the Organizational Structure

A number of factors led to a change in the original organizational management structure during the fourth year. Because the NPS assistant manager served under the BLM monument manager, the NPS did not have true jurisdiction over NPS lands within Parashant, as required under the proclamation. The NPS proposed that an NPS superintendent position be created, equal in authority to the BLM manager, such that NPS lands within the monument would be adequately and fairly represented, and to ensure that NPS laws, regulations, and policies were followed on NPS lands. Some within the BLM were initially opposed to this proposed change, believing it was a violation of the "new model" of management. The NPS asserted that the new model of management was still being achieved, in that the staffs were still integrated, and that the NPS and BLM managers would still supervise employees of both agencies. It was not viewed as abandoning the original vision, but rather as a way to strengthen the collaborative management. In the end, it was agreed that the NPS superintendent position be established, creating equal authorities for both the BLM and the NPS. This organizational revision, though different from the original model, is still unique and the only one of its kind in either the BLM or the NPS.

The dual management structure reflects an even greater cooperative and collaborative approach to management, because both agencies enjoy shared leadership and decision-making. However, it remains to be seen whether this, or some other organizational structure, is the most appropriate for the monument. In this interagency experiment, it is particularly important to continually evaluate the effectiveness of the organization to ensure that the original vision and goals for Parashant are being accomplished, and that both agencies have the opportunity to contribute to managing the values for which the monument was proclaimed. The monument's managers recently took a closer look at the skills mix within the staff, to better align Parashant's core mission with its most efficient future target organization.

Interagency Challenges

The joint BLM and NPS management of Parashant has often been referred to as a shotgun wedding. It's been a mixed bag of opportunities and successes, challenges and frustrations. BLM has a history of multiple-use management, which has been dominated by meeting the needs of commodity users such as livestock grazing and mineral interests. The agency is customer-service oriented, always trying to accommodate the user while managing resources. Wilderness, endangered species, and preservation are often viewed by some as a hindrance to meeting public demand. The National Park

Service's mandate, on the other hand, is to protect natural and cultural resources unimpaired for future generations. The BLM is more oriented towards managing resources and commodity uses, while the NPS gears its management more toward protection of resources and visitor management. Trying to mesh these two very different cultures and missions has been an interesting challenge.

A simple example illustrates this key philosophical difference between the two agencies. Several years ago, the BLM and NPS Parashant managers were on an all-terrain vehicle (ATV) field trip in the monument. After an exhilarating ride up an extremely rough and rugged old mining route, the managers from the two agencies began discussing how the area should be managed for the future. The BLM managers thought the route should be managed for ATV users, and the NPS managers remarked what a great hiking trail it would be! One agency was considering how the area could be made available for a wider array of public use, and the other was thinking about how to best protect the area and its resources, while still allowing for limited access.

Differences such as these have provided opportunities for each agency to learn from the other and to think about what "niche" Parashant should fit into in terms of resource management and public use. Babbitt's vision for the new monument was that it should not be managed as BLM multiple-use land, nor as a national park, but somewhere in between, within the context of the Antiquities Act and each agency's authorizing legislation. Having a monument jointly managed by both agencies is one of the best ways to accomplish this.

Vision Statement and Goals

Shortly after Parashant was proclaimed, the two agencies convened and spent many hours developing the following vision statement and monument management goals. These goals prioritize protection of the resources as called for in the presidential proclamation, while simultaneously trying to capitalize on the strengths of each agency.

Vision. Grand Canyon–Parashant National Monument is a model of land management that conserves the natural, scientific, and historic resources, and includes ecological restoration, rugged recreation, and ranching, while honoring the history and living traditions of the people who came before us—"The Place Where the

West Stays Wild."

Goals. In all activities undertaken to reach the goals of the monument, the first priority is to achieve the overriding purpose: the conservation and protection of the historic and scientific objects described in the proclamation.

- The monument serves as a model of efficient interagency coordination and cooperation, incorporating the strengths of each agency.
- The monument plan will be developed within a regional context, building upon existing plans, and using a collaborative planning process that will provide clear direction for Parashant's management.
- Natural and social settings will be managed to preserve the remote and unspoiled landscape character while providing opportunities for visitors to experience adventure, beautiful vistas, and a sense of discovery through a variety of sustainable backcountry activities.
- Protection of cultural, social, biological, and physical resources for which the monument was created will remain the highest priority in planning and management.
- Existing land use authorizations will be monitored and no new mineral sales, leases or mining claims, or non-scientific vegetative sale permits will be issued, so as to maintain the sustainability of the resource and aesthetics of the landscape.
- Through a system of designated routes, a variety of backcountry driving experiences and access to key destinations and features will be provided, while managing to protect resource values.
- Cooperation with all affected stakeholders will be sought by involving the public in monument planning and management.
- The monument acts as a model for scientifically based, ecological restoration. Research and investigative studies will guide in the restoration of healthy native ecosystems, natural fire regimes, and cultural landscapes.
- The infrastructure footprint will be the minimum necessary to provide for public safety and enjoyment and to protect the values upon which the monument is based.
- Design standards will be developed for signs, kiosks, facilities, and other developments across the monument to help ensure energy efficiency, sustainability, quality, and consistency with the purposes of the monument proclamation.

- Sustained, well-managed ranching operations and associated interpretive activities will showcase the monument's historical living and working landscape and enhance visitor experience.
- Conservation and restoration of a habitat mosaic that supports sustainable levels of a full range of native species, including predators, will be emphasized. The recovery and protection of special-status species will remain a primary focus.
- A proactive information and education program will provide diverse audiences with information about the monument. Audiences will understand the purpose of the monument and its resources and receive the information they need to have a safe and enjoyable experience.
- The preservation of natural quiet will be emphasized in areas identified as key recreational destination points and other concentrated-use areas possessing this value.

In addition to these written goals, the NPS and the BLM spent a considerable amount of time discussing other ways that the monument could be managed as similarly as possible by both agencies. The original goals were lofty indeed, including one filing system, one budget, one computer system, one procurement and contracting process, and one manager for both agencies. We have since discovered that each agency's laws, systems, and procedures are so ingrained from the very top and down through the organization, that it is essentially impossible to attempt to function as one unit at the local level. We have spent an incredible amount of time simply trying to mesh the two individual systems to enable them to work as well together as they do. A case in point is our computer systems, which prevent shared access due to firewalls. Yet, in order to do our jobs, we have to find ways to share equipment and access each other's systems and software. Another example is our very different budget systems and timelines. Since staff work across agency lines, many are required to know both systems, which requires an inordinate amount of time and effort to maintain and respond to data calls. Despite these external barriers, in general the staff is dedicated to making the monument work.

Management Plan

One of the first major challenges that faced the two agencies was to develop a plan for how the monument should be managed over the next 15–20 years. Both agencies have a long history of preparing management plans, with numerous differences in format, detail, and protocols. The challenge has been preparing a management plan that complies with the proclamation, meets both agencies' requirements and expectations, and is responsive to the protection of resources and the need for public use. This has been a difficult and demanding process due to the complexity of monument issues, joint management, and the fact that the Parashant plan is being prepared in conjunction with planning for the remaining two million acres of Arizona Strip BLM lands. The monument plan addresses several controversial issues, including wilderness, grazing, and access. A particularly challenging component of the plan has been the designation of routes in the monument, with proposals for over 1,800 miles of routes that are open, closed, or limited (with respect to motorized use). Some of the other issues needing resolution were the level of plan detail, differences in opinion regarding appropriate resource management and tools for accomplishing work (particularly for wildlife and vegetation management), wilderness management, use of management zones, environmental compliance and impairment analysis, planning budgets, the schedule of the plan, and reviews by each agency's higher-level offices.

Wherever possible, we tried to combine or adopt each other's processes. For example:

- The BLM agreed to adopt the NPS process for identifying purpose, mission, and significance statements. This has proved to be a critical and worthwhile exercise to ensure that we are complying with the proclamation and our respective core missions.
- A compromise between NPS management zones and BLM allocation units was reached, creating "management units" rather than traditional NPS management zones. These management units differ from NPS zones in that they serve primarily as guidelines for visitor management. Management goals were developed for the units that guide various use allocations and management actions.
- The NPS adopted the BLM's use of "visual resource management areas" to plan for and protect viewsheds.
- The NPS adopted the BLM's process to create management units for areas that should be managed for their wilderness character.

In other cases, the differences were either too significant or agency laws prohibited the agencies from managing in the same way, such that each agency retained its own management prerogatives. For example:

- The level of detail and format of the plan will appear much like a traditional BLM plan because the plan also covers the Vermilion Cliffs National Monument (which is under sole BLM jurisdiction) and the remaining BLM lands on the Arizona Strip. This may present some challenges to a reader who is more familiar with NPS plans and formats, as the organization is substantially different, and the level of detail significantly greater, than a traditional NPS plan.
- Impairment analysis, required for the NPS but not the BLM, will be conducted only for NPS lands.

Specific proposed management actions were made as cohesive as possible, such as combining NPS and BLM visitor impact inventory and monitoring, interpretive planning, and commercial use permitting. Again, in other cases, differences in agency law or jurisdictions prohibited proposing these joint management actions. For example, regarding wildlife management, on BLM lands the BLM manages habitat, while the state manages wildlife. On NPS lands, the NPS manages both habitat and wildlife, in cooperation with the state. The BLM authorizes water developments and habitat improvement projects, while the NPS generally does not. The collection of shed deer antlers is allowed on BLM lands, but not permitted on NPS lands.

Signage

Shortly after proclamation of the monument, temporary signs were placed along the boundary to alert the public of its location. These signs were simple, displaying both the BLM and NPS logos. As time passed, it became necessary to erect more permanent signs. Nationally, both agencies have expended considerable resources and money to establish name recognition by "branding," via the NPS Messaging Project and the BLM Imaging Project. Internally, the policy of each agency is that all signs should have a consistent "look," and be the same across NPS or BLM land. Our challenge was to develop a sign that would meet both agencies' policies and management direction, while still relaying to the public that the monument is one unit, despite the involvement of two agencies.

With the approval of our Washington offices, the Parashant staff met with that of Craters of the Moon National Monument in Idaho (another jointly managed monument) to pursue agreement on a joint sign design. Collectively, a design was agreed upon that preserves components of each agency's identity. The sign is square on one side (an NPS element) and trapezoid on the other (a BLM element), with a dark band across the top (like the NPS "unigrid" park brochures), and a landscape scene across the bottom (like the logo of BLM's National Landscape Conservation System, or NLCS). The joint sign identity effort is a good example of blending the two agencies' policies to meet the needs of the monument and the public. The public will be able to identify the signs and know that they are entering a special place to be treated with respect.

Comprehensive Interpretive Plan

One of the successes of our joint management has been the draft development of an interagency comprehensive interpretive plan. We convened an interagency and interdisciplinary group of staff from within and outside the monument to work on this strategy that will guide the interpretive and educational program of the monument. In light of the difficulty of physical access to the monument, the plan places particular emphasis on means of off-site interpretation, so that the public has the opportunity to learn about the monument and appreciate its values, regardless of whether they are able to physically visit.

Operational Issues

Both agencies hired law enforcement rangers for the monument. Even though they have the same title, their delegations of authority originate from different laws and regulations. A cross-designation of law enforcement authorities was prepared shortly after the monument's proclamation, allowing our rangers to work across the monument regardless of land ownership. This was necessary because law enforcement officers routinely travel across each other's lands during their official duties and may encounter violations in progress that require immediate law enforcement action. The agreement called for training and briefings on laws, regulations, policies, and procedures of both agencies. Inconsistencies in BLM and NPS regu-

246 / Sidles & Curtis

lations within Parashant quickly became apparent in matters such as the use of firearms, metal detectors, wildlife management, and off-road vehicles, as well as the acceptability of pets.

In order to deal with these inconsistencies in laws and regulations, the boundary between NPS land and BLM land is marked with signs. Our goal is to manage the monument as seamlessly as possible, but due to existing laws and regulations, we may not always be able to do so. In each instance, we confer and discuss the advantages and disadvantages of whether to try to harmonize policies and regulations changes. Policies have been relatively easy to propose for joint management, whereas changes in law would be difficult because they require a lengthy federal rule-making procedure. Currently, management is analyzing the laws governing ATV use to consider a rule change that would make ATV management more consistent between the NPS and BLM lands, ultimately helping to provide more consistent management to the public.

Dual Recognition of Joint Management

Another unanticipated challenge is that the state, regional, and Washington offices of both agencies sometimes fail to recognize that Parashant is managed jointly. Specific agency directives typically do not account for joint management and may nòt conform to the other agency's policies. It is an ongoing effort to educate others that Parashant is a partnership, that decisions cannot be made unilaterally, and that compromises may be necessary. An example of this is a directive that printed media must have a certain format to ensure consistency within the agency. Another example is the continuing effort of the BLM Arizona State Office to ensure consistency within their own field offices and NLCS units, resulting in directives that are oftentimes incompatible with the NPS partnership in Parashant.

Another more revealing example of this lack of recognition is that the NPS portion of Parashant is not officially recognized as a unit within the national park system, as is the BLM portion of the monument within the NLCS. The NPS Washington Office continues to consider Parashant to be part of Lake Mead National Recreation Area, despite the fact that Parashant has its own national monument status and proclamation, different management goals and objectives, line-item budget, and separate staff. Establishment of the

NPS superintendent position (described previously) has helped to raise the visibility of the monument within both agencies, but lack of recognition of the NPS portion of Parashant as an NPS unit has hurt the credibility of the monument, resulting in a lost opportunity to showcase its unique joint management.

Budget

Working with two very different budgets and budget processes has been both a challenge and an opportunity. The challenge is precisely that there are separate budget processes and submissions, and our integrated staffs need to have some understanding of both processes. Learning just one of these systems, much less both, is quite challenging, particularly since they seem to change each year. NPS and BLM budget requests are also not coordinated at the same time of year, so an inordinate amount of time is spent on preparing budgets. The positive aspect of having two budgets is that when one is insufficient, the other may have some funds to help compensate. For certain projects, funds can be requested through both processes, but those funds are typically limited to the requesting agency or may be tied to specific projects that are not transferable to the other agency's land.

Transition to Full Management Responsibilities by Monument Staff

Before the proclamation of Parashant, both agencies were actively managing their portion of the monument area independently. Funds were being expended, projects were underway, and plans existed to manage the area. After the monument was proclaimed, it was decided to continue the management and projects that were consistent with the interim management policy. Existing BLM field office staff and NPS Lake Mead staff have continued working in the area, while the Parashant staff concentrated on completing a joint management plan for the monument. This arrangement worked well for the first couple of years, but as time went by, it was agreed that these projects and management would be turned over to the Parashant staff as capabilities allow. The transition has been a little rocky due to a feeling of ownership and not wanting to let go on the part of both the Arizona Strip and Lake Mead staff. Some of the non-monument staff have almost refused to acknowledge Parashant, and would prefer to continue doing things as if nothing had changed. There has also been some reluctance on the part of the Parashant staff to accept more work, when their plates are already full.

Lessons Learned

Communications. Prior to the monument's proclamation, lines of communication were in place between Lake Mead NPS and Arizona Strip managers. They met at least twice a year to discuss common issues and become better acquainted. Once Parashant was proclaimed, monthly meetings were held with managers from both agencies and their staff. There were no limitations on who could attend: all staff members were welcome. The first meetings were well attended, filling the conference rooms. The open meetings helped employees stay informed and built support for developing a new model of monument management.

One of the mistakes we made was not adequately orienting new employees who joined the monument staff several years after it was created. As a result, these newer employees lack personal involvement and understanding about managing Parashant under this new model, and about the benefits of a jointly managed monument. Consequently, their feelings about joint management are less than enthusiastic.

Another mistake concerns upper management support. Shortly after monument designation, a meeting should have been held between the Arizona BLM state director and the Pacific West Region NPS director to help them understand the ramifications of a jointly managed monument. Getting support and understanding at that level early on would have resolved some of the later problems of receiving one-sided directions from each agency.

Community support. Grand Staircase–Escalante National Monument, established four years before Parashant and managed entirely by the BLM, is a close neighbor, and we were able to learn much from their experiences. Shortly after Parashant's proclamation, we invited key members of their staff to a meeting where they shared their "lessons learned." They provided insights on how to deal with the public and how to get the management plan focused and started. An unusual side benefit of having them in close proximity was that they deflected a lot of the public outrage regarding the creation of these monuments by presidential proclamation. The negative public reaction against the designation of Parashant was minor compared with that against Grand Staircase–Escalante.

Organizational structure. The original concept of having one manager report to two different agencies and represent their mandates and policies simultaneously was extremely difficult to carry out, as the two agency's missions and cultures differ significantly. If the individual was truly a joint manager for both agencies, thorough knowledge and fair representation of each agency's laws, regulations, and policies would be necessary. In addition, the manager would have to represent both agencies in separate management meetings, conferences, and workshops, plus receive and respond to all the correspondence targeted for that level of manager. Because of these overwhelming responsibilities and expectations, the Park Service assistant monument manager ended up assuming a lot of the NPS management responsibilities and functioning as a quasi-superintendent, rather than as an assistant manager with responsibility only for visitor services and cultural resources. The establishment of the NPS superintendent position helped to clarify the responsibilities and expectations of both the NPS and BLM managers.

More thought and consideration should have gone into the original organizational structure in order to brainstorm all possible shortcomings that might occur with a shared monument manager position. Theoretically, it sounded like a good idea. On the ground, given our particular circumstances in time and space, it did not work.

As stated earlier, our current model for jointly managing the monument is still in the experimental phase. Only time will tell how well it works. One thing is clear: in order for joint management to be a success, the personalities of the involved parties are absolutely critical—they must truly *want* to work together as a team. They need to understand and respect each other's differences, work together to come to consensus, and have fair and equitable representation, authorities, and decision-making responsibilities.

Conclusion

Our shotgun wedding has not been a rose garden, but neither has it been a disaster. We continue to learn from each other every day, to be more patient, to laugh, and to try to find ways to be "seamless," at least in the public's eye. We have stopped trying to force consistency in absolutely everything we do; sometimes it is just not appropriate or legal for us to manage in the same way, and that's a good thing. We have learned that while combining systems such as our budget, information technology, personnel, and administrative procedures might be a nice idea, there is no mechanism or support from the top for us to do that. While we are one monument and one team, we are learning to celebrate our differences and learn from each other. At the same time, we recognize that we are different from any other NPS or BLM unit, and that this gives us the opportunity to be better. We are history in the making, and we are committed to figuring it out together.

15

Application of the Antiquities Act to the Oceans
Something Old, Something New, Something Borrowed, Something Blue

Brad Barr and Katrina Van Dine

"Stroke of the pen. Law of the Land. Kinda cool."
Paul Begala, former Clinton advisor,
The New York Times, July 5, 1998

FEW PLACES ATTRACT MORE CONTROVERSY than those described as "the commons"—places owned by all, but owned by none—and not many other "commons" are more prone to bringing out as much open hostility and disagreement as the oceans. Perhaps it is livelihoods so closely tied to something that is not owned (in the traditional sense of fee-simple ownership) or under any direct control of that person. Perhaps it is the type of person who is drawn to the sea for his or her vocation or recreation. Perhaps it is tradition, built on historical principles of international law, including the right of a coastal nation to control the band of coastline immediately adjacent to its shores and the right of freedom of navigation and fishing on the historically defined high seas beyond the three-mile limit. Freedom of the seas is deeply rooted in maritime cultures, and shifting that historical position does not happen easily. The open access standard of oceans is nationally and internationally entrenched and there is strong reaction when any constraints are overlaid upon waters that have always been "free." Controversy over attempts to protect pieces of the ocean is nearly universal, very vocal, and usually based on preconceptions that protection will unreasonably interfere with access to resources. Clearly the oceans are not the easiest place in the world to establish protected areas.

Yet, with such issues as depletion of marine species from over-fishing and by-catch, changing ecological regimes resulting from global climate change, and increasing pressures to exploit the resources from offshore areas, designating protected areas is necessary if any part of the ocean is to be preserved in its unaltered and naturally functioning state. The unavoidable controversy of these designations requires lengthy public processes, sometimes taking years or even decades, to achieve some consensus on what should be done to protect an area. Often, the result of these long and contentious processes is "too little, too late." The political will to overcome the "too little, too late" outcome is rarely in evidence.

Every now and then, however, there comes along a national leader who has a vision for preserving natural areas for future generations. Such a leader needs tools to implement that vision, and one of those tools is the Antiquities Act of 1906. Application of the Antiquities Act in ocean and coastal areas can be a bit tricky, but used strategically it has the potential to accomplish what may be considerably more difficult to do without it, and offers more certainty that effective protection will be achieved.

One such visionary leader was Theodore Roosevelt. Over the span of his presidency, he was responsible for the proclamation of 18 national monuments,[1] including the 800,000 acres that comprised Grand Canyon National Monument. While he did not designate the greatest number of monuments, nor the greatest area proclaimed, nor did he encounter great opposition, at that time, to the establishment of these monuments, he was the one who signed the law, set the precedent for broad interpretation of the authority (particularly with regard to "objects" of "scientific interest"), and was famously successful in implementing his vision of preserving significant natural areas for future generations.

Moving into the Water

The national monument designation authority has been used by thirteen presidents to protect sites of significant natural, historic, or scientific interest.[2] Designation of marine areas as national monuments has precedence. In 1938, pursuant to the Antiquities Act, President Franklin D. Roosevelt issued a proclamation reserving most of the Anacapa and Santa Barbara Islands, which were then federal lands, as Channel Islands National Monument; later, President Harry S Truman enlarged the monument to encompass one nautical mile surrounding the islands' shoreline. Santa Rosa Island National Monument off Florida was designated, also by FDR, in 1938. Buck Island Reef National Monument was proclaimed by President John F. Kennedy in 1961. President Bill Clinton proclaimed California Coastal National Monument in 2000 and Virgin Islands Coral Reef National Monument in 2001.[3] The California Coastal designation was massive, encompassing all islands, rocks, exposed reefs, and pinnacles above mean high tide within twelve miles of shore, and running the whole length of the California coast. However, the designation does not protect any federal submerged lands or the water column.[4] The Virgin Islands designation, and an expansion of Buck Island Reef National Monument, did protect the submerged federal lands and waters of these areas, and prohibited all extractive activities.[5]

The Tricky Part: What Constitutes "Owned or Controlled"?

The Antiquities Act is applicable to "lands owned or controlled by the Government of the United States." Full sovereignty over lands is based on the historic doctrine of discovery, where exclusive title was claimed by the discovering nation, including the exclusive right to grant the soil for settlement. Vast tracts of public lands were divided over time into various uses, including the ceding of federal lands to states. When these actions were undertaken, the federal government reserved certain lands and maintained full sovereignty and clear title to manage them. It also created a legally accountable relationship between the federal government and the various states.

Sovereignty and jurisdiction over the oceans originated from a very different set of precepts. At the inception of the Union neither states nor the federal government were sovereign over the coastal ocean. Federal rights in the marginal seas are not rooted in any inherent or exclusive right based on the territorial growth of the nation. This zone was defined as the range of a cannon ball's flight and came to mean that a nation exercises sovereignty over its marginal seas for as far seaward as its cannons can shoot. This rule, while not formalized, functioned as customary law for nearly two centuries until a 1988 presidential proclamation expanded the territorial sea to twelve miles. The colonial states acquired authority over the waters three miles from their shores as successors to the early federal position that there was a zone of neutrality surrounding the United States. This position has been repeatedly recognized and in fact memorialized through the Submerged Lands Act of 1953 (SLA). In that act, federal claims to ownership of coastal waters were held not to exist by authority of the Constitution, and the constitutional delegation of admiralty jurisdiction and commerce regulation was not a cession by the states of those waters or the submerged lands. In all but a few specific circumstances the federal role in coastal waters is essentially subservient to the coastal state.

Current ocean management includes a complicated range of overlapping state, federal, and international authorities and jurisdictions, including state tidelands and submerged lands, the outer continental shelf, the territorial sea, the contiguous zone, the exclusive economic zone (EEZ), and the high seas. The jurisdictions are used to describe areas of offshore ownership and sovereignty; various forms of mineral, fishery, and natural resources; and national security rights and regulatory controls. Based on international laws of the sea, claims of ownership are not as complete as the full sovereignty claimed over terrestrial lands. The qualification of sovereignty and the extent of jurisdiction over the oceans seems to be directly related to how far the area is from the shoreline, and the idea of restricting access to parts of the sea for a variety of purposes is only just emerging in the perceptions of the general public.

Adopted in 1982, the United Nations Convention on the Law of the Sea (UNCLOS III) developed the modern legal and political norms governing the use of oceans. Most provisions are accepted as customary international law, even in the United States, which has never ratified this treaty. While UNCLOS III identifies a number of different zones within the coastal ocean, the zones relevant to this discussion are territorial waters, the contiguous zone, and the EEZ. As discussed by Aaron Flynn, UNCLOS III recognizes a zone extending twelve nautical miles from the coast as the "territorial sea," where the coastal nation can claim full ownership and sovereignty.[6] Up to 24 nautical miles from shore, in the "contiguous zone," the country can impose regulations "to protect the territorial sea and to enforce customs, fiscal, and sanitary laws." The boundary of the EEZ is generally 200 nautical miles from the coast, where the coastal nation has the right to explore, exploit, conserve, and manage marine resources. While each of these zones prescribes, or perhaps implies, some measure of ownership and control to varying degrees, the full applicability of the Antiquities Act authority remains unresolved for at least the areas beyond territorial waters, and efforts to use the Act for ocean protection must recognize constraints including the implications of the SLA and the constraints of admiralty law.

The primary domestic complication for federal protection of the territorial sea relates to jurisdiction of the area generally extending three nautical miles from the shore (Florida and Texas possess "three nautical leagues," or about nine miles), which was conferred to the coastal states by the SLA.[7] The law confers state title to and ownership of "the lands beneath the navigable waters within the boundaries of the respective states and the natural resources within such lands and waters."[8] Therefore, in state territorial waters, the president may not have the authority to designate a national monument, at least unilaterally, without the cooperation and consent of the state.

As noted above, in 1988 the United States claimed its territorial sea through presidential proclamation. Beyond three miles to the limit of the territorial sea (twelve nautical miles), there are good arguments to be made regarding the applicability of the Antiquities Act. The 1988 proclamation contained a provision stating that "nothing in the Proclamation: (a) extends or otherwise alters existing Federal or State law or any jurisdiction, rights, legal interests, or obligations derived therefrom," suggesting that the extension to twelve miles was intended to apply for international purposes and not to interfere with domestic law. The use of the Antiquities Act in the contiguous zone and the EEZ, as Flynn concludes, "remains an unsettled issue" though a 1999 presidential proclamation claiming a U.S. contiguous zone also includes the provision that the declaration is not to amend or interfere with existing domestic legislation.[9] These provisions within the 1988 and 1999 proclamations create an opening for a creative argument that the Antiquities Act can be used in these areas.

"Where There's a Will ... "

Political support for marine protected areas ebbs and flows over time, and the tides of the desires, hopes, and dreams of the American people with regard to ocean and coastal conservation also change, although perhaps with a somewhat lesser amplitude.

Designation and management of protected areas requires substantial political will even when public support appears to be strong. Presidents who have been willing to use the Antiquities Act to designate national monuments have, on occasion, acted in the face of political opposition, opposition that is often spearheaded by groups who have a personal or financial stake in the area being protected, or simply by those who object to government intervention in management of the resources of the commons. Presidents who have exerted the political will to act in the face of such opposition seem to have history on their side. While Congress has spoken out in reaction to a president's use of his power to designate national monuments, only rarely has Congress abolished a monument.[10] Courts have had several opportunities to hold the Act invalid and have been deferential to the Executive's power to designate a monument established through the Antiquities Act. Upon several occasions courts found that the issue was actually a difference of opinion between Congress and the president and invited Congress to act upon the issue.[11] On one occasion a court has found the Act unconstitutionally vague; however, this opinion was addressing the criminal prosecution aspects of the Act.[12] The Supreme Court has upheld the ability of the president to create monuments of significant size and for diverse purposes, and sanctioned the presidential use of the Act to protect large landscapes as well as archaeological sites.[13]

Beyond Congress and the courts, there is the issue—perhaps the most important issue—of preserving ecosystem structure and function in the face of significant threats. Ecosystems can be irretrievably altered and resources depleted in a surprisingly short period of time. Precipitous declines in animal populations, in biodiversity, and in habitat integrity can occur in the time it takes to build the constituency of support, particularly local support, needed to generate the political will required to designate a protected area under most marine protected area authorities. In some cases, national marine sanctuary designations have taken more than five years just to get to the part of the designation process where a draft management plan is on the street for formal public review (largely because these processes are based on significant and intensive public involvement at all phases). The Antiquities Act authority, by virtue of the speed of its implementation, can be used to preserve threatened resources before an ecosystem is degraded to such a degree that recovery—if even possible—will take many years and require great sacrifices from those who rely on those areas for their livelihoods and recreation. The political will to move forward with a controversial proclamation of a national monument can buy time for building constituencies of support while ensuring that the ecosystem's structure and function are maintained.

Lessons Already Being Learned

Few would dispute that monuments proclaimed under the Antiquities Act are among the most treasured of our national park units and protected areas, and that they are the foundation of our modern system of national parks. Many of the original monuments have been subsequently converted into national parks by acts of Congress. It is this conversion of monuments that offers the opportunity for extensive stakeholder involvement, for the inclusive and transparent public process that was not conducted when the monument was proclaimed. Often, the most difficult step is getting the discussion on the table. The greatest potential value of creating a national monument in the ocean may be setting the stage and opening the door to a more open discussion, but making sure the resources of that area are preserved during the time needed to reach consensus on conservation goals and management strategies.

A current illustrative example, albeit one that ultimately did not involve the proclamation of a national monument, is the creation of the Northwestern Hawaiian Islands Coral Reef Ecosystem Reserve (NWHICRER).[14] In 2000 and 2001, during the closing days of the Clinton Administration, two executive orders (EOs) provided immediate protection for an area of nearly 100,000 square nautical miles, believed to contain more than 70% of the nation's coral reefs, along with native Hawaiian cultural resources of inestimable value and a predator-dominated ecosystem so unique that ecologists continue to find it difficult to understand how it operates (Figure 15.1). As Executive Order 13178 makes clear: "This is truly a unique and special place, a coral reef ecosystem like no place on earth, and a source of pride, inspiration, and satisfaction for all Americans, especially the people of Hawaii. It is fully worthy of our best efforts to preserve a legacy of America's natural wonders for future generations."

The executive orders establishing NWHICRER provide for "strong and lasting protection," but not through designation as a national monument. According to Matthew Chapman, "the use of an EO, rather than statutory tools like the Antiquities Act, was in a sense a compromise that sought to protect the unique resources while welcoming input from all affected stakeholders.... Clinton made extensive use of the Antiquities Act to designate significant portions of wilderness areas [sic] as national monuments. He was considering a similar designation for the Northwestern Hawaiian islands but chose instead to issue these EOs."[15]

There is little doubt that Clinton clearly understood the potential benefits and pitfalls of the application of the Antiquities Act, having used it so broadly, and some would say so effectively, on land. Chapman contends that the reason Clinton chose not to use the Antiquities Act for NWHICRER was to allow the agency with existing authority throughout the reserve area, the National Oceanic and Atmospheric Administration (NOAA), to continue to act as the lead agency. Had the president proclaimed the area a national monument, this would have made the Department of the Interior (DOI) the lead, and, perhaps more importantly, prohibited extractive uses throughout the reserve,[16] as occurred with designa-

Figure 15.1. A Hawaiian green sea turtle swims through the shallows at Mokumanamana in the Northwestern Hawaiian Islands. Ninety percent of all Hawaiian green sea turtles nest at French Frigate Shoals in the NWHICRER. Photograph courtesy of Andy Collins/NOAA NWHICRER.

tion of Virgin Islands Coral Reef National Monument. Given that commercial fishing was known to occur in the proposed reserve, such a prohibition would create immediate and significant opposition. Also, with DOI as the lead, the jurisdictional landscape would be significantly changed, and would perhaps overreach the expertise of DOI agencies who, although unquestionably the experts in terrestrial protected areas management, have limited (but growing) experience and expertise in protecting and managing ocean resources.

The executive order identified what was believed to be the most ecologically sensitive areas within the reserve and set them aside as reserve protection areas. The ban on extractive uses, including fishing, was limited to these areas, which accounted for a little less than 5% of the total reserve. The other major provision included in the executive orders directed NOAA to develop a reserve operations plan to guide interim management activities until such time as the area could be fully evaluated for designation as a sanctuary under the National Marine Sanctuary Act. By using the executive orders to provide interim protection for the area, a compromise was reached in that existing jurisdictional authorities were preserved, the most critical areas within the reserve were afforded interim protection, and the area would ultimately be reviewed under the very inclusive and transparent national marine sanctuary designation process. Time will tell whether the decision to use the executive order compromise approach in the NWHICRER was a better choice than invoking the Antiquities Act to protect this nationally significant and highly fragile ecosystem.

In Section 6(g) of the National Marine Sanctuary Amendments Act of 2000, Congress "authorized" President Clinton to create NWHICRER, and made clear its intent that the area be evaluated for designation as a national marine sanctuary. This provided a more solid statutory foundation to the executive order establishing the reserve but set conditions on how the designation process should proceed, requiring that the review be as open and transparent to the public as possible, including the establishment of a reserve advisory council. While Congress' intent in including this section in the amendments to the National Marine Sanctuary Act may have been to dissuade the president from using the Antiquities Act, which was one of the options being considered to preserve the northwest Hawaiian Islands,[17] there is no specific mention of any such intent

260 / Barr & Van Dine

in the *Congressional Record* passages documenting the debate on the bill in either the House (October 25, 2000) or the Senate October 17, 2000).

One downside to the approach used in the creation of NWHICRER is that executive orders are, as Chapman rightly points out, "ephemeral." Any new president can vacate an executive order from a previous administration the same way it was created—with a "stroke of the pen." Yet, an executive order related to a protected area designation is not really as easy to vacate as some others. Rarely can a new administration ignore the constituency of support that has developed, both in the public and within the implementing agency, particularly if the designation has been in place for any length of time and the protections have become institutionalized within the bureaucracy. Nonetheless, while an executive order can provide some interim resource protection and also direct that subsequent action be taken to evaluate the area under another marine protected area authority, the strength of proclamation as a national monument, where an actual law sustains the protection intended, offers better odds that the designation will become a legacy rather than a historical footnote.

The example of NWHICRER illustrates both the pitfalls and potential benefits of proclaiming national monuments in the ocean, as well as some interesting compromises and creative accommodations that could be used to address those pitfalls. The concern about jurisdiction is significant. There are legitimate legal issues related to the appropriate application of the Antiquities Act in various ocean areas such as state waters, territorial waters, the contiguous zone, and the EEZ. The language of "owned or controlled" in the Act will have to be clarified, perhaps through litigation or amendment of the Act establishing authorities for each of these zones. Creating administrative flexibility to designate the appropriate lead management agency is also important to make national monument designation a more useful tool in the ocean. As shown by the example of NWHICRER, putting DOI in the lead role in areas where NOAA agencies would normally have jurisdiction would complicate existing agency authorities and create confusion among users and stakeholders. The decision as to which agency can best lead should rest on judgments of who can most effectively manage and preserve these special ocean areas, based largely on agency expertise and existing jurisdictions. Both DOI and NOAA bring strengths, weaknesses, and expertise to the table. In the ocean realm, NOAA is the agency with the most experience, has the most extensive existing jurisdiction, and is arguably the most appropriate agency to be held accountable for effective management. However, the Antiquities Act does not currently allow NOAA to be given authority over national monuments, which arguably is the reason for the strategy adopted for NWHICRER. Where areas proposed for national monument designation are adjacent to islands or coastal areas that are, or could become, national parks or wildlife refuges, DOI might be better suited to take the lead managing role for the monument. While it may be most effective to vest management authority of an ocean monument jointly in NOAA and DOI through the National Park Service or the U.S. Fish and Wildlife Service, with both being equal partners, agency cultures have not yet evolved sufficiently to make such a collaboration work effectively.

The ocean is, for better and worse, widely exploited for its living and non-living resources. If an area is not being actively used, the fact that it could be exploited sometime in the future is, to some, a compelling reason to keep it in the commons and as unregulated as possible. Again, the freedom of the seas is a deeply held conviction for many in coastal communities. Users and potential users—as differentiated from members of the "general public" who rarely get involved in these discussions but are stakeholders nonetheless—are likely to be the most vocal, as well as politically active. Pressure from opponents may keep the protection of some areas from even getting put on the table for discussion. The great promise of the Antiquities Act for ocean areas is that a visionary president can jump-start the dialogue and define the rules of the game, similar to what President Clinton did with the NWHICRER executive orders, and not have to accept the potential sacrifice of imperiled resources to the "too little, too late" syndrome in order to get the job done.

Beyond the Horizon

The Antiquities Act is part of the rich conservation history of this country, a tool of bold and visionary leaders. While perhaps controversial in the short term, a national monument proclamation can provide protection while it opens doors to more collaborative and consensus-based processes, building (or perhaps rebuilding) essential community support. It is important that the Antiquities Act be there when a visionary leader wants to use it. The jurisdictional questions are the greatest potential liability, but bold and visionary leaders are rarely constrained by "gray areas," where legal issues can be overcome by broad interpretation of authorities. If Teddy Roosevelt was able to use a statute that protects "objects" of "scientific interest" to preserve the Grand Canyon, who can tell what lies ahead?

The views expressed here are those of the authors and do not necessarily reflect the views of the Department of Commerce, NOAA, or any of its sub-agencies.

Notes

1. National Park Service, "Antiquities Act of 1906," on-line at www.cr.nps.gov/history/hisnps/NPSHistory/antiq.htm.

2. See the Appendix to this volume.

3. Channel Islands: Proclamation no. 2281, 52 Stat. 1541 (April 26, 1938); enlargement, Proclamation no. 2825, 63 Stat. 1258 (February 9, 1949). Santa Rosa Island: Proclamation no. 2337, 3 CFR 88 (1938). Buck Island Reef: Proclamation no. 3443, 3 CFR 152 (1961). California Coastal: Proclamation no. 7264, 65 *Federal Register* 2821 (January 11, 2000). Virgin Islands Coral Reef: Proclamation no. 7399, 66 *Federal Register* 7364 (January 17, 2001).

4. Ranchod 2001.

5. Proclamation no. 7392, 66 *Federal Register* 7335 (January 17, 2001).

6. Flynn 2004.

7. Federal Submerged Lands Act of 1956, 43 U.S.C. secs. 1301–1303, 1311–1315.

8. Flynn 2004.

9. "Territorial Sea of the United States of America," Proclamation no. 5928, 54 *Federal Register* 777 (December 27, 1988); "Contiguous Zone of the United States," Proclamation no. 7219, 64 *Federal Register* 48701 (August 2, 1999).

10. The Appendix to this volume lists all the abolished monuments.

11. *Wyoming v. Franke,* 58 F.Supp. 890 (D. Wyo. 1945); *Alaska v. Carter,* 462 F.Supp. 1155 (D. Alaska 1978); *Anaconda Copper Co. v. Andrus,* 14 Env't Rep. Cas. (BNA) 1853 (D. Alaska 1980).

12. *U.S. v. Diaz,* 499 F.2d 113 (9th Cir. 1974). See also the chapters by McManamon and Watkins in this volume.

13. *Cameron v. United States,* 252 U.S. 450 (1920); *Cappaert v. United States,* 426 U.S. 128 (1976); *Alaska v. Carter,* 462 F.Supp. 1157.

14. "Northwestern Hawaiian Islands Coral Reef Ecosystem Reserve," Executive Order 13178, December 4, 2000; "Final Northwestern Hawaiian

Islands Coral Reef Ecosystem Reserve," Executive Order 13196, January 18, 2001.

15. Chapman 2002.
16. Chapman 2002.
17. Chapman 2002.

Part 5

The Act's First Century

An Assessment

The Antiquities Act
A Cornerstone of Archaeology,
Historic Preservation, and Conservation

David Harmon, Francis P. McManamon, and
Dwight T. Pitcaithley

IN MANY WAYS, the central story of the Antiquities Act revolves around intentions. What did the architects of the Act intend? A series of tiny sites protecting well-defined archeological and natural curiosities, covering the smallest possible area? Or did they truly mean to give the president more leeway? If they did mean to do that, have subsequent presidents stretched the original intent beyond all reasonable recognition? And how does one explain the fact that presidents as different as the imperial Theodore Roosevelt and the crabbed Calvin Coolidge have nevertheless used the Act to remarkably similar ends? In the years since its passage, the federal courts have found in the language of the Act sufficient justification for the broader, Rooseveltian interpretation. Moreover, the range of opinions expressed by proponents of one or another version of the legislation put forward between 1900 and 1906 included broad as well as narrow perspectives. These questions of motivation and meaning are what make the history of the Antiquities Act so fascinating.

To answer those questions, one must first understand where the law came from and why it took the form that it did. The Antiquities Act is very much a product of its time, the direct result of two streams of angst whose headwaters are to be found in the specific conditions that prevailed at that particular moment in history. As the nineteenth century wound down, civic-minded elites woke up to the disturbing fact that America was finite. The image of the endlessly expanding, always beckoning frontier, so important to the doctrine of Euroamerican expansionism, had been abruptly erased by the historian Frederick Jackson Turner in his famous 1893 paper "The Significance of the Frontier in American History." Turner's decisive pronouncement that the American frontier was now closed underscored what had become apparent to many during the previous decade—that the great open landscapes of the West were filling up with settlers or increasingly coming under the control of land speculators. The critical mythic spaces occupying the very heart of the national unification story were rapidly being piecemealed into a motley assortment of private uses.

Congress already had preserved several outstanding examples of the American landscape and cultural heritage by creating national parks or reservations at Yellowstone, Mackinac Island (later transferred to the control of the state of Michigan), Casa Grande Ruin (between Tucson and Phoenix in Arizona), Sequoia, General Grant, and Yosemite (the last three all in California's Sierra Nevada).[1] In this context, handing the president broad power to reserve parts of those landscapes for continuing public benefit and edification was an act of nation-building.

At the same time, mounting reports of settlers, curiosity seekers, newfangled tourists, and profiteers ransacking southwestern archaeological sites for building materials, curios, or treasures did not comport well with the received notion of an America based on justice and probity. As Ronald F. Lee notes in his chapter, the elite opinion leaders were no doubt dismayed that the destruction was truly a democratic activity, carried on by everyone from illiterate cowboys to some of their rival eastern establishment institutions and Ivy League colleagues bending to demands for artifacts to display and exhibit in universities and museums. It made sense for these influential people to support a law whereby the president could, with a stroke of his pen, put a halt to the unseemly business in certain select places.

Yet all was not straightforward and simple in finding support for the Antiquities Act. Rising local and regional elites in the Southwest and West sometimes resented eastern scholars poaching on their archaeological sites. Even within the national government, the General Land Office of the Department of the Interior and the Smithsonian Institution jousted over which should be responsible for archaeological sites on public lands.[2] The overall objective of protecting archaeological sites from looting, and preserving them until they could be investigated using the newly emerging scientific methods and techniques of archaeology, was agreed to by the Act's proponents. By contrast, who would oversee the protection, and perhaps more to the point, who would regulate the subsequent investigations, was vigorously disputed. These concerns and disputes, of course, fit into the broad context of American nationalism, the rise of the Progressive political movement, the emergence of government programs to force the assimilation of American Indians into mainstream society, and parallel efforts to record Native American traditions before they disappeared.[3]

For some, preserving archaeological ruins[4] was a subtle but tangible reminder of who the conquerors were, of whose civilization had "won" the West. Newly anointed, these national monuments spoke to the supposed demise of Native American civilization while at the same time proclaiming the permanence and benevolence of the power emanating from Washington.

Many factors contributed to the impetus behind the Antiquities Act. The storied elements of the American nation were both natural, in the form of supposedly untouched wilderness landscapes,[5] and cultural, in the vestiges of the country's ancient past. In his contribution to this book, Char Miller makes the insightful observation that creating national monuments is a type of civic consecration: "Through a secular legislative act, the nation-state, at Devils Tower and elsewhere, created a new kind of sacred space—national in name, sweep, and scope...." It is by these means that the Antiquities Act, in subtle but deeply permeating ways, shored up key parts of the dominant unifying narrative the federal government wished to tell.

Understanding this helps to explain the motivations of the two men most responsible for maneuvering the law into its final form: Edgar Lee Hewett and John Fletcher Lacey. They invested themselves in the effort to pass the Antiquities Act because they shared the concern for, and assumptions behind, the nation-building ideal. But each had his own personal reasons as well.

At the beginning of the twentieth century, Hewett was a man determined to make a mark, both scholarly and politically, on the fledgling profession of American archaeology. He also was a booster of the American Southwest and West who sought to balance the cultural and educational dominance of the eastern elite with a regional perspective. But what Raymond Harris Thompson also brings out in his profile is a less obvious point: Hewett's was a politics of place, grounded in his love for the Pajarito Plateau and northern New Mexico, a landscape that combined both of the mythic elements described above. As Thompson pinpoints, Hewett was operating on the principle that "the federal government has a statutory responsibility for the archaeological resources on the land it owns or controls." This notion of stewardship became the foundation for the profession, the bedrock to which all archaeology on public lands is anchored.

Although Hewett was personally interested primarily in archaeology, because he had imbibed the New Mexican landscape he readily saw the political—and symbolic—advantages of including the protection of "objects of scientific interest" alongside that of archaeological sites. The language of the Antiquities Act is a hybrid of natural and cultural concerns not because of ineptitude, but because of Hewett's perception that the competing interests among government agencies and the scientific community could be reconciled, along with his political skills in executing a compromise. As Thompson describes in his chapter, Hewett grasped the basic problem: the rivalry between the Department of the Interior, which wanted a means to create national parks and control the protection of archaeological sites on public lands, and the Smithsonian Institution, which wanted to control the investigation of archaeological sites. It was Hewett who recognized that their "dueling bills" strategy was going nowhere. Most important of all, it was he who understood that the two approaches could best be reconciled in one piece of legislation, and that the way to get it passed was by coming up with carefully phrased, low-key wording palatable to a Congress that was no doubt weary of the topic and wished to dispose of it as quickly and non-controversially as possible.

John F. Lacey's personal motivations, though certainly more obscure, seem to have been very different. Unlike Hewett, Lacey was incapable of falling in love with a landscape. His approach to life was cerebral: when confronted with something new, rather than assimilating it emotionally he focused all his concentration on it, framing it as a problem or an issue, studying it until he satisfied himself that he owned it. His mind was essentially acquisitive. And intense: Lacey was a man who, as a soldier, prided himself on being able to read a dry-as-dust legal treatise while siege guns roared around him. The picture Rebecca Conard paints is of a man who placed a premium on self-mastery. She was challenged to be able to paint anything at all, given the reticence of Lacey's personal papers. This reluctance to speak from the heart, even in private letters, only serves to reinforce the image of Lacey as iron-willed and rather ascetic. Then too, he was politically ambitious in ways that Hewett was not.

Lacey's Civil War experience forged in him a deep sense of duty to country, and it is here that we find the roots of his interest in conservation. Whether it was his support of the Yellowstone Protection Act and of President Cleveland's use of the forest reserve act, his own work on the migratory wildlife law that carries his name, or his ushering of the Antiquities Act through Congress, Lacey was driven by a belief that good government—meaning impartial, factually informed government—was needed to keep the appalling extremes of human behavior in check. The government, in essence, had to step in and impose order on people who, unlike himself, were unable to master their own worst tendencies.

Once the antiquities bill was passed, it had to be enacted, and the mantle of leadership passed from Hewett and Lacey to Theodore Roosevelt. Like Lacey, TR placed a high value on self-control and determination. Indeed, some of his most famous exploits were, in their way, exercises in will: one thinks of him sojourning in the North Dakota badlands in the 1880s, leading the charge up San Juan Hill in 1898, finishing a speech after an assassination attempt in 1912. Furthermore, as Miller highlights in his chapter, Roosevelt was a Progressive who "believed deeply in the capacity of government to mold the commonweal, present and future." He shared this Progressive philosophy with both Lacey and Hewett, and it is the common thread that binds their disparate personalities together. Roosevelt, of course, was a much larger performer performing on a much larger stage, but the Progressive kinship among the three central figures of the Act's passage—which was endorsed and shared by a majority of Congress and by key administrators at the Department of the Interior, such as W. A. Richards, commissioner of the General Land Office—informed the very nature of the law. Simply put, at the time of the Act's passage in June 1906 the key people in Washington believed in the Progressive vision of a technocratically competent, paternalistically beneficent government whose expertise would be placed at the service of (what were assumed to be) common ideals. Under those assumptions, it makes perfect sense to give the president broad power to proclaim national monuments. After all, he will be acting on expert recommendations that, precisely because they are expert, must by definition produce the best possible result. That logic carried the day. Outside of politicians and communities in the West whose commercial interests were the most likely to be affected by monument proclamations, few had philosophical qualms about it.

This review leads us to the conclusion that the language of the Antiquities Act was carefully chosen by ideologically informed men who were deeply concerned that an old order was passing away and wanted to do something about it. Hewett, Lacey, and others who contributed to the drafts of bills that became the final text of the Act had a clear vision about what kind of power should be vested in the president, and they thought that bestowing such power was a good thing. They shared an understanding of the cultural, educational, and historic values of archaeological, natural, and scientific resources and an agreement that these should be publicly protected and their use regulated. Western congressional interests were in dissent, and that dissent is reflected in the language referring to the "smallest area compatible with proper care and management of the objects to be protected." But the majority of Congress acceded to Hewett and Lacey's Progressive vision. Had Congress wanted to, it could have endorsed earlier antiquities bills that limited monuments to a few hundred acres; it did not. Even though Lacey himself promised western representatives that the Act would not be used to "lock up" large areas, the House and Senate knew exactly what sort of a man they were about to hand over these powers to. Unless they were incredibly naïve they also must have known what use he would likely make of them. Roosevelt's bully-pulpit track record was there for all to see, as was his keen interest in conservation. It cannot have come as a shock to any member of Congress when, in December 1906, TR declared the first large natural national monument, Petrified Forest, nor even when he outdid that by more than tenfold with an 800,000-acre Grand Canyon proclamation some thirteen months later.

In summary, the main cultural components of the Antiquities Act were a broad-based anxiety over the loss of key mythic elements of the putative national narrative, fused with a Progressive conviction in the ability of government to identify and maintain a commonweal. The result was a law uneasily embedded in a mixture of paradox and irony. Paradox, because the Antiquities Act was seen by its framers as an instrument to promote a unified citizenry, a cohesive nation-state, even though its methods were sure to alienate people (mostly in the West) whose economic aspirations were curtailed by new monument proclamations. Irony, because while both the eastern supporters of the Act and the western opponents of it were conscious of the passing away of a desirable old order, they seemed to be unaware that their visions of this order were not only very different, but in large part mutually exclusive.

The West's alienation from the Act disposed itself in legal flare-ups over the Mount Olympus and Grand Canyon proclamations, and discontent rose again in 1943 with the legal challenges posed by the Jackson Hole case. Progressivism had passed from the scene, driven from the field by the disillusionments of World War I and the Great Depression, but paternalism of a different sort was still very much in evidence. Looming metaphorically above the Tetons was the figure of an actual flesh-and-blood paterfamilias, an ultra-rich easterner—and hence an outsider both socioeconomically and geographically—who was hoarding most of the land down in the valley because he was certain its highest and best use was as part of the national park system. There can be little doubt that resentment of John D. Rockefeller, Jr., played an important role in Wyoming's decision to challenge Franklin D. Roosevelt's Jackson Hole monument proclamation: the lawsuit may have been filed against the Park Service, but in the minds of many locals the great magnate was an unindicted co-conspirator. The social and economic disparities of the two sides are a virtual subtext to Hal Rothman's account of the controversy. In his summing-up, Rothman gets right to the heart of the matter: this was an early battle between the Old West of resource extraction and the New West of services and tourism.

In seeking the Rockefeller lands for the new monument, the Park Service was looking to garner a complete range of life zones from the high peaks of the Grand Tetons down to and across the valley floor—a valley which included much valuable ranchland. That was the crux of the issue. Although Wyoming argued that its sovereignty had been traduced and the Park Service had not properly identified scientific or historic objects that would justify the monument, the real reason for the outcry was that tax revenues, grazing fees, and potentially developable land would be lost. However, these objections would not (and probably could not) be adjudicated. The Park Service mounted a typical legal defense, first trying to get the suit summarily dismissed on procedural grounds and then, after that failed, enlisting expert witnesses to testify at trial to the monument's ecological and historic importance. The trial judge, as so often happens, ended up dismissing the lawsuit for technical reasons and did not even rule on the merits of the proclamation. In terms of clarifying the limits of presidential authority under the Act, the lawsuit accomplished nothing, though some years later it did induce the government to negotiate away the president's authority to use the Act in Wyoming as a way to get the delegation's support for incorporating most of Jackson Hole National Monument into Grand Teton National Park.

Had Congress been compelled to seek similar quid pro quos elsewhere, the landscape of the West would look very different today, and nowhere more so than in Alaska. The unique circumstances surrounding the disposition of Alaska's public domain came to a head in the late 1970s, and the problem of what to do landed on the desk of Secretary of the Interior Cecil D. Andrus. In his account of the Carter monument proclamations (written in collaboration with his colleague John C. Freemuth), Andrus leaves no doubt as to his convictions on the matter. He was absolutely convinced then that using the Antiquities Act to secure protection of the so-called (d)(2) lands was right and necessary, and he and Freemuth remain convinced now. While Andrus and the rest of the Carter administration faced a definite precipice in the form of a pending expiration of the (d)(2) moratorium, their response was anything but precipitate. Carter's proclamations of December 1, 1978, were preceded by years of research and analysis, as well as extensive negotiations through various congressional channels. Alternatives to the use of the Antiquities Act, such as withdrawals under the Federal Land Policy and Management Act (FLPMA), were considered. Finally, when it looked as though the whole process was about to go over the cliff, Andrus advised Carter to act.

Yet both men knew that the proclamations were not the end of the story. They recognized that Antiquities Act designations were too inflexible to allow for the "subtle shades of management regimes" that would be desirable in Alaska. Although the Carter proclamations were vilified by critics as cramming a one-size-fits-all federalism down the throats of Alaskans, in truth they were a conscious tactic to get negotiations into an end game by removing any further incentives to stall. They produced exactly this effect, and in two years almost all the newly created national monuments were redeployed into other designations. Many went into a new status of "national park and preserve" in which the national park portion is open to traditional subsistence activities, while the national preserve portion is open to sport hunting and trapping, under federal regulation.[6] It is also worth noting, in case one is inclined to frame this issue in a partisan way, that the Democrat Andrus was working within a framework of withdrawals established by his Republican predecessor in the Nixon administration, Rogers C. B. Morton. Furthermore, one of the main opponents of the Carter proclamations was Alaska Senator Mike Gravel, a Democrat.

Accusations of partisan politics resurfaced again—with a vengeance—in 1996. There is no question that proclaiming Grand Staircase–Escalante National Monument was a calculated election-year move by President Bill Clinton, one sure to win him favor nationally while costing him nothing in the electoral college, since Utah was irretrievably Republican. But, as Mark Squillace goes on to explain in his chapter, Clinton's second-term proclamations were not only politically astute, but strategic in a different way: they were based on carefully crafted and ecologically significant recommendations by Secretary of the Interior Bruce Babbitt. Not only did Babbitt offer to visit potential new monuments and meet with the local congressional delegation before making a recommendation to the president—discussions that often sparked changes in the monument proposal—he also encouraged delegations to preempt the process by developing their own alternative plans for protecting areas that were under consideration as potential monuments. "This last concession resulted in legislation protecting several remarkable areas that would not likely have received congressional attention without indications from the secretary that these areas were being considered for national monument status," notes Squillace. By allowing local interests the leeway to develop their own protection strategies for these lands, presumably the results would be more in tune with their needs and desires than a monument designation.

Babbitt was painted as an uncompromising ideologue by his opponents, but Squillace details just how much he was concerned with accommodating local objections and certain commercial requests (such as for utility rights of way across Sonoran Desert National Monument). Nor was Babbitt interested in exposing the Antiquities Act to possible amendment or repeal by recklessly using it—which may be why he did not push Clinton to proclaim the Arctic National Wildlife Refuge as a national monument. In light of continued attempts to open portions of the refuge to oil drilling, environmentalists may well point to Babbitt's decision (and that of Andrus before him) as a matter of deep regret, although the additional protections monument status would have added may not be enough to prevent Congress from authorizing drilling anyway.

However much Babbitt and Clinton were willing to voluntarily engage with local opponents of monuments, they were not ready to support proposals to amend the Act to require public consultations before proclamations are made. This brings up a fundamental issue of fairness, the analysis of which is the crux of James R. Rasband's contribution to the book. It is not enough, he argues, for the monuments to have achieved—as virtually all of them have—widespread *ex post facto* acceptance, even among former local opponents. No matter how overwhelmingly positive the Act's accomplishments, Rasband says, the process by which they were achieved is deeply, perhaps fatally, flawed because it is undemocratic and therefore runs counter to the entire basis of American government, which is founded on the free consent of an informed citizenry. This is a serious criticism, and cannot be ignored.

Rasband is not denying that the Act has been beneficial; for him, "the critical question is whether the same or similar results could be achieved by a process that does not so thoroughly disregard the input and interests of rural communities and state and local governments." He thinks they could, and he wants to see an amendment to the Act requiring local consultation and impact studies prior to proclamation. He goes on to rebut a number of arguments that are often made against amending the Act, pointing out that the Federal Land Policy and Management Act can now be used to achieve many of the same goals. For Rasband, FLPMA has rendered the Antiquities Act largely (though not completely) superfluous. He closes his argument by asking whether the paternalistic decision-making structure of the Act—what he calls "conquest by certitude," borrowing a phrase from Charles Wilkinson—is really appropriate today, particularly given the fact that public participation and impact studies are so firmly enshrined in the rest of natural resources law.

On purely ethical grounds it really is difficult to disagree with Rasband, and he may be right that FLPMA can substitute for the

Antiquities Act in many cases. Even so, several counterarguments can be made. One is based on the assumption that sometimes, even in a democracy, it is good for the president to be able to make unilateral decisions on crucial issues. At the risk of drawing disproportionate parallels, think of the leeway given to the president in setting foreign policy, or in nominating members of the cabinet. While these are subject to some measure of congressional oversight and even formal approval, by custom the president is usually allowed to exercise strong leadership in these realms. This is so precisely because the potential for paralyzing fractiousness is so high under any other scenario. One could plausibly argue that conservation policy, with respect to the management of public lands, is a like category, both in terms of its momentousness and the potential for decision-making to become mired in the quicksand of partisan politics. The story told by Andrus and Freemuth about the Carter monuments is a case in point. Furthermore, the special nature of land withdrawals tends to pit local interests against national ones, and to the extent that members of Congress are reluctant to override objections to a proposed withdrawal from the delegation of the state involved, the process is hog-tied. If that is considered undesirable, then it is a good thing for the president to be able to cut this Gordian Knot using the power bestowed by the Antiquities Act.

Part of Rasband's argument is that the ends do not justify the means, and that the process of the Act does not live up to the wilderness ideals that its resulting monuments promote. Yet one can respond that the quality of the ends achieved is, in fact, important to consider. Moreover, wilderness values are not the only ones being protected by large natural-area monuments. David Harmon brings out both these points in his chapter. Arguing from the concept of ecological significance, he shows how the monuments variously exemplify rarity, superlativeness, representivity, and ecological integrity. The full worth of these qualities emerges only when placed in a larger systems context. For example, the features preserved in the geological and cave monuments are interesting in themselves, but they disclose added value when considered as contributors to worldwide geodiversity. Similarly, individual World Heritage sites are spectacular places to visit, yet their importance truly blossoms only when they are understood as parts of a global system of recognition of places of outstanding universal value. The same holds for monuments as components of ecoregional representivity schemes and as units in a network monitoring the "Vital Signs" of ecological integrity. In all these areas the Act has made crucial contributions to the evolving practice of nature conservation.

Another argument against amending the Act is that its most recent uses *are* more flexible and more cognizant of local interests— that application of the law is evolving to meet new needs and desires. The three chapters exploring "New Horizons for the Act" all testify to this. As told by Elena Daly and Geoffrey B. Middaugh, the Bureau of Land Management's new National Landscape Conservation System is positioning itself to become a systematic exemplar of the "new paradigm" of protected areas. A major shift in conservation theory, the new paradigm holds that the future expansion of protected areas will come less and less from new Yellowstone-model exclusionary parks and more and more from protected landscapes and managed resource extraction areas.[7] These are essentially multiple-use areas with a stronger preservationist/protectionist management overlay than that found on lands as traditionally managed by the BLM. Whether the bureau can make the new paradigm work in an American political context, and whether it can establish a true distinction between its new monuments and other BLM lands, remains to be seen. But clearly, armed now with an organic act (FLPMA, passed in 1976) and charged with a newfound mission of creating a different kind of national monument, the BLM is poised to transcend its lineage as the bureau in charge of the leftover lands nobody wanted.[8]

The BLM has also been given the task of co-managing two new national monuments along with the National Park Service (NPS). The field report from one of them, Grand Canyon–Parashant National Monument, is largely a story of the difficulties in getting two very different agency cultures to mesh. The authors, Parashant co-superintendents Darla Sidles (NPS) and Dennis Curtis (BLM), candidly admit that many field staff from both sides looked at co-management as the bureaucratic equivalent of a shotgun wedding. Indeed, the first organizational structure for Parashant did not work and had to be replaced. But persistence is beginning to pay off: Sidles and Curtis give us a supervisor's-eye view of how the monument is drawing from both BLM and NPS policies and practices to come up with innovations in such basic park functions as signage, interpretive planning, vehicle use management, and more. Parashant is an unfinished experiment, but that is precisely the point: there is nothing in the Antiquities Act that prohibits flexibility in how protection is achieved, or by whom. While most monuments are still under the exclusive jurisdiction of the National Park Service, thanks to the Carter and Clinton proclamations several are now managed or co-managed by the BLM, U.S. Forest Service, U.S. Fish and Wildlife Service, and, in one instance, the Armed Forces Retirement Home. We can expect that as these new monuments mature, the respective managing agencies will place their own stamp on them.[9] It is even conceivable that we will see new national monuments that are co-managed by one or more federal partners in concert with nonfederal entities, such as tribal, state, or local governments, or with nonprofit organizations.

We might also witness the application of the Antiquities Act to an entirely new frontier: the oceans. Conservation of the sea is fundamentally different from that on land, for a variety of biophysical, ecological, political, social, and legal reasons. Brad Barr and Katrina Van Dine endorse the notion that tools such as the Act need to be available to visionary leaders so that they may look beyond the concerns of the moment to the needs of future generations, especially in the ocean realm. Marine ecosystems can be irreparably damaged in a surprisingly short time. The conventional course toward designating a new national marine sanctuary can takes years because of public involvement requirements—during which lag time fisheries can collapse, seabeds may be devastated by bottom-trawling, and ecosystem structure can be seriously compromised. The authors observe that "the political will to move forward with a controversial proclamation of a national monument can buy time for building constituencies of support" while simultaneously safeguarding marine ecosystems. Used strategically, Barr and Van Dine conclude, the Antiquities Act "has the potential to accomplish what may be considerably more difficult to do without it, and offers more certainty that effective protection will be achieved."

In assessing the overall value of the Act, we must emphasize again that it is about more than just national monuments. The chapters by Francis P. McManamon, Jerry L. Rogers, and Joe E. Watkins establish the indisputable importance of the Act to the development of archaeology and historic preservation in America. McManamon makes the critical point that there was nothing foreordained about the basic policies governing the public interest in archaeological sites—as he puts it, "the need for well-qualified indi-

viduals with sufficient institutional support to conduct archaeological investigations, and the fundamental commemorative, educational, and scientific values of archaeological resources." We take
these for granted today, but in 1906 Congress could just as well have
"solved" the looting problem by adopting a less comprehensive,
more commercially oriented approach that emphasized recovery
and display, or even the sale, of individual items rather than preservation of whole sites in context. Congress could have ignored the
requirement for careful recording, analysis, and reporting as essential elements of archaeological investigations and overlooked the
requirement of public interpretation and stewardship of collected
artifacts and data. In 1906 it would have been a defensible position
to take; after all, American archaeology was in its infancy and had
no long-standing tradition of professional standards. As we can
clearly see now, that would have been a far less satisfactory solution.
Beyond this, McManamon sees a vigorous legal lineage extending
from the Antiquities Act through later federal historic preservation
law. However, as he goes on to point out, several court cases in the
1970s deemed the Act too vague to be used to prosecute criminal
looting. To remedy this, Congress could have amended the Act.
Significantly, it chose to leave the venerable law intact, instead passing a new, targeted statute, the Archaeological Resources Protection
Act of 1979.

Watkins provides a different perspective on the Act. He associates it with the federal government's campaign to make American
Indians disappear, both physically (through military action) and
culturally (by "de-Indianizing" them). After all, during the Act's
formative years economic, social, and political tensions also produced the Wounded Knee massacre, the expropriation of American
Indian lands by the Jerome and Dawes Commissions, and the
destruction of tribal sovereignty by the Curtis Act, although there
are no direct contemporary links between the Act and these tragic
events. The Antiquities Act, in recognizing the developing professionalism in American archaeology, privileged archaeologists, historians, and scientists, putting American Indian objects and sites, as
well as their interpretation in the public domain, under the control
of non-Indian experts in museums and universities. Unfortunately,
the experts too often reduced Native American cultures, and to
some degree Indian people themselves, to the status of data to be
described, organized, and salvaged before they disappeared. Then

too, some of the natural-area national monuments proclaimed under the Act also subverted Indian culture by disregarding their status as sacred sites. Watkins concludes that "in some ways the Antiquities Act of 1906 can be seen to be a continuation of government policies that were aimed at erasing the image of the contemporary American Indian from the landscape in favor of the 'dead and disappearing culture' destined to exist only in museums or to be engulfed in mainstream America." Yet he too acknowledges the Act as the direct ancestor of newer laws that have given rise to, among other things, a burgeoning number of autonomous tribal historic preservation offices.

Like McManamon and Watkins, in his chapter Rogers also traces the source of systematic historic preservation back to 1906 and the Antiquities Act, which, along with the Historic Sites Act of 1935 and the National Historic Preservation Act of 1966, "launched a national idea of historic preservation." In addition, these laws "consolidated federal leadership of the field in the National Park Service, and spread their effects throughout an amazingly extensive and effective network in the United States." Importantly, he also emphasizes how the field of historic preservation, like that of nature conservation, is not remaining static. Innovations in identifying intangible cultural heritage and protecting cultural landscapes—which draw from some of the same ideas as does the "new paradigm" of protected areas—challenge the National Park Service and other monument-managing agencies in ways not seen before. Rogers specifically calls on the Park Service to abandon its bunker mentality with respect to the Clinton-era monuments assigned to other agencies. Rather, NPS should try to constructively influence the others' management standards and philosophies. Doing so calls for a "bold leadership posture" that risks "the security of past gains for the possibility of greater future gains." Here again we see the effects of the Antiquities Act playing out in fresh and unexpected ways.

What, then, can we conclude about this remarkable law—still so controversial a hundred years after its passage? To some, it has been a callous abuse of presidential power; to others, a triumph of presidential vision. To American Indians, it has had a unique and often troubling meaning. The most basic question, however, is this: Is the Antiquities Act a bad law, or a good law?

One way to answer that question is to pose some others: think of what the American landscape would look like today had the Act never been passed. Would anything at all be left of Chaco, Wupatki, Bandelier, and a host of other pre-Columbian sites in the Southwest? Would the irreplaceable earthworks of Effigy Mounds or Hopewell Culture still be intact? Would the shorelines of Acadia and Olympic have long since been sold off for vacation homes? Would the public be able to enjoy the fantastic landscapes and rock formations of Arches, Zion, Bryce Canyon, Capitol Reef, or Rainbow Bridge? Would the Grand Canyon be bordered by rim-side trophy houses of the rich and shot through with private trails, toll roads, and spurious mine claims? Would we have preserved such ecologically important (but less obviously scenic) places as Joshua Tree, Saguaro, and Organ Pipe Cactus? Or the paleontological treasures of Dinosaur? Would we have missed out on preserving Edison's laboratory, the historic towpaths along the Potomac at C&O Canal, and the Japanese-American internment camp at Minidoka? What would have become of Katmai—the fabled Valley of Ten Thousand Smokes? of Glacier Bay? of Wrangell–St. Elias and tens of millions of other acres of public land in Alaska?

The Antiquities Act, like other legal landmarks of American archaeology, historic preservation, and nature conservation, is the product of intentions and actions that don't always measure up to, and sometimes contradict, our stated national ideals. But the conservation of the country's natural and cultural heritage always has been a work in progress. It must continue to be, for it is a job that by its very character can never be finished. Effective conservation requires constant self-evaluation and a willingness to accept criticism. It is important, therefore, to honestly criticize the Antiquities Act for failing to achieve a better record in fostering democratic participation in decision-making, for not going about the protection of "objects of historic and scientific interest" in a more systematic manner, for contributing to the "Imperial Presidency," for failing to adequately acknowledge the interests of local communities, for helping to dispossess Native Americans of their past. Important to criticize, and seek to improve—but not to condemn. For if we insist on holding the Act to an impossibly high standard, and are willing to seriously weaken or even annul it on these grounds, we must be prepared to do the same for a great many other laws whose effects reach into every corner of American life.

A more judicious approach is to assess, to the best of our ability, whether the benefits of the Act have outweighed the drawbacks. As just noted, this assessment must forever be provisional, always remaining subject to periodic re-evaluation in the light of new facts and new sensibilities. All we can do is pass interim judgment from a particular point in time. From where we sit in 2006, our judgment is that, on balance, the Antiquities Act has served this country very well. An America without the Antiquities Act would be one with a much shallower perspective on the past. It would have far less capacity to correct this problem, for it would lack the professional cultural heritage expertise necessary to do so. It would be much less beautiful, with much less ecological integrity. It would be far more commercial, and burdened with a meaner civic spirit.

When the Act was passed in 1906, the clock was running down on the first, expansionist phase of American history. Now, a hundred years later, a momentous century looms ahead. It may yet prove to be a Century of Limits, whose main challenges will involve a downward adjustment of expectations. The world is becoming evermore crowded with people, and pressures on archaeological sites, historic resources, and the few remaining natural areas are only becoming more dire. With isolationism becoming less and less viable, the need for citizens to appreciate and value the full diversity of the American past, and of the people (both ancient and modern) who contributed to it, has never been greater. The protections realized by the Antiquities Act have left us in a much better position to deal with these challenges. Over the past century, more inclusive ideals and new ways of thinking have exposed many flaws in the foundations of American archaeology, historic preservation, and nature conservation, flaws that must be accounted for and fixed if at all possible. Yet the edifice that stands on the foundation, the legal framework that protects and helps us understand America's natural and cultural heritage, is indispensable. The Antiquities Act, for all its own flaws, is a cornerstone of that structure. That is reason enough to celebrate its first hundred years of achievement and to look forward to new and innovative uses being made of it in the century to come.

Notes

1. NPS 2005.
2. See the chapter by Lee in this volume; Snead 2001; and *Preservation of Historic and Prehistoric Ruins, Etc.,* hearing before the Subcommittee of the

Committee on Public Lands, April 20, 1904, Senate Document no. 314, 58th Cong., 2nd Sess.

3. Hays 1959; Limerick 1987; McManamon 2003.

4. As Native Americans now point out, the use of the term "ruins" (along with other common descriptors of ancestral sites, such as "abandoned") implies that these ancient ancestral sites are no longer of any value, when in fact they are often still part of a tribe's living traditions. For a discussion, see Salazar-Halfmoon 2006.

5. Several recent studies have made the point that landscapes had to be de-inhabited, stripped of their Native American cultural associations, before they could be reconstructed as being purely natural and then transformed into national parks; see Catton 1997; Keller and Turek 1998; Spence 1999.

6. Norris 2004.

7. Categories V and VI, respectively, in the IUCN international category system. The new paradigm has roots in, among other things, the British conception of national parks, international work in cultural landscapes, and interdisciplinary theories of "sense of place." In international protected area work, the new paradigm is gaining in influence. For an introduction, see Phillips 2003. For protected landscapes and category VI areas generally, see Brown et al. 2005.

8. The role of the BLM's predecessor, the General Land Office (GLO), is an interesting side story to all of this. As Daly and Middaugh note, the GLO can hardly claim a stellar record for good government, nor was it ever consistently a conservation leader among federal agencies. Nonetheless, a good deal of credit has to be given to the two GLO commissioners active just before the passage of the Antiquities Act, Binger Hermann and W. A. Richards, for proactively withdrawing several key areas pending permanent preservation, among them Mesa Verde (which was made a national park by congressional legislation three weeks after the Act was passed) and Chaco Canyon. Hermann and Richards' repeated attempts to induce national park proposals are an underappreciated chapter in the history of American land conservation.

9. In the early years of its existence the National Park Service grossly underfunded the national monuments, paying their managers salaries on the order of $1 per month, and consequently the level of protection the monuments were afforded was vastly inferior to that given to places designated as national parks. Today, while considerable discrepancies remain among the budgets of individual parks, all of them—no matter how designated—are managed according to a basic set of policies (NPS 2000a) that provide for much more consistency across the national park system. For example, the quality and philosophical approach of resource management being done in Bryce Canyon (which is now a national park but began as a national monument) should not in practice differ substantially from that

being carried out in comparably sized Bandelier (which began as and remains a national monument). In the new BLM monuments under the National Landscape Conservation System, there is also a basic consistency in that most visitor infrastructure is to be located outside the boundaries in adjacent towns. By contrast, the handful of national monuments under the Forest Service differ greatly in management. For example, the intensity of visitor services and preservationist orientation of Mount St. Helens National Volcanic Monument make it "much more like a national park than a national forest," while at Admiralty Island and Misty Fiords National Monuments in Alaska, management is not much different from that of the adjacent Tongass National Forest. For the Forest Service's management of its monuments, see Williams 2003.

Appendix

Essential Facts and Figures on the National Monuments

The following table includes basic information on every national monument proclaimed under the Antiquities Act. Other national monuments, created by congressional action, are not included here. Some presidents have also used the Antiquities Act to declare relatively minor boundary expansions to existing national monuments (e.g., at Katmai in 1931, 1942, and 1969; see Norris 1996). Such decrees are not included here.

Acreages are rounded to the nearest whole acre. The "Acreage at time of proclamation" column includes all acreage within proclaimed monument boundaries, whether federal or non-federal. The "Current federal acreage" column excludes non-federal lands; hence, the current figures for some monuments are lower than the originally proclaimed acreage. Current (as of 2003) acreage data for NPS units are on-line at www2.nature.nps.gov/stats/acrebypark03.pdf. Current (as of 2001) acreage for BLM units are on-line at www.blm.gov/NM_Details.pdf (both accessed September 1, 2005).

Areas marked with an asterisk (*) are also World Heritage sites.

Sources

The table is based upon earlier ones compiled by Rothman (1989) and Squillace (2003), and on data from the Cornell University Law School Legal Information Institute website: http://straylight.law.cornell.edu/uscode/html/uscode16/usc_sec_16_00000431----000-notes.html (accessed September 1, 2005). Additional information from Szasz 1977; Hogenauer 1991; NPS 2000b; Santucci and Hughes (undated).

Name at time of proclamation	Date proclaimed	Acreage at time of proclamation	Current status (managing agency)	Current federal acreage
Administration of Theodore Roosevelt				
Devils Tower (Wyo.)	Sept. 24, 1906	1,194	Devils Tower National Monument (NPS)	1,347
El Morro (N.Mex.)	Dec. 8, 1906	160	El Morro National Monument (NPS)	1,040
Montezuma Castle (Ariz.)	Dec. 8, 1906	161	Montezuma Castle National Monument (NPS)	841
Petrified Forest (Ariz.)	Dec. 8, 1906	60,776	Petrified Forest National Park (NPS)	93,533
Chaco Canyon (N.Mex.)	Mar. 11, 1907	10,643	Chaco Culture National Historical Park* (NPS)	32,840
Cinder Cone (Calif.)	May 6, 1907	5,120	both incorporated 1916 into Lassen Volcanic National Park (NPS)	106,368
Lassen Peak (Calif.)	May 6, 1907	1,280		
Gila Cliff Dwellings (N.Mex.)	Nov. 16, 1907	160	Gila Cliff Dwellings National Monument (NPS/USFS)	533
Tonto (Ariz.)	Dec. 19, 1907	640	Tonto National Monument (NPS)	1,120
Muir Woods (Calif.)	Jan. 9, 1908	295	Muir Woods National Monument (NPS)	523
Grand Canyon (Ariz.)	Jan. 11, 1908	808,120	most of monument incorporated 1919 into Grand Canyon National Park* (NPS)	1,180,863
Pinnacles (Calif.)	Jan. 16, 1908	1,320	Pinnacles National Monument (NPS)	17,874
Jewel Cave (S.Dak.)	Feb. 7, 1908	1,275	Jewel Cave National Monument (NPS)	1,274
Natural Bridges (Utah)	Apr. 16, 1908	120	Natural Bridges National Monument (NPS)	7,636

Name at time of proclamation	Date proclaimed	Acreage at time of procla- mation	Current status (managing agency)	Current federal acreage
Lewis and Clark Cavern (Mont.)	May 11, 1908	160	abolished 1937; incorporated into Lewis and Clark Cavern State Park	—
Tumacacori (Ariz.)	Sept. 15, 1908	10	Tumacacori National Historical Park (NPS)	46
Wheeler (Colo.)	Dec. 7, 1908	300	abolished 1950; incorporated into Rio Grande National Forest (USFS)	—
Mount Olympus (Wash.)	Mar. 2, 1909	639,200	Olympic National Park* (NPS)	913,529

Administration of William Howard Taft

Navajo (Ariz.)	Mar. 20, 1909	not specified	Navajo National Monument (NPS)	360
Oregon Caves (Oreg.)	July 12, 1909	466	Oregon Caves National Monument (NPS)	484
Mukuntuweap (Utah)	July 31, 1909	16,000	incorporated 1919 into Zion National Park (NPS)	143,073
Shoshone Cavern (Wyo.)	Sept. 21, 1909	210	abolished 1954; lands now under BLM jurisdiction	—
Gran Quivira (N.Mex.)	Nov. 1, 1909	160	Salinas Pueblo Missions National Monument (NPS)	985
Sitka (Alaska)	Mar. 23, 1910	57	Sitka National Historical Park (NPS)	112
Rainbow Bridge (Utah)	May 30, 1910	160	Rainbow Bridge National Monument (NPS)	160
Big Hole Battlefield (Mont.)	June 23, 1910	5	Big Hole National Battlefield (NPS)	655
Colorado (Colo.)	May 24, 1911	13,466	Colorado National Monument (NPS)	20,534
Devils Postpile (Calif.)	July 6, 1911	798	Devils Postpile National Monument (NPS)	798

Name at time of proclamation	Date proclaimed	Acreage at time of proclamation	Current status (managing agency)	Current federal acreage
Administration of Woodrow Wilson				
Cabrillo (Calif.)	Nov. 14, 1913	<1	Cabrillo National Monument (NPS)	160
Papago Saguaro (Ariz.)	Jan. 31, 1914	2,050	abolished 1930; land transferred to state of Arizona and local agencies	—
Dinosaur (Colo./Utah)	Oct. 4, 1915	80	Dinosaur National Monument (NPS)	205,686
Walnut Canyon (Ariz.)	Nov. 30, 1915	960	Walnut Canyon National Monument (NPS)	3,289
Bandelier (N.Mex.)	Feb. 11, 1916	23,352	Bandelier National Monument (NPS)	32,831
Sieur de Monts (Maine)	July 8, 1916	5,000	Acadia National Park (NPS)	45,956
Capulin Mountain (N.Mex.)	Aug. 9, 1916	640	Capulin Volcano National Monument (NPS)	793
Old Kasaan (Alaska)	Oct. 25, 1916	43	abolished 1955; incorporated into Tongass National Forest (USFS)	—
Verendrye (N.Dak.)	June 29, 1917	253.04	abolished 1956; now a National Historic Landmark under the state of North Dakota	—
Casa Grande (Ariz.)	Aug. 3, 1918	480	Casa Grande Ruins National Monument (NPS)	473
Katmai (Alaska)	Sept. 24, 1918	1,088,000	Katmai National Park and Preserve (NPS)	4,017,041
Scotts Bluff (Nebr.)	Dec. 12, 1919	2,054	Scotts Bluff National Monument (NPS)	2,952
Yucca House (Colo.)	Dec. 19, 1919	10	Yucca House National Monument (NPS)	34

Name at time of proclamation	Date proclaimed	Acreage at time of procla-mation	Current status (managing agency)	Current federal acreage
Administration of Warren G. Harding				
Lehman Caves (Nev.)	Jan. 24, 1922	593	Great Basin National Park (NPS)	77,180
Timpanogos Cave (Utah)	Oct. 14, 1922	250	Timpanogos Cave National Monument (NPS)	250
Fossil Cycad (S.Dak.).	Oct. 21, 1922	320	abolished 1956; incorporated into South Dakota Resource Area (BLM)	—
Aztec Ruins (N.Mex.)	Jan. 24, 1923	5	Aztec Ruins National Monument (NPS)	257
Mound City Group (Ohio)	Mar. 2, 1923	57	Hopewell Culture National Historical Park (NPS)	955
Hovenweep (Utah)	Mar. 2, 1923	286	Hovenweep National Monument (NPS)	785
Pipe Spring (Ariz.)	May 31, 1923	40	Pipe Spring National Monument (NPS)	40
Bryce Canyon (Utah)	June 8, 1923	7,440	Bryce Canyon National Park (NPS)	35,833
Administration of Calvin Coolidge				
Carlsbad Cave (N.Mex.)	Oct. 25, 1923	719	Carlsbad Caverns National Park* (NPS)	46,427
Chiracahua (Ariz.)	Apr. 18, 1924	3,655	Chiracahua National Monument (NPS)	11,982
Craters of the Moon (Idaho)	May 2, 1924	22,652	Craters of the Moon National Park & Preserve (NPS/BLM)	714,727
Castle Pinckney (S.C.)	Oct. 15, 1924	4	abolished 1956; privately owned	—
Fort Marion (Fla.)	Oct. 15, 1924	19	Castillo de San Marcos National Monument (NPS)	20
Fort Matanzas (Fla.)	Oct. 15, 1924	1	Fort Matanzas National Monument (NPS)	299

Name at time of proclamation	Date proclaimed	Acreage at time of proclamation	Current status (managing agency)	Current federal acreage
Fort Pulaski (Ga.)	Oct. 15, 1924	20	Fort Pulaski National Monument (NPS)	5,365
Fort Wood (Statue of Liberty) (N.Y.)	Oct. 15, 1924	10	Statue of Liberty National Monument* (NPS)	58
Wupatki (Ariz.)	Dec. 9, 1924	2,234	Wupatki National Monument (NPS)	35,422
Meriwether Lewis (Tenn.)	Feb. 6, 1925	50	incorporated 1938 into Natchez Trace Parkway (NPS)	51,861
Glacier Bay (Alaska)	Feb. 26, 1925	1,379,316	Glacier Bay National Park and Preserve* (NPS)	3,281,424
Father Millet Cross (N.Y.)	Sept. 5, 1925	<1	abolished 1949; incorporated into Old Fort Niagara State Historic Site	—
Lava Beds (Calif.)	Nov. 21, 1925	45,590	Lava Beds National Monument (NPS)	46,560
Administration of Herbert Hoover				
Arches (Utah)	Apr. 12, 1929	4,520	Arches National Park	76,353
Holy Cross (Colo.)	May 11, 1929	1,392	abolished 1950; incorporated into White River National Forest (USFS)	—
Sunset Crater (Ariz.)	May 26, 1930	3,040	Sunset Crater Volcano National Monument (NPS)	3,040
Great Sand Dunes (Colo.)	Mar. 17, 1932	35,528	Great Sand Dunes National Park and Preserve (NPS)	82,106
Grand Canyon "II" (Ariz.)	Dec. 22, 1932	273,145	incorporated 1975 into Grand Canyon National Park * (NPS)	1,180,863
White Sands (N.Mex.)	Jan. 18, 1933	131,487	White Sands National Monument (NPS)	143,733
Death Valley (Calif./Nev.)	Feb. 11, 1933	848,581	Death Valley National Park (NPS)	3,323,772

Name at time of proclamation	Date proclaimed	Acreage at time of proclamation	Current status (managing agency)	Current federal acreage
Saguaro (Ariz.)	Mar. 1, 1933	53,510	Saguaro National Park (NPS)	87,526
Black Canyon of the Gunnison (Colo.)	Mar. 2, 1933	10,288	Black Canyon of the Gunnison National Park (NPS)	30,244
Administration of Franklin D. Roosevelt				
Cedar Breaks (Utah)	Aug. 22, 1933	5,701	Cedar Breaks National Monument (NPS)	6,155
Fort Jefferson (Fla.)	Jan. 4, 1935	47,125	Dry Tortugas National Park (NPS)	61,481
Joshua Tree (Calif.)	Aug. 10, 1936	825,340	Joshua Tree National Park (NPS)	768,886
Zion "II" (Kolob Section) (Utah)	Jan. 22, 1937	49,150	incorporated 1956 into Zion National Park (NPS)	143,073
Organ Pipe Cactus (Ariz.)	Apr. 13, 1937	330,690	Organ Pipe Cactus National Monument (NPS)	329,365
Capitol Reef (Utah)	Aug. 2, 1937	37,060	Capitol Reef National Park (NPS)	241,234
Channel Islands (Calif.)	Apr. 26, 1938	1,120	Channel Islands National Park (NPS)	79,019
Fort Laramie (Wyo.)	July 16, 1938	214	Fort Laramie National Historic Site (NPS)	832
Santa Rosa Island (Fla.)	May 17, 1939	9,500	incorporated 1946 into Gulf Island National Seashore (NPS)	99,617
Tuzigoot (Ariz.)	July 25, 1939	43	Tuzigoot National Monument (NPS)	58
Jackson Hole (Wyo.)	Mar. 15, 1943	210,950	incorporated 1950 into Grand Teton National Park (NPS)	307,691

Name at time of proclamation	Date proclaimed	Acreage at time of procla-mation	Current status (managing agency)	Current federal acreage
Administration of Harry S Truman				
Effigy Mounds (Iowa)	Oct. 25, 1949	1,000	Effigy Mounds National Monument (NPS)	2,526
Administration of Dwight D. Eisenhower				
Edison Laboratory (N.J.)	July 14, 1956	2	Edison National Historic Site (NPS)	21
Chesapeake and Ohio Canal (Md. / D.C. / W.Va.)	Jan. 18, 1961	5,264	incorporated 1971 into Chesapeake and Ohio Canal National Historical Park (NPS)	14,448
Administration of John F. Kennedy				
Russell Cave (Ala.)	May 11, 1961	310	Russell Cave National Monument (NPS)	310
Buck Island Reef (V.I.)	Dec. 28, 1961	850	Buck Island Reef National Monument (NPS)	19,015
Administration of Lyndon B. Johnson				
Marble Canyon (Ariz.)	Jan. 20, 1969	32,547	incorporated 1975 into Grand Canyon National Park (NPS)	1,180,863
Administration of Jimmy Carter				
Admiralty Island (Alaska)	Dec. 1, 1978	1,100,000	Admiralty Island National Monument (USFS)	1,006,370
Aniakchak (Alaska)	Dec. 1, 1978	350,000	Aniakchak National Monument and Preserve (NPS)	577,039
Becharof (Alaska)	Dec. 1, 1978	1,200,000	Becharof National Wildlife Refuge (USFWS)	1,157,000

Name at time of proclamation	Date proclaimed	Acreage at time of procla- mation	Current status (managing agency)	Current federal acreage
Bering Land Bridge (Alaska)	Dec. 1, 1978	2,590,000	Bering Land Bridge National Preserve (NPS)	2,537,672
Cape Krusenstern (Alaska)	Dec. 1, 1978	560,000	Cape Krusenstern National Monument (NPS)	588,242
Denali (Alaska)	Dec. 1, 1978	3,890,000	Denali National Park and Preserve (NPS)	6,028,763
Gates of the Arctic (Alaska)	Dec. 1, 1978	8,220,000	Gates of the Arctic National Park and Preserve (NPS)	8,214,302
Kenai Fjords (Alaska)	Dec. 1, 1978	570,000	Kenai Fjords National Park (NPS)	601,839
Kobuk Valley (Alaska)	Dec. 1, 1978	1,710,000	Kobuk Valley National Park (NPS)	1,669,913
Lake Clark (Alaska)	Dec. 1, 1978	2,500,000	Lake Clark National Park and Preserve (NPS)	3,436,167
Misty Fiords (Alaska)	Dec. 1, 1978	2,285,000	Misty Fiords National Monument (USFS)	2,294,739
Noatak (Alaska)	Dec. 1, 1978	5,880,000	Noatak National Preserve (NPS)	6,276,090
Wrangell–St. Elias (Alaska)	Dec. 1, 1978	10,950,000	Wrangell–St. Elias National Park and Preserve* (NPS)	11,665,271
Yukon–Charley Rivers (Alaska)	Dec. 1, 1978	1,720,000	Yukon–Charley Rivers National Preserve (NPS)	2,183,173
Yukon Flats (Alaska)	Dec. 1, 1978	10,600,000	redesignated 1980 Yukon Flats National Wildlife Refuge (USFWS)	8,630,000

Administration of Bill Clinton

Grand Staircase– Escalante (Utah)	Sept. 18, 1996	1,885,800	Grand Staircase– Escalante National Monument (BLM)	1,870,800
Agua Fria (Ariz.)	Jan. 11, 2000	71,100	Agua Fria National Monument (BLM)	71,100

Name at time of proclamation	Date proclaimed	Acreage at time of proclamation	Current status (managing agency)	Current federal acreage
California Coastal (Calif.)	Jan. 11, 2000	883	California Coastal National Monument (BLM)	883
Grand Canyon–Parashant (Ariz.)	Jan. 11, 2000	1,054,264	Grand Canyon–Parashant National Monument (BLM/NPS)	1,024,425
Giant Sequoia (Calif.)	Apr. 15, 2000	327,769	Giant Sequoia National Monument (USFS)	327,769
Canyons of the Ancients (Colo.)	June 9, 2000	182,422	Canyons of the Ancients National Monument (BLM)	163,892
Cascade–Siskiyou (Oreg.)	June 9, 2000	85,173	Cascade–Siskiyou National Monument (BLM)	52,947
Hanford Reach (Wash.)	June 9, 2000	195,000	Hanford Reach National Monument (USFWS)	195,000
Ironwood Forest (Ariz.)	June 9, 2000	189,731	Ironwood Forest National Monument (BLM)	129,022
President Lincoln and Soldier's Home (D.C.)	July 7, 2000	2	President Lincoln and Soldier's Home National Monument (AFRH/NPS)	2
Craters of the Moon "II" (Idaho)	Nov. 9, 2000	754,863	expansion of Craters of the Moon National Monument (NPS/BLM)	754,863
Vermillion Cliffs (Ariz.)	Nov. 9, 2000	294,160	Vermillion Cliffs National Monument (BLM)	280,324
Carrizo Plain (Calif.)	Jan. 17, 2001	246,048	Carrizo Plain National Monument (BLM)	204,107
Kasha–Katuwe Tent Rocks (N.Mex.)	Jan. 17, 2001	5,394	Kasha–Katuwe Tent Rocks National Monument (BLM)	4,114
Minidoka Internment (Idaho)	Jan. 17, 2001	73	Minidoka Internment National Monument (NPS)	73

Name at time of proclamation	Date proclaimed	Acreage at time of proclamation	Current status (managing agency)	Current federal acreage
Pompeys Pillar (Mont.)	Jan. 17, 2001	51	Pompeys Pillar National Monument (BLM)	51
Sonoran Desert (Ariz.)	Jan. 17, 2001	496,337	Sonoran Desert National Monument (BLM)	486,603
Upper Missouri River Breaks (Mont.)	Jan. 17, 2001	494,451	Upper Missouri River Breaks National Monument (BLM)	374,976
Virgin Islands Coral Reef (V.I.)	Jan. 17, 2001	12,708	Virgin Islands Coral Reef National Monument (NPS)	12,708
Governors Island (N.Y.)	Jan. 19, 2001	22	Governors Island National Monument (NPS)	22

Bibliography

AAAS [American Association for the Advancement of Science]. 1900. *Proceedings of the American Association for the Advancement of Science: Forty-Ninth Meeting, Held at New York, N.Y., June, 1900.* Easton, Penn.: The Permanent Secretary of the AAAS.

Albright, Horace, and Robert Cahn. 1985. *The Birth of the National Park Service.* Salt Lake City: Howe Brothers.

Ames, Michael. 1992. *Cannibal Tours and Glass Boxes.* Vancouver: University of British Columbia Press.

Anonymous. 1998. "Western Lawmakers Targeting Antiquities Act." *Common Ground* 3:1, 4–6.

Bailey, Robert G. 1995. *Description of the Ecoregions of the United States.* 2nd ed. Miscellaneous Publication no. 1391. Washington, D.C.: U.S. Department of Agriculture–Forest Service.

———. 1998. *Ecoregions Map of North America: Explanatory Note.* Miscellaneous Publication no. 1548. Washington, D.C.: U.S. Department of Agriculture–Forest Service.

Bandelier, Adolph F. 1881. "A Visit to the Aboriginal Ruins in the Valley of the Rio Pecos." *Papers of the Archaeological Institute of America, American Series* 1:2, 34–135.

———. 1883. *Report on the Ruins of the Pueblo of Pecos.* Papers of the Archaeological Institute of America: American Series, 2d ed. Boston: Cupples, Upham and Co. (Reprint of Bandelier 1881.)

Benedetto, Richard, and Linda Kanamine. 1996. "President Protects Utah Lands." *USA Today,* September 19.

Bieder, Robert E. 1989. *Science Encounters the Indian, 1820–1880: The Early Years of American Ethnology.* Norman: University of Oklahoma Press.

Bond, Frank. 1912. "The Administration of National Monuments." In *Proceedings of the National Park Service Conference Held at Yellowstone National Park, September 11 and 12, 1911.* Washington, D.C.: U.S. Government Printing Office, 85–86.

Brown, Jessica, and Brent Mitchell. 2000. "The Stewardship Approach and Its Relevance for Protected Landscapes." *The George Wright Forum* 17:1, 70–79.

Brown, Jessica, Nora Mitchell, and Michael Beresford, eds. 2005. *The Protected Landscape Approach: Linking Nature, Culture and Community.* Gland, Switzerland, and Cambridge, U.K.: IUCN.

Brubaker, Sterling, ed. 1984. *Rethinking the Federal Lands.* Washington, D.C.; Resources for the Future.

Cameron, Jenks. 1922. *The National Park Service: Its History, Activities and Organization.* Institute for Government Research, Service Monographs of the United States Government no. 11. New York: D. Appleton and Co.

Cart, Julie, and Elizabeth Shogren. 2002. "Colorado: New Energy Project at Monument Exploration—Advocates for the Environment Assail the Bush Administration's Plan for the Canyons of the Ancients in Colorado." *Los Angeles Times*, August 13.

Catton, Theodore. 1997. *Inhabited Wilderness: Indians, Eskimos, and National Parks in Alaska*. Albuquerque: University of New Mexico Press.

Chapman, Matthew. 2002. "The Northwestern Hawaiian Islands Coral Reef Ecosystem Reserve: Ephemeral Protection." *Ecology Law Quarterly* 29, 347–370.

Chauvenet, Beatrice. 1983. *Hewett and Friends: A Biography of Santa Fe's Vibrant Era*. Santa Fe: Museum of New Mexico Press.

Childs, S. Terry, and Eileen Corcoran. 2000. *Managing Archaeological Collections: Technical Assistance*. Washington, D.C.: Archeology Program, NPS, 2000. On-line at www.cr.nps.gov/archeology/collections/ (accessed September 2005).

Claus, Robert. 1945. "Reference Service Report: Information about the Background of the Antiquities Act of 1906." Unpublished manuscript on file at the Office of Archeology and Historic Preservation, NPS, Washington, D.C.

Clawson, Marion. 1983. *The Federal Lands Revisited*. Washington, D.C.: Resources for the Future.

Clemensen, A. Berle. 1992. *Casa Grande Ruins National Monument, Arizona: A Centennial History of the First Prehistoric Reserve, 1892–1992*. Denver: Denver Service Center, NPS. On-line at www.nps.gov/cagr/adhi/adhi.htm (accessed May 2005).

Collins, R. B., and M. P. Michel. 1985. "Preserving the Past: Origins of the Archaeological Resources Protection Act of 1979." *American Archaeology* 5:2, 84–89.

Connally, Ernest Allen. 1986a. "Origins of the National Historic Preservation Act of 1966, Part I." *CRM Bulletin* 9:1. On-line at http://crm.cr.nps.gov/archive/09-1/9-1-all.pdf (accessed September 21, 2005).

———. 1986b. "Origins of the National Historic Preservation Act of 1966, Part II." *CRM Bulletin* 9:2. On-line at http://crm.cr.nps.gov/ archive/09-2/9-2-all.pdf (accessed September 21, 2005).

Cutright, Paul Russell. 1985. *Theodore Roosevelt: The Making of a Conservationist*. Urbana: University of Illinois Press.

Dalton, Kathleen. 2002. *Theodore Roosevelt: A Strenuous Life*. New York: Alfred A. Knopf.

DiMeglio, Steve. 2000. "Clinton Looks West in Search of a Legacy." *Gannett News Service*, May 29.

Dixon, Roland B. 1928. "Frederic W. Putnam." In *Dictionary of American Biography*. Allen Johnson, ed. New York: Charles Scribner's Sons, 15:276–278.

DOI [Department of the Interior], Office of the Secretary. 1900. Records of the Office of the Secretary of the Interior, Lands and Railroads Division, Letter Received, 1900, file 1633.

DOI. 1904. *Circular Relating to Historic and Prehistoric Ruins of the Southwest and Their Preservation.* Washington, D.C.: U.S. Government Printing Office.

Eaton, Marietta. 2001. "Consultation on Grand Staircase–Escalante National Monument from Planning to Implementation." *American Indian Quarterly* 25:1, 28–34.

Fagette, Paul. 1996. *Digging for Dollars: American Archaeology and the New Deal.* Albuquerque: University of New Mexico Press.

Fairfax, Sally K. 2005. "When an Agency Outlasts Its Time—A Reflection." *Journal of Forestry* 103:5, 264–267.

Ferdon, Edwin Nelson, Jr. 1993. "Introduction: Edgar L. Hewett: The Nature of the Man." In Edgar Lee Hewett, *Ancient Communities in the American Desert.* Albert Henry Schroeder, ed. Archaeological Society of New Mexico Monograph Series no. 1. Albuquerque: Archaeological Society of New Mexico, 11–19.

Fewkes, J. Walter. 1896. "Two Ruins Recently Discovered in the Red Rock Country, Arizona." *American Anthropologist* (o.s.) 9:8, 269–270.

Fine-Dare, Kathleen S. 2002. *Grave Injustice: The American Indian Repatriation Movement and NAGPRA.* Lincoln: University of Nebraska Press.

Flynn, Aaron. 2004. *Marine Protected Areas: Federal Legal Authority.* Congressional Research Service Report no. RL32486. Washington, D.C.: Congressional Research Service, 2004.

Foss, Philip O., ed. 1987. *Federal Lands Policy.* Westport, Conn.: Greenwood Press.

Fowler, Don D. 1986. "Conserving American Archaeological Resources." In *American Archaeology Past and Future: A Celebration of the Society for American Archaeology, 1935–1985.* David J. Meltzer, Don D. Fowler, and Jeremy A. Sabloff, eds. Washington, D.C.: Smithsonian Institution Press, 135–162.

———. 1999. "Harvard versus Hewett: The Contest for Control of Southwestern Archaeology, 1904–1930." In *Assembling the Past: Studies in the Professionalization of Archaeology.* A. Kehoe and M. B. Emmerichs, eds. Albuquerque: University of New Mexico Press, 165–211.

———. 2000. *A Laboratory for Anthropology: Science and Romanticism in the American Southwest, 1846–1930.* Albuquerque: University of New Mexico Press.

Fowler, Don D., and Barbara Malinkey. 2005. "The Origins of ARPA: Crafting the Archaeological Resources Protection Act of 1979." In *Preserving Archaeology in the Courts.* Sherry Hutt and Marion Forsyth, eds. Walnut Creek, Calif.: AltaMira Press, in press.

Fowler, John M. 1974. "Protection of the Cultural Environment in Federal Law." In *Federal Environmental Law*. Erica L. Dolgin and Thomas G. P. Guilbert, eds. St. Paul, Minn.: Environmental Law Institute, West Publishing Co., 1466–1517.

Gallagher, Annette, C.H.M. 1981. "Citizen of the Nation: John Fletcher Lacey, Conservationist." *Annals of Iowa* 46, 9–22.

Gates, Paul W. 1968. *History of Public Land Law Development*. New York: Public Land Law Review Commission.

Glass, James A. 1990. *The Beginnings of a New National Historic Preservation Program, 1957 to 1969*. Nashville: American Association for State and Local History.

Graubard, Stephen. 2005. *Command of Office: How War, Secrecy, and Deception Transformed the Presidency from Theodore Roosevelt to George W. Bush*. New York: Basic Books.

Gray, Murray. 2004. *Geodiversity: Valuing and Conserving Abiotic Nature*. Chichester, U.K.: John Wiley & Sons.

Gulliford, Andrew. 2000. *Sacred Objects and Sacred Places: Preserving Tribal Traditions*. Boulder: University of Colorado Press.

Hales, David F. 1984. "The World Heritage Convention: Status and Directions." In *National Parks, Conservation, and Development: The Role of Protected Areas in Sustaining Society*. (Proceedings of the 4th World Parks Congress.) Jeffrey A. McNeely and Kenton R. Miller, eds. Washington, D.C.: Smithsonian Institution Press, 744–750.

Haury, Emil Walter. 1983. "Foreword." *Those Who Came Before: Southwestern Archeology in the National Park System*. Robert Hill Lister and Florence Cline Lister, eds. Tucson: University of Arizona Press and Southwest Parks and Monuments Association, 8–10.

Haycox, Stephen W. 1992. "The Politics of Environment: Cecil Andrus and the Alaska Lands." *Idaho Yesterdays* 36:3, 28–36.

Haynes, Henry W. 1900. "Progress of American Archaeology During the Past Ten Years." *American Journal of Archaeology*, 2nd ser., 4, 19.

Hays, Samuel P. 1959 [1999]. *Conservation and the Gospel of Efficiency: The Progressive Conservation Movement, 1890–1920*. Cambridge, Mass.: Harvard University Press. (2nd ed.; Pittsburgh: University of Pittsburgh Press, 1999.)

Hellman, Geoffrey T. 1967. *The Smithsonian: Octopus on the Mall*. Philadelphia: J.B. Lippincott.

Hewett, Edgar Lee. 1904a. "Government Supervision of Historic and Prehistoric Ruins." *Science*, n.s., 20, 723.

———. 1904b. "Memorandum Concerning the Historic and Prehistoric Ruins of Arizona, New Mexico, Colorado and Utah, and Their Preservation." In *Circular Relating to Historic and Prehistoric Ruins of the Southwest and Their Preservation*. Washington: U.S. Government Printing Office.

———. 1905. "General View of the Archaeology of the Pueblo Region." *Smithsonian Institution Annual Report for 1904*, 583–605.

———. 1906. "Preservation of American Antiquities: Progress during the Past Year; Needed Legislation." *American Anthropologist*, n.s., 8, 109–114.

Higham, John. 1955. *Strangers in the Land: Patterns of American Nativism, 1860–1925*. New Brunswick, N.J.: Rutgers University Press.

Hodel, Donald Paul. 1986. *The Secretary of the Interior's 20th Anniversary Report on the National Historic Preservation Act*. Washington, D.C.: NPS.

Hogenauer, Alan. 1991. "Gone But Not Forgotten: The Delisted Units of the U.S. National Park System." *The George Wright Forum* 7:4, 2–19.

Holmes, W. H. 1889. "Debasement of Pueblo Art." *American Anthropologist* 3, 320.

Hough, Walter. 1893. "Columbian Exposition in Madrid, 1890." *American Anthropologist* 6, 271–272.

———. 1908. "Otis Tufton Mason." *American Anthropologist*, n.s., 10, 664.

Hutt, Sherry, Elwood W. Jones, and Martin E. McCallister. 1992. *Archaeological Resource Protection*. Washington, D.C.: National Trust for Historic Preservation—The Preservation Press.

Ickes, Harold L. 1935. "Statement by Hon. Harold L. Ickes, Secretary of the Interior." In *Preservation of Historic American Sites, Buildings, Objects, and Antiquities of National Significance*. Hearings before the Committee on the Public Lands, House of Representatives, on H.R. 6670 and H.R. 6734, April 1, 2, and 5, 1935. Washington, D.C.: U.S. Government Printing Office.

Ise, John. 1961. *Our National Park Policy: A Critical History*. Baltimore: Johns Hopkins Press (published for Resources for the Future).

IUCN. 1979a. "IUCN Review of Grand Canyon World Heritage Nomination." On-line at http://whc.unesco.org/archive/advisory_body_evaluation/075.pdf.

———. 1979b. "IUCN Review of Kluane/Wrangell–St. Elias World Heritage Nomination." On-line at http://whc.unesco.org/archive/advisory_body_evaluation/072.pdf.

———. 1981. "World Heritage Nomination—IUCN Technical Review: Olympic National Park." On-line at http://whc.unesco.org/archive/advisory_body_evaluation/151.pdf.

———. 1992. "World Heritage Nomination—IUCN Summary: Glacier Bay National Park and Preserve (U.S.A.) (Extension to Existing Wrangell-St. Elias–Kluane Site)." On-line at http://whc.unesco.org/archive/advisory_body_evaluation/072.pdf.

———. 1995. "World Heritage Nomination—IUCN Summary: Carlsbad Caverns National Park (USA)." On-line at http://whc.unesco.org/archive/advisory_body_evaluation/ 721.pdf.

Johnson, Allen, ed. 1928. *Dictionary of American Biography*. New York:

Charles Scribner's Sons.

Keller, Robert H., and Michael F. Turek. 1998. *American Indians & National Parks*. Tucson: University of Arizona Press.

Kennedy, Roger G. 1994. *Hidden Cities: The Discovery and Loss of Ancient North American Civilization*. New York: The Free Press.

Kopkind, Andrew. 1988. "O.K., Bruce, That's a Wrap—Next." *The Nation*, February 27.

Krakauer, Jon. 1997. *Into Thin Air*. New York: Villard.

Landau, Patricia M., and D. Gentry Steele. 1996. "Why Anthropologists Study Human Remains." *American Indian Quarterly* 20:2, 209–228.

Lange, Charles H., and Carroll L. Riley, eds. 1966. *The Southwestern Journals of Adolph F. Bandelier, 1880–1882*. Albuquerque: University of New Mexico Press.

Larmer, Paul. 2001. "Mr. Babbitt's Wild Ride." *High Country News*, February 12, 1.

LaVor, Marty. 1993. "The New Secretary of the Interior—Bruce Babbitt." *High Country News* 25:1 (January 25).

Lee, Ronald F. 1970. *The Antiquities Act of 1906*. Washington, D.C.: National Park Service, Office of History and Historic Architecture, Eastern Service Center. (Reprinted, *Journal of the Southwest* 42:2 (2000), 198–269. Electronic edition on-line at www.cr.nps.gov/aad/PUBS/LEE/index.htm; accessed April 2005).

Leopold, Aldo. 1949 [1970]. *A Sand County Almanac*. New York: Oxford University Press. (Reprinted, New York: Ballantine Books, 1970.)

Leshy, John D. 1998. "Putting the Antiquities Act into Perspective." In *Visions of the Grand Staircase–Escalante*. Robert B. Keiter, Sarah B. George, and Joro Walker, eds. Salt Lake City: Utah Museum of Natural History and Wallace Stegner Center.

———. 2000. "The Babbitt Legacy at the Department of the Interior: A Preliminary View." *Environmental Law* 31, 199–227.

———. 2001. "Water Rights for New Federal Land Conservation Programs: A Turn of the Century Evaluation." *University of Denver Water Law Review* 4, 271ff.

Limerick, Patricia Nelson. 1987. *The Legacy of Conquest: The Unbroken Past of the American West*. New York: W. W. Norton.

Lurie, Nancy O. 1988. "Relations between Indians and Anthropologists." In *Handbook of North American Indians*. Volume 4: *History of Indian–White Relations*. Wilcomb E. Washburn, ed. Washington, D.C.: Smithsonian Institution Press, 548–556.

Lyon, Edwin A. 1996. *A New Deal for Southeastern Archaeology*. Tuscaloosa: University of Alabama Press.

Mackintosh, Barry. 1985. *The Historic Sites Survey and National Historic Landmarks Program*. Washington, D.C.: NPS.

―――. 1986. *The National Historic Preservation Act and the National Park Service*. Washington, D.C.: NPS.

―――. 1991. *The National Parks: Shaping the System*. Washington, D.C.: NPS.

Mark, Joan. 1980. *Four Anthropologists: An American Science in Its Early Years*. New York: Science History Publications.

Marshall, Robert. 1937. "The Universe of Wilderness Is Vanishing." *Nature Magazine* 29, 236–238.

Matero, Frank. 1999. "Lessons from the Great House: Condition and Treatment History as Prologue to Site Conservation and Management at Casa Grande Ruins National Monument." *Conservation and Management of Archaeological Sites* 3, 203–224.

Mattison, Ray H. 1955. "Devils Tower National Monument: The First Fifty Years." On-line at www.nps.gov/deto/first50_text.htm.

McDermott, John Dishon. 1966. "Breath of Life: An Outline of the Development of a National Policy for Historic Preservation." Unpublished manuscript on file at the Office of Archeology and Historic Preservation, National Park Service, Washington, D.C.

McDonagh, Eileen L. 1999. "Race, Class, and Gender in the Progressive Era: Restructuring State and Society." In *Progressivism and the New Democracy*. Sidney M. Milkis and Jerome M. Mileur, eds. Amherst: University of Massachusetts Press, 145–184.

McGimsey, Charles R. 1972. *Public Archaeology*. New York and London: Seminar Press.

McManamon, Francis P. 1991. "The Federal Government's Recent Response to Archaeological Looting." In *Protecting the Past*. George S. Smith and John E. Ehrenhard, eds. Boca Raton, Fla.: CRC Press.

―――. 1996a. "The Antiquities Act—Setting Basic Preservation Policies." *CRM* 19:7, 19–23.

―――. 1996b. "90 Years of Archeology and Historic Preservation." *CRM* 19:7, 17.

―――. 2001. "Cultural Resources and Protection under United States Law." *Connecticut Journal of International Law* 16, 247–282.

―――. 2003. "Archaeology, Nationalism, and Ancient America." In *The Politics of Archaeology and Identity in a Global Context*. Susan Kane, ed. Boston: Archaeological Institute of America.

Merryman, John H. 1985. "Thinking about the Elgin Marbles." *Michigan Law Review* 83, 1881–1923.

Mihesuah, Devon A. 1996. "American Indians, Anthropologists, Pothunters, and Repatriation: Ethical, Religious, and Political Differences, in Repatriation: An Interdisciplinary Dialogue." *American Indian Quarterly* 20:2, 229–250.

Milner, George R. 2004. *The Moundbuilders: Ancient Peoples of Eastern North America*. London: Thames and Hudson.

Moore, Charles. 1928. "Charles Eliot Norton." In *Dictionary of American Biography*. Allen Johnson, ed. New York: Charles Scribner's Sons, 13:569–572.

Morris, Edmund. 2001. *Theodore Rex*. New York: Random House.

Muir, John. 1992. *The Eight Wilderness Discovery Books*. Seattle: Diadem.

Nash, Roderick. 1967. *Wilderness and the American Mind*. New Haven: Yale University Press.

National Association of Tribal Historic Preservation Officers. 2005. "THPO's Contact List." On-line at www.nathpo.org/THPO_Members/state_list.-htm.

National Park System Advisory Board. 2001. *Rethinking the National Parks for the 21st Century*. Washington, D.C.: National Geographic Society.

Nelson, Robert H. 1995. *Public Lands and Private Rights: The Failure of Scientific Management*. Lanham, Md.: Rowman & Littlefield.

Nie, Martin A. 1999. "In Wilderness Is Dissension." *Forum for Applied Research and Public Policy* 14:2, 77–83.

Nordenskjöld, G[ustav]. 1893. *The Cliff Dwellers of the Mesa Verde, Southwestern Colorado: Their Pottery and Implements*. D. Lloyd Morgan, trans. Stockholm: P.A. Norstedt and Soner.

Nordland, Rod. 1997. "The Gods Must Be Angry." *Newsweek*, May 26, 44.

Norris, Frank B. 1996. *Isolated Paradise: An Administrative History of the Katmai and Aniakchak NPS Units*. Anchorage, Alaska: NPS.

————. 2004. "A Historical Overview of Consumptive Use Patterns in National Park Service Areas." In *Protecting Our Diverse Heritage: The Role of Parks, Protected Areas, and Cultural Sites*. David Harmon, Bruce M. Kilgore, and Gay E. Vietzke, eds. Hancock, Michigan: The George Wright Society, 326–327.

Norton, Charles Eliot, et al. 1885. *Sixth Annual Report of the Archaeological Institute of America, 1884–85*. Cambridge, Mass.: John Wilson and Son.

NPS [National Park Service]. 1930. *Glimpses of Our National Monuments*. Washington, D.C.: U.S. Government Printing Office.

————. Undated [1991]. *Held in Trust: Preserving America's Historic Places, The National Historic Preservation Act of 1966, 25th Anniversary Report*. Washington: NPS.

————. Undated [1993]. *National Parks for the 21st Century: The Vail Agenda*. Washington, D.C.: NPS.

————. 2000a. *National Park Service Management Policies 2001*. Washington, D.C.: NPS.

————. 2000b. *The National Parks: Index 2000–2003*. Washington, D.C.: NPS.

————. 2005. *The National Parks: Shaping the System*. Rev. ed. Harpers Ferry, W.Va.: Harpers Ferry Center, NPS.

————. Undated. "An Overview of Vital Signs Monitoring and Its Central Role in Natural Resource Stewardship and Performance Management."

On-line at science.nature.nps.gov/im/monitor/docs/Vital_Signs_Over-view.doc. (Accessed September 15, 2005.)

Omernik, James M. 1995. "Ecoregions: A Framework for Managing Eco-systems." *The George Wright Forum* 12:1, 35–50.

———. 2004. "Perspectives on the Nature and Definition of Ecological Regions." *Environmental Management*. On-line journal at www.springer-online.com.

Palmer, T. S. 1917. "The National Monuments as Wild-life Sanctuaries." In *Proceedings of the Fourth National Parks Conference*. Washington, D.C.: U.S. Government Printing Office, 208–225.

Pammel, Louis H., ed. 1915. *Major John F. Lacey Memorial Volume*. Cedar Rapids, Iowa: Torch Press for the Iowa Park and Forestry Association.

Phillips, Adrian. 2003. "Turning Ideas on Their Head: The New Paradigm for Protected Areas." *The George Wright Forum* 20:2, 8–32.

Pierson, Lloyd M. 1956. "A History of Chaco Canyon National Monument." Unpublished manuscript in the library of the Division of Archeology, National Park Service, Washington, D.C.

Pinchot, Gifford. 1910. *The Fight for Conservation*. New York: Doubleday, Page.

PLLRC [Public Land Law Review Commission]. 1970. *One Third of the Nation's Land: A Report to the President and the Congress*. Washington, D.C.: U.S. Government Printing Office.

Prucha, Francis Paul. 1976. *American Indian Policy in Crisis: Christian Reform-ers and the Indian, 1865–1900*. Norman: University of Oklahoma Press.

———. 1988. "United States Indian Policies, 1815–1860." In *Handbook of North American Indians*. Volume 4: *History of Indian–White Relations*. Wil-comb E. Washburn, ed. Washington, D.C.: Smithsonian Institution Press, 40–50.

———. 1990. *Documents of United States Indian Policy*. 2nd ed. Lincoln: Uni-versity of Nebraska Press.

Putnam, Frederic W. et al., eds. 1879. *Reports upon Archaeological and Ethno-logical Collections from Vicinity of Santa Barbara, California, and from Ruined Pueblos of Arizona and New Mexico, and Certain Interior Tribes*. Washington, D.C.: U.S. Government Printing Office.

Rana, Bhola. 1998. "Money Hitch to Clean Up Everest." *Bernama* [Malaysian National News Service], May 15.

Ranchod, Sanjay. 2001. "The Clinton National Monuments: Protecting Eco-systems with the Antiquities Act." *Harvard Environmental Law Review* 25, 535–589.

Rasband, James, James Salzman, and Mark Squillace. 2004. *Natural Resources Law and Policy*. New York: Foundation Press.

Reiger, John. 2000. *American Sportsmen and the Origins of Conservationism*. 3rd ed. Corvallis: Oregon State University Press.

Riding In, James. 1992. "Without Ethics and Morality: A Historical Overview of Imperial Archaeology and American Indians." *Arizona State Law Journal* (24):1, 11–34.

Righter, Robert W. 1982. *Crucible for Conservation: The Creation of Grand Teton National Park.* Boulder: Colorado Associated University Press.

Rodgers, Daniel T. 1998. *Atlantic Crossings: Social Politics in a Progressive Age.* Cambridge, Mass.: The Belknap Press of Harvard University Press.

Rogers, Edmund B., comp. 1958. "History of Legislation Relating to the National Park System through the 82d Congress." Collection of photostats, 108 volumes (Volume 4: The Antiquities Act). Washington, D.C.: Natural Resources Library, Department of the Interior.

Rogers, Jerry L. 1984. "The Integration of Law, Policy, and Technical Information in National Park Service Cultural Resource Programs." *CRM Bulletin* 7:3. On-line at http://crm.cr.nps.gov/ archive/07-3/7-3-all.pdf (accessed September 21, 2005).

———. 1986. "The National Historic Preservation Act—A Retrospective." *CRM Bulletin* 9:1. On-line at http://crm.cr.nps.gov/archive/09-1/9-1-all.pdf (accessed September 21, 2005).

———. 1987. "The National Register of Historic Places: A Personal Perspective on the First Twenty Years." *The Public Historian* 9, 91–104.

———. 1988. "Historic Preservation: New Threats, New Strategies." *History News* 43, 6–10.

———. 2004. Miki Crespi and the Origin of the National Park Service Ethnography Program." *Practicing Anthropology* 26, 7–11.

Rose, Jerome C., Thomas J. Green, and Victoria D. Green. 1996. "NAGPRA is Forever: The Future of Osteology and the Repatriation of Skeletons." *Annual Review of Anthropology* 25, 81–103.

Rothman, Hal K. 1989. *Preserving Different Pasts: The American National Monuments.* Urbana: University of Illinois Press. (Reprinted, University Press of Kansas, 1994. Electronic version on-line at www.cr.nps.gov/history/online_books/rothman/index.htm; accessed April 2005).

———. 1991. *Navajo National Monument: A Place and Its People, an Administrative History.* Professional Papers no. 40. Santa Fe, N.M.: NPS Southwest Cultural Resources Center.

———. 1999. "The Antiquities Act and National Monuments: A Progressive Conservation Legacy." *CRM* 22:4, 16–18.

Rowell, Galen. 1977. *In the Throne Room of the Mountain Gods.* San Francisco: Sierra Club Books.

Runte, Alfred. 1987. *National Parks: The American Experience.* 2nd ed. Lincoln: University of Nebraska Press.

Russell, Peter. 1992. *Gila Cliff Dwellings National Monument: An Administrative History.* Professional Papers no. 46. Santa Fe, N.M.: National Park Service Southwest Cultural Resources Center.

Salazar-Halfmoon, Virginia. 2006. "Changing Ideas and Perceptions." In *People, Places, and Parks: Proceedings of the 2005 George Wright Society*

Conference on Parks, Protected Areas, and Cultural Sites. David Harmon, ed. Hancock, Mich.: The George Wright Society.

Santucci, Vincent L. 2005. "Fossils, Objects of Antiquity, and the Antiquities Act (1906)." Unpublished manuscript. McLean, Va.: NPS.

Santucci, Vincent L., and Marikka Hughes. Undated. *Fossil Cycad National Monument: A Case of Paleontological Resource Mismanagement.* On-line at www2.nature.nps.gov/geology/paleontology/pub/grd3_3/focy1.htm. Accessed September 15, 2005.

Sax, Joseph L. 1980. *Mountains without Handrails: Reflections on the National Parks.* Ann Arbor: University of Michigan Press.

Schlesinger, Arthur M., Jr. 1989. *The Imperial Presidency.* 2nd ed. Boston: Houghton, Mifflin.

Sellars, Richard West. 2005. "Pilgrim Places: Civil War Battlefields, Historic Preservation, and America's First National Military Parks, 1863–1900." *CRM: The Journal of Heritage Stewardship* 2, 22–52.

Senge, Peter M. 1990. *The Fifth Discipline: The Art and Practice of the Learning Organization.* New York: Doubleday Currency.

Shafer, Craig L. 1999. "History of Selection and System Planning for US Natural Area National Parks and Monuments: Beauty and Biology." *Biodiversity and Conservation* 8, 189–204.

Shankland, Robert. *Steve Mather of the National Parks.* New York: Alfred A. Knopf, 1951.

Silverberg, R. 1968. *Mound-builders of Ancient America: The Archaeology of a Myth.* New York: Graphic Society.

Snead, James E. 1999. "Science, Commerce, and Control: Patronage and the Development of Anthropological Archaeology in the United States." *American Anthropologist* 101:2, 256–271.

———. 2001. *Ruins and Rivals: The Making of Southwest Archaeology.* Tucson: University of Arizona Press.

Spence, Mark David. 1999. *Dispossessing the Wilderness: Indian Removal and the Making of the National Parks.* New York and Oxford: Oxford University Press.

Spielberg, Steven. 1977. *Close Encounters of the Third Kind.* New York: Delacorte Press.

Sprague, Roderick, and Walter W. Birkby. 1970. "Miscellaneous Columbia Plateau Burials." *Tebiwa* 13:1, 1–32.

Squier, Ephraim G., and Edwin H. Davis. 1998 [1848]. *Ancient Mounds of the Mississippi Valley.* David J. Meltzer, ed. Washington, D.C.: Smithsonian Institution Press. (Originally published in 1848 as *Smithsonian Contributions to Knowledge*, vol. 1.)

Squillace, Mark. 2003. "The Monumental Legacy of the Antiquities Act of 1906." *Georgia Law Review* 37:2, 473–610.

Stamm, Alicia, and Ford Peatross. 1983. *Historic America: Buildings, Structures, and Sites.* Washington: Library of Congress.

Stocking, George W., Jr.. 1960. "Franz Boas and the Founding of the American Anthropological Association." *American Anthropologist* 62, 1–17.

Sullivan, Lynne P., and S. Terry Childs. 2003. *Curating Archaeological Collections: From the Field to the Repository*. Walnut Creek, Calif.: AltaMira Press.

Sullivan, Thomas Alan. 1947. *Proclamations and Orders Relating to the National Park Service up to January 1, 1945*. Washington: U.S. Government Printing Office.

Szasz, Ferenc M. 1977. "Wheeler and Holy Cross: Colorado's 'Lost' National Monuments." *Journal of Forest History* 21:3, 134–144.

Thomas, David Hurst. 2000. *Skull Wars: Kennewick Man, Archaeology, and the Battle for Native American Identity*. New York: Basic Books.

Thompson, Raymond Harris. 2000. "Edgar Lee Hewett and the Political Process." *Journal of the Southwest* 42:2, 260–318.

Thoreau, Henry David. 1849 [1939]. *Walden*. New York: The Heritage Press.

Thorsell, Jim, comp. 1992. *World Heritage Twenty Years Later*. Gland, Switzerland, and Cambridge, U.K.: IUCN.

Tolson, Hillory A. 1933. *Laws Relating to the National Park Service, the National Parks and Monuments*. Washington, D.C.: U.S. Department of the Interior.

Trigger, Bruce G. 1989. *A History of Archaeological Thought*. Cambridge, U.K.: Cambridge University Press.

Trope, Jack F., and Walter R. Echo-Hawk. 1992. "The Native American Graves Protection and Repatriation Act: Background and Legislative History." *Arizona State Law Journal* 24:1, 35–78.

Tsosie, Rebecca. 1997. "Indigenous Rights and Archaeology." In *Native Americans and Archaeologists: Stepping Stones to Common Ground*. Nina Swidler, Kurt E. Dongoske, Roger Anyon, and Alan S. Downer, eds. Walnut Creek, Calif.: AltaMira Press, 64–76.

Turner, Frederick. 1997. "Oh, Wilderness." *Outside* (April). On-line at http://outside.away.com/magazine/0497/9704fewild.html.

Ubelaker, Douglas H., and Lauryn Guttenplan Grant. 1989. "Human Skeletal Remains: Preservation or Reburial?" *Yearbook of Physical Anthropology* 32, 249–287.

UNESCO [United Nations Educational, Scientific, and Cultural Organization]. 2005. *Operational Guidelines for the Implementation of the World Heritage Convention*. Paris: UNESCO World Heritage Centre.

Utley, Robert M. 2004. *Custer and Me: A Historian's Memoir*. Norman: University of Oklahoma Press.

Van Valkenburgh, Sallie. 1962. "The Casa Grande of Arizona as a Landmark on the Desert, a Government Reservation, and a National Monument." *The Kiva* 27:3, 1–31.

Vincent, Carol Hardy, and Pamela Baldwin. 2001. *National Monuments and the Antiquities Act: Recent Designations and Issues*. Congressional Research Service Report no. RL30528. Washington, D.C.: Congressional Research Service.

Walter, Paul Alfred Francis. 1947. "Edgar Lee Hewett, Americanist, 1865–1947." *American Anthropologist* 49:2, 261–271.

Waterman, Laura, and Guy Waterman. 1993. *Wilderness Ethics*. New York: The Countryman Press.

Watkins, T. H. 1992. *Righteous Pilgrim: The Life and Times of Harold L. Ickes, 1874–1952*. New York: Henry Holt & Co.

Watkins, T. H., and Charles Watson. 1975. *The Land No One Knows: America and the Public Domain*. San Francisco: Sierra Club Books.

Watts, Sarah. 2003. *Rough Rider in the White House: Theodore Roosevelt and the Politics of Desire*. Chicago: University of Chicago Press.

Welch, David. 2005. "What Should Managers Do in the Face of Climate Change?" *The George Wright Forum* 22:1, 75–93.

Webb, Melody. 1987. "Cultural Landscapes in the National Park Service." *The Public Historian* 9, 77–89.

Wendorf, Fred, and Raymond Harris Thompson. 2002. "The Committee for the Recovery of Archaeological Remains: Three Decades of Service to the Archaeological Profession." *American Antiquity* 67:2, 317–320.

Wiebe, Robert H. 1967. *The Search for Order, 1877–1920*. New York: Hill & Wang.

The Wilderness Society. 2001. "The Antiquities Act: Protecting America's Natural Treasures." On-line at www.wilderness.org/Library/Documents/upload/The-Antiquities-Act-Protecting-Americas-Natural-Treasures.pdf.

Wilkinson, Charles F. 1999. *Fire on the Plateau: Conflict and Endurance in the American Southwest*. Washington, D.C.: Island Press.

Willey, Gordon R., and Jeremy A. Sabloff. 1993. *A History of American Archaeology*. 3rd ed. New York: W. H. Freeman and Co.

Williams, Gerald W. 2003. "National Monuments and the Forest Service." Unpublished manuscript, November 18.

Williss, G. Frank. 1985. *"Do Things Right the First Time": Administrative History—The National Park Service and the Alaska National Interest Lands Conservation Act of 1980*. Washington, D.C.: NPS. Available on-line at www.cr.nps.gov/history/online_books/ williss/.

Yozwiak, Steve. 1998. "To Keep It Wild." *Arizona Republic,* November 27.

About the Contributors

Cecil D. Andrus is the chairman of the Andrus Center for Public Policy at Boise State University, in Boise, Idaho (www.andruscenter.org). He was elected four times as governor for the state of Idaho, from 1971 to 1977, and again from 1987 to 1995. He was the secretary of the U.S. Department of the Interior, 1977–1981. He played a pivotal role in the passage of the Alaska National Interest Lands Conservation Act, the Surface Mining Act of 1977, and the acts that created the Frank Church River of No Return Wilderness Area, Hells Canyon National Recreation Area, and Snake River Birds of Prey area. He is the author, with Joel Connelly, of *Cecil Andrus: Politics Western Style*.

Brad Barr is senior policy advisor in the Office of the Director of the National Oceanic and Atmospheric Administration's National Marine Sanctuary Program. His primary area of responsibility is federal interagency coordination for the National Marine Sanctuary System. He sits on the board of directors of the Coastal Zone Canada Association, and of the Science and Management of Protected Areas Association. His publications have focused on a wide range of issues related to marine protected areas, and his current research interest is the identification and preservation of ocean wilderness.

Rebecca Conard is professor of history and director of public history at Middle Tennessee State University. In addition to teaching, she is an associate of Tallgrass Historians L.C. of Iowa City, Iowa, a cultural resource consulting firm she co-founded with Jan Olive Nash in 1993. Conard is a past president of the National Council on Public History. Her publications include several articles on protecting and managing cultural resources, as well as the books *Places of Quiet Beauty: Parks, Preserves, and Environmentalism* and *Benjamin Shambaugh and the Intellectual Foundations of Public History*.

Dennis Curtis is the manager of Grand Canyon–Parashant National Monument for the Bureau of Land Management, overseeing various resource uses and management of over 800,000 acres of public land. These uses include recreation, livestock grazing, ponderosa pine restoration and research, rangeland improvement projects, wilderness use, transportation and facility maintenance, and other related activities. He has worked for BLM for 37 years, 25 as a manager or supervisor, serving as assistant district manager, area manager, planning team leader, and project manager. He graduated from the University of Utah with a Master's degree in geography.

Elena Daly is the director of the Bureau of Land Management's National Landscape Conservation System (NLCS). The NLCS consists of 31 national monuments and conservation areas, 148 designated wilderness areas, 604 wilderness study areas, 36 wild and scenic river segments, 10 national historic trails, and 2 national scenic trails. In addition to developing policy for these diverse units, she is BLM's primary contact for partnership and stewardship development. During her 22-year career she has worked in California, Oregon, and Idaho as well as Washington, D.C. Ms. Daly holds both a B.A. and an M.A. in American history, and a Juris Doctorate.

John C. Freemuth, Ph.D., is a senior fellow with the Cecil D. Andrus Center for Public Policy, and professor of political science and public administration, Boise State University, where his emphasis is on natural resource and public land policy and administration. He has authored an award-winning book, *Islands under Siege: National Parks and the Politics of External Threats*, as well as numerous articles on natural resource policy. He was chair of the Science Advisory Board of the Bureau of Land Management, where he worked on policies to improve the use of scientific information for land managers as well as improve the relationship between science and democratic decision processes. Dr. Freemuth was named the Carnegie/CASE Professor of the Year for Idaho in 2001.

David Harmon is the executive director of the George Wright Society, an association of researchers, resource managers, administrators, and other professionals advancing the scientific and heritage values of parks and other protected areas. He also is vice chair for North America of IUCN's World Commission on Protected Areas. He has written on a wide range of topics related to parks and also maintains a strong research interest in the relationship between biological and cultural diversity. His most recent books are *Managing Mountain Protected Areas: Challenges and Responses for the 21st Century* (co-edited with Graeme L. Worboys), *The Full Value of Parks: From Economics to the Intangible* (co-edited with Allen D. Putney), and *In Light of Our Differences: How Diversity in Nature and Culture Makes Us Human.*

Ronald F. Lee (1905–1972) spent his career with the National Park Service after undertaking doctoral studies in history at the University of Minnesota. As NPS chief historian from 1938 to 1951, he played an important role in developing the nation's historic preservation policy in the aftermath of the passage of the Historic Sites Act of 1935. Lee later served as assistant director of the agency, and, in the 1950s, was in charge of NPS's division of interpretation, where he contributed significantly to the expansion of museum and interpretive services under the Mission 66 program. Aside from his pioneering history of the Antiquities Act, Lee also authored *Family Tree of the National Park System,* a valuable brief administrative history of the NPS.

Francis P. McManamon is the chief archaeologist of the National Park Service and departmental consulting archaeologist for the Department of the Interior. He is involved in the development of policy, regulations, and guidance for NPS and government-wide archaeological programs. His office also provides professional and public information about archaeology (www.cr.nps.gov/archeology). He provided technical assistance on the Kennewick Man case and the New York City African Burial Ground project, and for U.S. delegations to UNESCO negotiations on illegal artifact trafficking and the protection of underwater archaeological resources. McManamon co-authored *Archaeology and You,* promoting public involvement in archaeology. He graduated from Colgate University and earned his Ph.D. at the State University of New York at Binghamton. He has worked in the NPS Washington headquarters office since 1986.

Geoffrey B. Middaugh recently retired as first deputy director of the Bureau of Land Management's National Landscape Conservation System (NLCS). Prior to becoming the deputy in 2003, he was the group manager for wilderness, rivers, and national historic and scenic trails on the NLCS staff. He has 32 years of BLM experience in such positions as deputy project manager of the BLM/U.S. Forest Service Interior Columbia Basin Ecosystem Management project, associate district manager, budget analyst, outdoor recreation planner, and multi-resources staff chief. He has a Bachelor of Science in forestry from the University of Missouri and a Master of Science from Utah State University.

Char Miller is professor of history and director of urban studies at Trinity University in San Antonio; in 2002, he was named a Piper Professor, a state-wide award for excellence in teaching and service to higher education in Texas. He is the author of *Gifford Pinchot and the Making of Modern Environmentalism,* which won the Charles A. Weyerhaeuser Book Award, the Independent Publishers Biography Prize, and the National Outdoor Book Contest Award for History and Biography, among other awards. He has also published *The Greatest Good: 100 Years of Forestry in America, Deep in the Heart of San Antonio: Land and Life in South Texas, The Atlas of U.S. and Canadian Environmental History,* and *Fifty Years of the Texas Observer.*

Dwight T. Pitcaithley is college professor of history at New Mexico State University. He retired from the National Park Service in June 2005 after serving as chief historian for ten years. During his thirty-year career with the NPS, he served in Santa Fe, Boston, and Washington, D.C., where he focused on issues relating to historic preservation and the interpretation of historic sites. He holds a Ph.D. in history from Texas Tech University, has served as president of the National Council on Public History, and is currently president of the George Wright Society. His most recent publications include chapters in *Preserving Western History, Public History and the Environment,* and *Seeing and Being Seen: Tourism in the American West.*

James Rasband is a professor of law and associate dean of academic affairs at Brigham Young University's J. Reuben Clark Law School where he teaches courses in public lands and natural resources law, wildlife law, water law, and international environmental law. Prior to entering law teaching, he practiced law at the Perkins Coie law firm in Seattle, Washington, where his practice focused on Indian treaty litigation. Professor Rasband has published a number of articles on a variety of natural resource topics, with a particular focus on the public trust doctrine, the Antiquities Act, and wilderness issues. He is the co-author of *Natural Resources Law and Policy* (with James Salzman and Mark Squillace), a legal casebook.

Jerry L. Rogers is a member of the executive council of the Coalition of National Park Service Retirees. As National Park Service associate director for cultural resources from 1981 through 1994, he was responsible for leading cultural resource management in the national parks, federal agencies, states, tribes, local governments, and the private sector. He has also served as director of Texas Tech University's Ranching Heritage Center and president of the New Mexico Heritage Preservation Alliance. After chairing "Discovery 2000," a conference to develop vision for national parks in the 21st century, he retired in 2001 and now lives in Santa Fe, New Mexico.

Hal Rothman is professor of history at the University of Nevada–Las Vegas. He is the author of *Preserving Different Pasts: The American National Monuments*; *Devil's Bargains: Tourism in the Twentieth Century American West*, which received the 1999 Western Writers of America Spur Award for Contemporary Nonfiction; as well as numerous other books. He has also written histories of fifteen national park areas, two of which, *LBJ's Texas White House: "Our Heart's Home"* and *The New Urban Park: Golden Gate National Recreation Area and Civic Environmentalism,* were later published as university press books. In 2004, he received the Harry Reid Silver State Research Award from the University of Nevada–Las Vegas.

Darla Sidles is the National Park Service superintendent of Grand Canyon–Parashant National Monument. Sidles has worked for the NPS for sixteen years in such parks as Zion, Denali, Big Bend, and Arches. Her previous positions included chief planner, vegetation management specialist, biological technician, maintenance laborer, dispatcher, and wilderness ranger. She has also served as the acting associate to the NPS director, and as legislative assistant to Senator Daniel Akaka (Hawaii), both in Washington, D.C.

Mark Squillace is professor of law and director of the Natural Resources Law Center at the University of Colorado School of Law. Before coming to Colorado, Professor Squillace taught at the University of Toledo College of Law and at the University of Wyoming College of Law. He is a former Fulbright scholar, and the author or co-author of numerous articles and books on natural resources and environmental law. In 2000, Professor Squillace took a leave from teaching to serve as special assistant to the solicitor at the Department of the Interior. In that capacity he worked with Secretary of the Interior Bruce Babbitt on a variety of legal and policy issues, including the designation of national monuments.

Raymond Harris Thompson retired in 1997 as director of the Arizona State Museum and Fred A. Riecker Distinguished Professor of Anthropology at the University of Arizona, where he taught for 41 years. He received the Public Service Award of the Department of the Interior for his efforts to protect the nation's archaeological resources. He has contributed to national initiatives to improve the care and management of museum collections and to develop policies for the repatriation of cultural objects and the control of cultural heritage. He played a modest role in the passage of the Archaeological Resources Protection Act of 1979 and the development of the network of law and regulation for archaeological and historic preservation in Arizona.

Katrina Van Dine, Esq., has extensive experience working in marine science and policy, beginning with marine mammal studies at the College of the Atlantic to her most recent project preparing a legal white paper for the National Oceanic and Atmospheric Administration's Marine Protected Areas Center. Her ocean policy experience has involved working with a broad range of stakeholders, managers, and scientists, and she has participated extensively in the national discussion of changes to ocean management through a variety of scientific, technical, and legal conferences. Ms. Van Dine is currently research counsel at the Roger Williams University School of Law Marine Affairs Institute, collaborating with Rhode Island Sea Grant and the University of Rhode Island Marine Affairs Program.

Joe E. Watkins, an associate professor of anthropology at the University of New Mexico, received his Bachelor's degree from the University of Oklahoma and his Master's and Doctor's degrees from Southern Methodist University. His study interests include the ethical practice of anthropology and anthropology's relationships with descendant communities and Aboriginal populations. He is a member of the Board of Directors of the Society for American Archaeology. His book *Indigenous Archaeology: American Indian Values and Scientific Practice* is in its second printing. His latest book, *Sacred Sites and Repatriation*, a text oriented toward high school students, was published in 2005.

Index